"But what will y

In 1978 a 37-yea

leaves husband a

pioneer Donner Trail. She walks... Alone.

From her original raw journal we feel her ordeal of incapacitating foot pain, bewilderment, and fears of a woman alone in cities, back roads, deserts, wilderness...

And then, as surely as the stars come out above her at night, the American people emerge one by one in a proud pageant of characters. From a dirt poor, aging Nebraska couple: "Here now, you just come on in. It's all right to cry. Set right down here in our special rocking chair. Would the davenport be better? How about a root beer float?"

More sobs.

She meets hobos, wetbacks, madams and cowboys, vibrant all. America shines turbulent and roiling, yet ultimately benevolent. Even the crazy Nevada woman who padlocks her in a shack and the police who strip search her in mistaken identity--all are deftly and humanely introduced.

Buoyed by the tender kindness of strangers, she painstakingly grows into her expanding world of hog judging, cattle branding, and arrowhead hunting. She comes to revel in being alone, sleeping miles from the nearest human.

Trekking deeper through the grand western landscape, we too thrill with her on seeing the languid grace of a mountain lion, marvel at the desert mirages, and come to regret the killing of furious rattlesnakes.

But what of the Donner Party who inspired her journey? Their ghostly 1846 footsteps, faint at first, echo louder as she approaches California . After following their path and schedule for six searing months, she joins them in memorial before the great wall of the Sierra which had become their death trap. After a brief pause she triumphantly completes the journey to Sacramento 's Sutter's Fort in honor of the many who never reached it but so gruesomely died trying.

WESTWARD WOMAN

My Two Thousand Mile Trek
Of Raw Discovery
Along The DONNER TRAIL

Barbara Maat

Little Nest Press

1. adventure travel, 2. women's solo , 3. Donner Party, 4. western pioneer trails, 5. modern American cultural history, 6. Women's Liberation

References and quotations from other sources include : **Ordeal by Hunger** by George R. Stewart, 1960 ; **The Gathering of Zion** by Wallace Stegner, 1964, University of Nebraska Press; **The Women's Room** by Marilyn French, 1977; **Spiritual Midwifery** by May Gaskin , 1975; **The Seven Pillars of Wisdom** by T.E. Lawrence, 1922 ; **Home from the Hill** by The Kingston Trio, 1960; **On The Trail** by Grofe Ferde from **Grande Canyon Suite**, 1931; **God Bless America** by Irving Berlin, 1918; **Sing Down the Moon** by Scott O'Dell , 1976; **Happy Trails** by Dale Evans, 1950; **I Can See for Miles** by Peter Townshend, 1967; **Sunshine on My Shoulders** by John Denver, 1973; **The Wayward Bus** by John Steinbeck, 1947; **Carousel** by Oscar Hammerstein, II, 1945; **Staying Alive** by The Bee Gees, 1977, **America The Beautiful** by Katherine Lee Bates, 1910, **Trails West** by National Geographic Society, 1979; R16.

ISBN 146373882X

DEDICATION

In 1846   to the memory of the toiling,
           suffering, animals of the Donner
           Party.

In 1978   to all those who smiled and waved...
           thank you.

In 2010   for Paul Kardos, my loyal brother,
           and for Bob Duncan, the optimist.

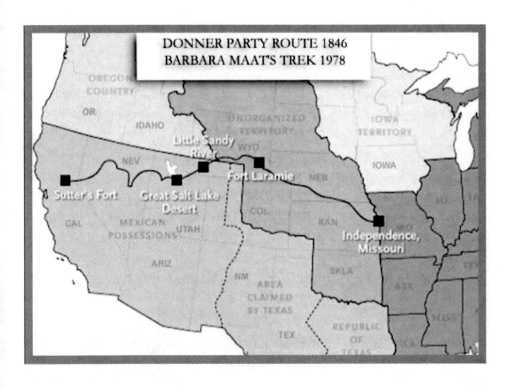

DONNER PARTY ROUTE 1846
BARBARA MAAT'S TREK 1978

Contents

ACKNOWLEDGEMENTS

In 1978 at the end of the trek I had 92 names tucked in my pack of people I had met along the way who joined me at least in spirit for the journey. At the end I sent each a Donner State Park postcard expressing thanks for "our" victory of completion.

But for 34 long years I was unable to recall the name of the generous man who had started it all for me with his gift of Donner artifacts. In 2010 a small scrap of paper fell from an old notebook with his name and address. With pounding heart I prayed that at last I might finally thank him and personally credit him with changing my life. But alas, it was too late. He had died. Edward C. Merkle, thank you, wherever you are...

Now in 2010 I have a new group who have carried this book project. Thank you all, Sharon Skolnik, Sue Williams, Patty Spielman, Kenneth Ditmer, Thatcher Hogan, Cathy Smith-Hogan, Eleanor Sweeney, Sarah Fagan Greenberg, David Hiser, Steve Moore, Warren Stephen, Sue Shellar, Susan Fazekas, Quentin Kardos, Dóra Bényi, Maureen Kardos, Donald Kardos, Mark Koons, Susan Fazekas and Cindy Aykroyd.

Thank you, Paula and Cliff. And thank you Howard, my husband, who, after all, really did "let" me go.

INTRODUCTION

Still, after 164 years, the excruciating story of the 1846 Donner Party stimulates fascination. Our human desire to "get our minds around it" produces ever-expanding archaeology, research, speculation, and arguments. Movies, documentaries, poetry, books, articles… our Donner Party shelves are already groaning. My book yields no new facts. In fact, the knowledgeable reader will notice my historical inaccuracies consistent with 1978's flawed understanding.

Although back then I intended to have the emigrant experience foremost as my focus, the immediacy of my challenges consumed me for much of my journey. And yet, I hope that my experiences contribute to feeling the similar sense of time and distance, physical stress, and intermittent mental collapse that many pioneers also lived. Scorching heat, gnawing hunger, grand western landscapes unfolded daily, weekly, monthly, all accompanying the chore of churning on and on, day after tiring day, with rattlesnakes, sunburn… joy… thirst… hope…

Even more than echoes of 1846, this journal of modern history is a celebration of heartland America 1978 with all its cultural turmoil in the Women's Liberation Movement amid the stubborn American values of idealism, independence, and kindness. As always the vivid characters of individual people are the stars.

Now in 2010 we look back at 1978 startled to see how quickly our lives have become accustomed to Google maps, cell phones, digital cameras, GPS, and computer searches, all so unimaginable to me a short 32 years ago. Oh, how the swift seasons roll!

One day early in 2010 my phone rang, and a man's friendly voice asked, "Are you the woman who walked the Donner Trail in 1978?"

"Yes," I answered, flabbergasted.

"My name is Bob Duncan. My girlfriend and I were in a blue pick-up truck at Alder Creek near Donner State Park when we saw a woman pulling a golf cart. It was cold and stormy so we offered a ride to Truckee. She answered, 'No,' but a few days later we saw her interviewed on TV. Was that you? Do you remember me?"

Truthfully I could not recall the incident, but "Dunc" had skillfully with persistence tracked me down with the help of Kristin Johnson of Utah, the current Donner Party authority. Thus a new journey slowly began: the re-birth of this book.

A personal note about the fragility of memory: at the insistence of Bob Duncan, I found and re-read my 1978 journal which had languished for more than three decades in the attic. Shockingly, I had forgotten almost everything about my journey. The memories have since inched back, but gaps remain. Clear as a bell's sound, however, are the voices of some sentences, important or not, uttered by people along the way. I see their faces, their clothes, the wallpaper behind them. But other journal jottings, often brief (thinking at the time the events were indelible), tell me nothing today. Those events, even whole days, are irretrievably gone.

I wrote the book shortly after my return, selecting the most telling experiences. I used italics for passages lifted whole (and sometimes embarrassing) from my original trail journal. The rest of the text is primarily from my skimpier journal notes but expanded for clarity. Photos are dated 1978 from the original trip or 1979 when I retraced the route by car with Eleanor Sweeney, a photographer friend. Photographers are noted with their pictures in order of book appearance:

ES Eleanor Sweeney
SS Susan Shellar
MK Mark Koons
BM Barbara Maat
HM Howard Maat
WS Warren Stephen
DH David Hiser
MB Melinda Berge
MK Mickey Pfleger
PM Paula Maat

My day by day itinerary can be found in the Appendix. Gleaned from my original journal, it contains many of the flaws and confusions of the trek itself.

Fair warning... patience... a slow start for a long haul ahead... oh, what a time! (If impatient to hit the trail, jump to chapter 4 to begin walking with me.) Those were the days, my friend...

Barbara Maat
September, 2010

1

INSPIRATION

My babies stirred sleepily in the next room as I gripped my book. And suddenly I wasn't reading. My eyes had stilled. The last word blurred. My fingertips and lips numbed in horror.

The book that changed my life, *Ordeal by Hunger,* by George R. Stewart, is a true narrative about the Donner Party, a group of 87 pioneers who emigrated to California in 1846. I had identified with the individuals, especially the women. I tensed my muscles reading of their back-breaking struggle through the Wahsatch (original spelling) Mountains and worked my mouth for saliva as they strained thirst-crazed across the Great Salt Desert. Through a hundred calamities I walked with them across the pages. Despite incredibly difficult circumstances, they came within a hairsbreadth of their goal, Sutter's Fort in California, but were stopped by early winter snowstorms in the great mountainous wall of the Sierras. With credulity stretched taut, I hovered with them through the narration of that unspeakable winter in their wet hovels under the 30-foot deep snow. Death by starvation and the bitter poignancy of mothers frantically striving to keep their children alive riveted me to their story of horror.

INSPIRATION

My own moment of truth in the Donner saga came over an incident no more or less crucial than any number of similar horrors. Recitation of death and cannibalism had passed before my intense eyes, but when a carefully cached food store was found to be rifled and eaten by wild animals during a desperate rescue effort, well, that was too much. It was then that my eyes halted and blurred, my fingers and lips numbed, and my perception of the world and the human spirit was forever altered. I laid aside *Ordeal by Hunger* and reentered my own world of diapers and baby food, but the pall lingered.

―――――――

A couple of years later in 1966, our family moved to California for two years. A born and bred northeasterner, I was stirred by the big sky and flat expanses as early in our westward trip as Ohio. By the time we reached South Dakota, my amazement and awe at the treeless emptiness bordered on panic. I felt downright irresponsible traveling with two small children in the terrifying vacant expanse. The car seemed an inadequate and too slow vehicle to deliver us across the endlessness. What if it broke down? We'd sizzle to death like hotdogs in a frying pan, no trees for shade, no hills for hiding, no water for cooking, no people for comfort, and no doctors. (When my children were young, I viewed doctors as an essential tool for survival.) Behind the panic lurked the guilt. Dear God, just let us get across these eternal plains and I promise I'll never do anything to risk my children's lives so foolishly again.

"Howard, go faster!" I irrationally ordered my puzzled husband.

"The thing that gets me," he retorted changing the subject "is how in hell the pioneers crossed this country in slow, lumbering, covered wagons. Sometimes, I understand, they made only eight miles a day."

2

INSPIRATION

For the rest of the trip I immersed myself in imagining the infinitely more frightening situation the pioneer mother faced. My son, Cliff, developed an allergic reaction to an insect bite, and Paula, my daughter, got an earache. Hour after hour we rode across the plains, my fear and panic for myself turning to awe, respect, and admiration for my imagined pioneer mother. An almost imperceptible hump in the distance would hover within her vision a whole day, while we would speed past it within ten minutes. How did she endure it?

We arrived in California after a relatively slow 15-day crossing of the country. (To a pioneer, it would have been unimaginably fast.) California life swept away my Great Plains moods and thoughts, but the seed of fascination for emigrant crossings had been planted. After two years we returned to the east where my children grew to teenagers.

———————

In 1976, in a bicentennial spirit, we pulled the children from school and went on a four-month camping trip throughout the west. I was determined that they get a dose of Americana and history, a smell of the land, and an eye for the landscape of this nation. As usual the adults probably soaked up more than the kids. As a crusty old rancher in Nevada said, "History is too precious to squander on the young. Like great literature, history should be reserved for the mature adult when there's more experience under the belt to appreciate it." Maybe so...

While camping in Death Valley, a garrulous retired man[*] began relating tales of his fervent love of history. A friend of his had flown over the Great Salt Desert in a private plane and had located what was left of pioneer wagons abandoned in 1846. "And only two weeks ago, I

_____

[*] See Acknowledgements

3

stood on the very spot where these ravaged pioneers were forced to abandon their wagons. Ahhhh, I felt their despair as I looked around at the desolation."

His emotional recitation was moving. My pulse quickened as half-forgotten memories stirred. "Was it the... ones that got snowed in the Sierras? ... the Donner Party?!"

"Yes!" he exclaimed, delighted to meet another who at least had heard of them, "and you can still see the wagon ruts from 130 years ago, but," he cautioned, "it's dangerous out there."

By this time the memories of the book, *Ordeal by Hunger,* were flooding me, and I spilled a torrent of questions. There we stood in the scorching heat of Death Valley, two united kindred spirits jabbering in a state of mutual excitement; only seconds before we'd been total strangers. He led me to his camper where he dragged forth a box of relics he'd retrieved from the desert wagon mounds. I approached as if approaching a shrine. There were pieces of wood, metal, and oxen bones; but the most heartrending was a tight wad of covered wagon canvas ripped and balled with desert salt. In a spontaneous burst of generosity he reached down and grabbed an oxen bone and piece of wood which he extended to me. "Here, these are for you because you appreciate and love these great pioneers as much as I do." I was humbled and honored. I still am.

The next day we left Death Valley through desert similar to that on the more northerly Donner Trail. On the seat beside me cushioned in a tissue box rested the Donner oxen bone and salt-twisted wood. I stared motionless at the bleak desert landscape through the windows of the humming car. It would take a whole day for a wagon train to cross the horizon I was scanning. I imagined a line of rocking lumbering white-topped wagons, their movement barely perceptible against the distant mesas and buttes. The oxen toiled under the broiling sun while some of the weary

4

women must have stared resignedly from under the sun bleached fabric. So many days, so many weeks, so many nights and horizons, minor and major crises, so much tedium, yet it all added up to crossing a country. What must it have been really like? What did it really FEEL like? How was it to breathe new air daily and to travel through changing scenes... to be an emigrant pioneer? To cross a country? And then with a stunning bolt of recognition I KNEW that someday I would walk the Donner Trail myself. I KNEW it suddenly and completely, and that certain knowledge wafted over me in waves and chills of alternating joy and fear. I shivered and giggled and cried and flinched and sweated and tried to come to grips with my newly revealed knowledge. From that instant there was never any doubt I would do it; the only question was when.

To explain my strange behavior I merely told my family that I was excited about my Donner relics. The truth was still too new, fragile, and precious to be spoken aloud.

I felt a need and an urge to track down the Donner story immediately while we were still in the west, so we decided to drive the extra 300 miles north to Salt Lake City, the closest major city right on the Donner Trail. Our brief search there revealed no Donner information, so we turned away from thoughts of the Donner Party and pulled out the campground guide to find the nearest cheap tenting spot. It was 40 miles away, a place called East Canyon Reservoir. As navigator, I held the open book on my lap reading aloud the directions from the guide, "East Canyon... Dixie Hollow..."

As we headed into the Wahsatch Mountains, I picked up another book I had been reading, *The Gathering of Zion* by Wallace Stegner. On page 164 I suddenly found myself reading about the decidedly non-Mormon group, the Donner Party. My languid perusal flared to an avid interest as their struggle through the Wahsatch was described.

Wahsatch! The mountains we were now driving through. As the car shifted to a lower gear, I glanced up from the book just as we passed a tiny road sign, Dixie Hollow. One of my kids had just asked for the graham crackers, which I passed to the back seat as I resumed reading the Stegner book: "then seven miles of equally stiff down along the side hill into what is now called Dixie Hollow…" and "up what Pratt called Canyon Creek (now East Canyon Creek) for six exhausting miles." Puzzled, I glanced to my left knee where I re-read the guide's directions to... what campground again?   EAST CANYON.   ...   DIXIE HOLLOW.   ... WASATCH MOUNTAINS.   It was one of those rare moments in time and fate when stunning coincidences collide, and what an impact it was!

I had been drawn to Salt Lake City in search of Donner information only to find nothing. Then, having given up, we blindly but unerringly stumbled over their very path camping that night within a stone's throw of their campsite 130 years before. The catalyst for this Donner knowledge had been a book about Mormons, a campground guide, and graham crackers. It seemed a final affirmation of my intention to retrace the Donner Trail.

I have been pressed hundreds of times to explain why I, a presumably normal 37-year old mother, decided to leave home for seven months and retrace on foot the route of the Donner Party. I have here described the series of occasions over the years which eventually led to the first naive steps, but the why remains not satisfactorily answered.

It was, no doubt, partly to revel in a pioneer experience, to feel alkali dust in the wind, to see the desert mirage, to hear the coyotes howl after a storm, and to feel the hunger of a hard day on the trail satisfied. It was to get a hint of the 1846 sense of time and distance so greatly different from 1978's. As a Nevada Mormon woman suggested, it was "to pay a little reverence" to the pioneers, my own personal pilgrimage of honor and respect, especially for the women.

But yet, the sum of all small reasons does not equal a full answer of why. In the end the reasons remain hidden and inscrutable. Yet I am as deeply confident now as when on the trail that it was the right thing, the perfect thing for me to be doing at that time. I never wavered in that conviction. It felt right, always, every step.

It mattered to lots of people that I have a definite reason for the journey, but it never mattered to me. I just did it.

2

GETTING READY

"Indeed, if I do not experience something far worse than I have yet done, I shall say the trouble is all in getting started."   Tamsen Donner

I anticipated the trip would be the greatest experience of my life, almost a pilgrimage. I assumed I would share it with one or two other women, for it had been the women pioneers who had moved me so deeply. After careful deliberation I wrote to an old friend inviting her to share this journey. She had recently converted to Mormonism, and much of the Donner Trail later became the Mormon Trail. With a sense that I had honored her, I waited eagerly and naively for the return mail …

I approached the mailbox with tingling anticipation … but it was empty. The next day my heart jumped ... but the white letter was only a phone bill. I felt strangely embarrassed. Days passed, and I stared in disbelief as the mailbox yawned empty of the letter I sought. Four months later my answer came tacked as a P.S. at the end of a Christmas card, "Oh yes, about your trip — no thanks." Chastened I approached a few other friends and shyly invited them to join me. "Are you kidding? And not have my hot shower every night?" "You must be crazy. I can't take the time." "Oh, Barbara, don't go: you'll miss the height of the selling season." (I was a real estate broker.) I was wounded when people did not take me or my plans seriously. It shook my fragile confidence. I became secretive about the trip. Then I faced the truth. I would have to go alone or not at all… I chose to go alone.

Early March in Massachusetts when the dusk is a rainy gray and the cold seeps inside along the leaky windowsill, reality crowded out the vague sunny visions I'd had of the trip ahead. Until then I had hummed *The Grand Canyon Suite*, "We're on the trail. My mule and I, we haven't a care" while envisioning an amble through waving tall grasses with a road a safe distance on the left and a river, the Platte, vaguely to my right. "Clippity, clippity, clippity clop, over the rim of a hill" I'd hum as a yellow butterfly darted jaggedly across my imaginary path.

The mule went away in my mind before March but not without a fight. "My mule and I" was too romantic an image to give way easily to the reality of impracticability, but admittedly, I knew nothing about mules.

Now my departure date was less than six weeks away, and I opened my eyes to the real world around me. I frowned. I'd be outside there in Kansas next month where it got dark like now here and rained and where some little towns wouldn't have campgrounds or motels or friends, and then just exactly what would I do? ... It was my first panic attack. When night fell out there and I was alone, where would I hide? Visions of my sneaking behind sheds or crouching in back yards crowded me as I searched outside my own Massachusetts window. The houses on our street looked cozy and warm behind the lighted windows, but I was watching the imaginary me, cold and frightened, outside on the menacing dark street. With the dreadful sinking feeling that I wouldn't be able to cope, that my precious trip was a delusion, that I'd bitten off more than I could chew, I all but gave it up right then.

But there is security in conviction, and my conviction was firm; I would do the trip, period. The moment of gut-wrenching fear subsided slowly. If the pioneers did it in the wilds of 1846, I'd do it in 1978. Then solutions came. I stopped mentally crouching out there in fear and defeat and went to the police station or the nearest church parsonage or the town clerk or mayor or librarian or ... suddenly towns seemed full of nice safe people who'd let me sleep on a porch or in a yard. The panic attack passed. It was the first and not the last, but a tiny seed of coping confidence had been planted.

For a while I felt compelled to envision every possible eventuality so as to mentally prepare, but the situations were limitless. What would I do if a pack of half-wild dogs attacked while I camped alone? What if my trick back went into spasm in the wilderness and I couldn't move? A co-worker said testily, "Tell me just exactly what you are going to do when two burly truck drivers pull up and say, 'Honey, get in the truck?" And then I realized the futility of imagining, let alone preparing, for every possible problem. A heavy burden slipped away with the realization that I could not expect to anticipate every contingency but would have to rely on my own ability to cope as the trip unfolded. Absolved of that responsibility, I breathed easier as dreary Massachusetts March passed to still leafless April.

From other people I needed practical help, such as maps and equipment. I also thought I needed supportive approval and enthusiasm, so I peppered the mails with 35 letters to western trail experts, rangers, friends, historians, and transportation departments. I briefly described my plans, asked for help and signed my name ambiguously "B. Maat" to foil any anti-women prejudice. I met a wall of indifference and discouragement which unhappily armored and numbed me.

One day a letter came from the ranger at Donner Memorial State Park, Steve Moore. "Dear Ms. or Mr. Maat," it read. "Ms!" I loved him already. I held my breath. A long, thoughtful, and encouraging letter followed. Alone in the house, I leaped with joy, giggled, and kissed the letter. I twirled on tiptoes girlishly about the room. I sat on the floor and reread it. My eyes brimmed with tears realizing how deprived of encouragement I had been and how sorely I had needed it. I hugged the letter to myself. It was almost as good as having a friend go with me.

Inevitably the few people who knew about the trip inquired about how I was going to protect myself. Everyone assumed I'd carry a gun or mace or bring a dog to repel assault. A colleague shook his head, "Barbara, why don't you stay home where you belong? You'll be subjecting yourself to all kinds of danger."

I approached a friend, a captain in the Massachusetts State Police. Somewhat belligerently I said, "Now don't tell me to stay home because I AM going, but what kind of protection should I carry, a gun?" I braced for his disapproving lecture.

With a twinkling amused smile he replied, "Naw, you can't carry a gun. It's against the law in many states, and besides, there's not much you can do against a determined attacker anyway. Why don't you forget all this talk about weaponry. Go ahead with your trip, and have a wonderful time. It's something you'll be talking about for the rest of your life. As for danger, it'll be no different from walking down the street of your own town." (A questionable comfort.) Thank you, State Trooper. I never could picture how the quick draw would have worked anyway. Ludicrous. It's just not my style.

With the gun issue settled and the burro image gone I began researching and collecting in earnest equipment for backpacking. Good boots and pack were items of supreme importance. I would pay any price for either. A poor selection of either would jeopardize the trip. The pack selection was easiest. I chose the one that was most comfortable when loaded with sandbags. It hugged tightly against my back with the weight on shoulders and riding on hip sides. It was $75, a Jan Sport Great Sack II, internal frame. I was outraged that for the price it was not waterproof, but as for comfort, I never had a complaint.

I've always been a sneaker person but "backpacking

with sneakers? HA! HA! HA! You've got to be kidding!" said the muscled young salesman half my age. Ouch. Sometimes these outdoors mountaineering and backpacking people can be very intimidating, so I stole into the boot department like a thief in the night. "I'd like some very light weight hiking boots," I said with what I hoped was an assertive voice.

"What are you going to be using them for?" he parried.

Gulp. There I stood feeling feeble and inadequate before the outdoorsie young man. "Oh, just walking on the flat," I half lied. At that point I could not even faintly imagine my skinny legs and bony feet propelling me 2,000 miles across plains and mountains and deserts. To give away my secret was unthinkable. If he laughed … why, it might evaporate. My dream was still dangerously fragile. I protected and guarded it from laughter, ridicule, or doubt.

I bought a second pair of $43 boots (the first pair had given severe blisters) and faced the immediate problem of money. As a real estate broker I needed one more sale to give me the money I'd need for the trip. Luckily I was working with a pleasant young couple motivated to buy, easy to please, and financially able. But as my departure date neared, and time pressures increased, the sale eluded me. For the last three weeks I ate up valuable conditioning time squiring around my exasperating young couple who never did buy.

In my free hours I walked up and down the streets of my town with my bright new pack and new fancy Italian hiking boots. How silly I felt! There was something worse than feeling silly, however, and that was feeling pain. A pinched nerve in my shoulder needled me mercilessly. My leg muscles ached and quivered with fatigue on the slightest upgrade, and, unmistakably, the sore spot on my heel was topped by a small fluid-filled lump. But I persevered and increased my miles from two a day to eleven, the average per day needed to complete the trip. On the day I did eleven, I staggered into my real estate office and collapsed into a chair too pained and stiff to even remove the pack. "How many miles did you do today?" said my upbeat colleague. "Eleven." I whispered.

"Hey! Great!" He chortled. "Now you've got it made!"

I'm forever indebted to him for his optimism. The fact that it took two days to recover was never mentioned. "Oh well," I secretly rationalized, "the pioneers were all kinds of people. Some were conditioned, but many had to become trail toughened while on the way." I'd be one of those.

All in all I don't think a less qualified specimen ever attempted a pioneer trail. I had never backpacked. I was not conditioned. I suffered for years from intermittent severe muscle spasms in my back. I was also prone to Meniere's Syndrome, periodic attacks of incapacitating dizziness. I did not have adequate funds. My maps were incomplete. I was walking out on my two teenage children who, I was told, would need their mother at this crucial teen stage. My old house was only half renovated and barely livable for my family whom I was leaving behind. I was rather sheltered and naive, plunging ahead with conviction and faith backed by scant experience and shaky confidence.

But in truth, is there ever a right time or a convenient time for such a trip as this? I would have waited in vain for the perfect time to work it in. This year was as good, or bad, as any, I thought, so I carved it out of or into my life and made the time.

My real estate office gave me a surprise party, singing "Happy trails to you, until we meet again. Happy trails to you. Keep smiling until then. Happy trails to you, till we meet again." The broker who had oozed contempt the day before, "Do you have any idea at all how hot it is in the desert? Obviously you don't," had a tear in his eye. It was a touching send-off for a seemingly impossible dream.

LEAVING HOME

"The longest journey begins with a single step."   Lao-tzu

The transition from sleep to wakefulness was instantaneous, but I didn't dare open my eyes yet. I wasn't sure I wanted to start the day, the day I would break away from home, from my own safe bed, from the familiar smell of the guinea pig cage, and the street light that nightly irritated me, and the thousand little things that suddenly made home so dear. I lay with my eyes tightly closed, alert, and then with horror I felt my back tighten to the verge of spasm. Dear God NO! "Easy, easy, relax," I commanded myself as I finally opened my eyes with slow deliberation. "Deep breath," but not too deep. Wait ... wait ... pause. "Now, sit up, straight up, don't twist, keep going ... now stand." With the exquisite controlled deliberation of defusing a bomb, I worked my back away from the edge of spasm, every movement down to the finger tips cautious and minutely measured. No one must ever know that my trip teetered so close to the edge of disaster before it had even begun.

I crept downstairs avoiding any glance to the right, for it was there that my half loaded pack sat propped against the wall. But its presence dominated the whole room. Through breakfast its yellow canvas hovered menacingly just out of sight as my back twinged threateningly. The situation rapidly escalated to ludicrous proportions. I, about to begin a 2,000-mile trek... was afraid of my pack. Numbly I approached it head on and fumblingly crammed in the last minute odds and ends, maps, food, water, but I couldn't lift it into the car. The fear of it dominated me. My friend had to carry it for me.

The car crept away from the house, forlorn and

unnoticed. At the intersection another car stopped, and out hopped Helen Bruni, a woman I scarcely knew but who had heard of my trip. She dashed across the street, reached impulsively through the open window of the car and kissed me fervently wishing me an emotional "good luck."

At the bus station I again lost the battle of will and nerve and had my pack carried right on to the bus and placed in the seat next to me. I would have to come to terms with it later.

I waved goodbye and sat staring as beloved Boston passed by and behind. The spring buds on the trees were still tightly compact. They would bloom and fall before I'd see them again. The streets would ooze tar in the summer heat and skim with ice in the fall before I'd return.

I was on my way.

I planned a stop to see my grandfather in Bridgeport, Connecticut, another stop to see Father Russo, a trail enthusiast in Yonkers, New York, and a last stop in Missouri to see Gregory Franzwa who had generously offered his valuable trail maps to copy. Only after all that would come my first step on the trail.

After pulling in and out of nameless and faceless bus stations distinguished only by their varying degrees of squalor, we pulled into Bridgeport. Time ran out for the reconciliation with my pack. It was just as well. I had no choice. I picked it up gingerly at first, heaved it onto my back and marched into the scary dark city. My back never even quivered.

My grandfather has always been a symbol of pioneering heritage and pride to me. Having come to the United States from Hungary at the age of 19 with $3.00 in his pocket, he managed to learn the language, raise a fine family, and put in an honest and honorable 45 years with

General Electric. Sometime in my formative years he must have found time to instill in me his own respect for "pioneer stock." My grandmother always had hovered subserviently in the background. Her "old country" long skirts and incomprehensible language mingle intimately in my memory with the aroma of Hungarian pastries which she pressed upon us insistently. I looked forward to my visit with Grandpa as a kind of affirmative acknowledgement of his immigration 71 years before and my journey as a tribute to and a continuation of his pioneering spirit.

I walked up his long and creaky backstairs in the dark, past the initials my father had carved in the banister as a boy. My knock was answered after a long wait. An old man, my grandfather, peered at me with a worried, bewildered expression. "Hello Grandpa," I said. "It's Barbara. Remember? I called earlier to tell you I was coming."

The old eyes struggled to peer through the fogs of age and reflected the mental effort to orient himself. Ever the decent gentleman, he invited me in. "Who are you?" He asked.

"I'm Barbara. I'm your son Louie's daughter." Long pause.

"Do you know my children?" he asked visibly brightening at the mention of his children.

"Yes. I'm your son Louie's daughter. Do you remember that Louie had two children?"

"Yes."

"And one of them was a little girl?"

"Oh yes! Little Barbara!" he smiled joyfully.

"Yes!" I excitedly exclaimed, "and that's me!" But the light of recognition that had flared briefly faded. Later my Aunt Lillian arrived. My grandfather turned to my aunt and gestured to me saying, "Who is this woman? I don't know her."

17

LEAVING HOME

I had arrived too late in a life weighted with distant memories and a mind revisiting the early years. Age and time had slipped a curtain between us before I had even known it was happening. With a wistful sadness and vague guilt I boarded the bus for Yonkers and Father Russo.

Later from a Y.M.C.A. room in Yonkers I wrote my first letter home.

April 21, 1978

Dear Howard, Paula, and Cliffie,

No matter what happens on this trip, even if my back breaks and I get chickenpox in the middle of the desert, this day alone will have made it all worthwhile.

I've spent the last 5 hours – it seems like 5 days worth of experience – at the Catholic Parish, Our Lady of Mt. St. Carmel, a declining small urban church in Yonkers. There is no way I could ever describe Father Dominic Russo and if I could, you'd never believe it. He must be the most authentic ball of fire on earth, an eccentric nut. I love him.

He said that until about nine years ago, he had no interests, and then he found "the answer to a dream and a prayer", the WEST!! He took me to his 2 rooms in the rectory where he has books, maps, records, souvenirs, pictures of himself in western costumes, bottles of water from famous rivers, rocks from famous passes, all in a personal shrine from floor to ceiling. The religious stuff runs a poor second in quantity and enthusiasm. He leaped from object to object in a breathless frenzy, unable to stay on any one topic long enough even to finish a sentence. When I left, the place looked like it had been ransacked, maps and books and horse shoes and records stacked on chair edges and slipping into heaps on the floor. The impressive thing is that everything was so ordered when I arrived, but his enthusiasm had him darting in 50 directions and thinking of 50 things to show me at once and SHOUTING at me the

18

whole time, gesticulating wildly.

Interwoven with all this from my point of view was my own fascination of being behind the scenes in a real ethnic Catholic Church. I felt privileged to get this glimpse and almost (but not quite) guilty since I have some anti-Catholic prejudices. The priests are waited on, buzzed, and called for dinner and coffee breaks, and served in an elegant dining room. I'm getting ahead of myself. Anyway, Father Russo was buzzed for a coffee break, and we and others had coffee and cake. The cook and her daughter and the cook's husband were enthralled with the idea of my trip. The daughter, about my age, has never been anywhere but mentioned how much she likes "pretty scenery on TV" and begged me to take a camera. She had tears in her eyes and was awed to think anyone could do something as wonderful as my trip sounded to her. Everyone was wonderful to me and seemed happy. Then back to the Russo rooms for another exhausting session. (Everyone had tried on my pack. It was fun.)

Another buzzer at 6:00 o'clock and the three priests and I were served dinner in a beautiful room. No one ever asked my religion. All repeatedly expressed amazement "that your husband would LET you do this." My gently pointed answer was, "Well, I LET HIM go on trips too!" The Monsignor loosened up after I repeatedly (and sincerely) admired his bonsai collection. He then expressed with deceiving calmness his distress at the disheartening (to him) trends in the community. He was born and raised in this parish in 1913 and spent his life as an army chaplain, to return to these, his boyhood streets, to be the Monsignor. The Italians are moving out. The Arabs from Jordan are moving in. Some are Catholics but have their own Arab speaking priest. He ate in their home once and was disturbed by their customs, women hiding in the background, men sitting and eating out of a huge common platter heaped with rice and chunks of pork "as big as your fist" and all eating "WITH THEIR HANDS", (enunciated with quiet horror). The women then crept forward after the men finished eating.

The table talk was sprinkled with harried comments about church duties, confessions to be heard that evening, confirmations to be done in the morning, funeral arrangements, what time the bishop would arrive, what time the cook would put in the turkey, displeasure that it would be stuffed with only "Stove Top" stuffing. I then again felt honored when the Monsignor invited me to see his other bonsai outside, and I again (with sincere honesty) expressed that they were much more beautiful than those at the Boston Flower Show, so he warmed to his subject and talked of each tree, how this one is 35 years old, how that one gets its first leaves pulled off each spring (a maple) so that the second leafing will produce tiny leaves, how he plans to wire and trim another, how his bonsai teacher suggested he shape another or leave alone another since its character was formed. In the Orient some are 300 years old and still tiny. Then, another honor, I felt: he took me to see more plants in his very elegant and tastefully decorated suite.

Father Russo then ushered me hurriedly back to his room and in a rush before hearing confessions pressed some gifts on me: a cross with turquoise colored stones, a lovely poem he has mass-printed, a bookmark, a patriotic American flag tile. He insisted with the authority that only a Catholic priest can press that he pay the $10 for my room at the "Y" which he drove me to. I'm now in my "Y" room in downtown Yonkers, and it is perfect: no pretension, cracked plaster, peeling paint, Goodwill 1940's style odds and ends of furniture in an ancient building, clean and rather like a college dorm, friendly and non-critical. The real topping for the day was a remark from Father Russo at the end. There he sat in his car, very short, stout middle, in his fluttering black robe saying, "Monsignor was really nice to let you in the rectory. I've known other priests who are as queer as ducks, believe me!"

He wanted your address. He'll be writing to you. He wants to visit our "home" – shudder terror – FIX IT UP! I'm sure we'll be right down there with the Arabs to him in its present state.

Love,
Euphoric
Barbara

There was a playful tease from a black woman at the switchboard, "You're going to do WHAT? ALONE!!? Honey, I just might not let you go!" Chuckle ...

As I was leaving New York for the long ride to Missouri, I wrote the first lines in my journal:

Waiting for the bus at the Port Authority was like drowning in numbing misery. The tears were an eyelash away, nothing in particular, just too much feeling pressing me. I felt brave, pathetic, privileged, misunderstood, exalted, and overlooked, thankful and resentful. As the bus pulled out of New York, the tears squeezed out, and then the trip was on. Within 20 minutes some of the physical stress and mental agony began magically to disappear. Stomach ache and nausea and dizziness and sore back receded. My backpack no longer seemed like a threatening bomb ready to trick my back into spasm. I took charge of my predicament for the first time, arranged the maps and food and water bottle and bus seat. The 24-hour ride which I had looked at as an ordeal became pure pleasure. The slow deep beat of satisfaction about travel got me together again.

The bus had one person for every two seats and there was marked isolation between passengers. Despite 20 hours together, each of us remained separated rigidly. Near the end of the trip I felt calm enough to approach the man across the aisle to inquire how he liked his philosophy book. Electrically, within seconds we were marveling at the coincidence of our travel plans. He had just given up serious plans to walk across the country. He had even perused the L.L. Bean equipment catalog. Here at last was a person who spoke my language about the appropriateness of setting out with purpose but not details, with a sense of exploring self along with the physical world. This young man was a professional intellectual and student, a type I generally have contempt toward as self-absorbed and self-centered, yet he tuned in immediately to my trip with total understanding. He said repeatedly and prophetically, "If you have your goal clearly in mind, you will certainly succeed. You might follow unforeseen paths or be temporarily diverted, but the only essential ingredient for success is for you to hold a steady vision of your goal."

He said that my body would also be a guide for me if I learned to heed its messages. He was on his way to Los Angeles after breaking away from the spirit-killing effects of four years in New York City. He had no idea where or what he'd do when he reached Los Angeles but had complete faith that when he arrived, his body and instinct would tell him what to do, where to go, etc. I was trying to remain flexible, but he was awesome (and an inspiration) to me in his lack of concern for the details of the future. Suddenly people all over the bus were talking. Two who had overheard us came and asked me about my trip and wished me luck with great warmth. One older woman's brother had just walked all over Europe for nine and one half months. She gave me her phone number for when I pass her Kansas town. The bus buzzed with unaccustomed chatter, and then abruptly, the trip was over. We disembarked in St. Louis, said Goodbyes, and I caught a quick bus to Gerald, Missouri, where Greg Franzwa had his precious maps for me to copy.

The bus stopped in Gerald momentarily, long enough for me to hop out. It was one of those tiny towns where they hang out a flag on the gas station pump to signal the bus driver whether or not to stop. Immediately I ran into my first crisis, no motels, no hotels, no guest houses, and . . . no Greg Franzwa. He wasn't home. I had walked the three miles to his rural setting, my pack sagging painfully, my mind churning in disbelief with the suddenness of my unexpected predicament. Night was rapidly falling as I walked into the nearby woods and sat disconsolately on a log. I had little time for self pity as huge black rain clouds rolled in and the first sprinkle hit, so in a flurry I went into my storm routine and found that my sleeping bag cover leaked like a pitcher. It was too cold to apply seam sealer and the tube was nearly empty anyway. I also discovered a total of five ticks on my pack, in my sleeping bag, and on my clothes. I was sure they were also on my body, "but the hell with them for now." With the ticks and rain assaulting me I had no time to indulge bug phobias or my old claustrophobic fear of being zipped blindly into my bivy bag. I wiggled in and ... zipped. I clutched the flashlight all night and awoke next morning with a fine feeling of confidence and triumph. To save weight I carried no tent, no pad, no air mattress, no ground cloth (except the bivy bag, a sleeping bag cover.)

But my problem persisted. The weather was cold and wet. The Franzwa house sat maddeningly empty for two days while I hid bewildered in the woods. Had I been forgotten? Did he mark his calendar May 24 instead of April 24?

My greatest torment has always been waiting in helpless passivity, and after waiting and waiting and watching and listening for two days and pushing down tears, I finally said, "what the hell" and gave in completely, sobbed and moaned and made crying tunes and blubbered in a wonderful wallow of self-pity. Things seemed much better after the cry; in fact, things seemed just fine and downright comfortable. Just after dark, dozing comfortably in the woods, I heard cars and people calling. It was the Franzwas. I crawled out of my sleeping bag and went to them feeling very foolish, my eyes swollen nearly shut from my earlier bout of sobbing. He had, indeed, forgotten to check his calendar after all.

The next day I traced Greg's Oregon Trail maps onto my own. I had about 80 county maps, one half inch to the mile. As I made the first tracings with my red-orange crayon, a tremendous shiver of excitement ran up my spine. I was almost, really almost, on my way. For the first time, the beginning of my dream seemed at hand.

The following day I waited at the little gas station where the tiny flag was hung out to signal the bus to stop for me. I was coming to terms with my backpack. It no longer intimidated me. It felt almost comforting. In fact, it was a little bit like carrying my home on my back.

My final bus ride to Independence, Missouri, was not uneventful. I vomited on the bus. I arrived in the strange city after dark. I found a cheap hotel and incredibly, ridiculously, tipped a bellhop to carry my backpack fifty feet down the hall. Oh well, what's 50 feet out of 2,000 miles...

The next morning the sun sparkled, and I took my first step of my longest journey alone and unnoticed in Independence Square.

4

FIRST STEPS

April 28 – April 30
(34 Miles)

"Fools rush in where angels fear to tread."   Alexander Pope

" ....for amber waves of grain..."   Bates 1895   1979 ES

I tried to look as if I knew what I was doing, but in truth my maps looked incomprehensible. The red line that I had copied as the Oregon Trail wound diagonally across the city blocks without proper regard for 1978 street layouts. I suspected it was heading into the heart of a frightening neighborhood, but the maze of streets on the map gave no clue. Every few steps I'd pull out my map again and gaze anew at the tangled mess.

A startling sight came into view as I resumed my anxious wandering. A neat little building sat squarely on my path behind a sign reading Trail Restoration Society. I knocked tentatively on the door, and despite the early hour, an elderly man in a conservative dark blue suit opened the door of the tiny religious-looking museum. It was a historic building for a splinter group of the Mormon Church. I asked for help with my maps, and the kindly gentleman slowly and carefully rerouted me with a crayon around the scary section where my map would have led me. My unsuspected stumble into the historic trail building just as I was on the verge of becoming lost was a soothing reprieve from my rush into fear. The appearance of the benign religious man lent the whole episode an aura of benevolent fate. I left the little building breathing easier and headed for the gently curving boulevard. My troubles were not over, however, for my pack was feeling heavy and the day was heating rapidly.

I walked on the grassy edge of the fine old road, experiencing for the first time the intense scrutiny of hundreds of passing motorists. Dozens of people slowed or stopped to shout ride offers. My first unsure day on the trail made me jumpy and suspicious. A large dump truck circled and passed me repeatedly, and I tensed until a friendly man hopped out, smiling and cheerful, and tried to help me. When I explained that I was on my first day of a 2,000-mile walk, he looked incredulous and I felt embarrassed. I saw myself through his eyes, staggering, sweating, overheated with flaming face, collapsing on the grass frequently for panting rests, rolling backward unbalanced with the weight of my pack, skinny and out of place in the city. But he smiled encouragingly and wished me well and periodically circled back to check my progress.

Rare early photo with backpack   1978

The day became a blur of shoulder pain and thirst
and cheeks pulsating with heat. At one point I walked
through a dirty area of old warehouses and junkyards, and
then I saw a tiny, well-worn path that led down a steep
brushy hill toward a market. My body seemed feverishly hot
as I followed visions of grape juice and started down the
dirt path to the store. As I began picking my way through
the assorted whiskey bottles, I looked up and stopped short.
Ahead under the shade of the brush were lolling some
scruffy-looking hobos. I was too tired to even re-climb the
short hill, so I merely continued down the hill making a

slight detour around the hobo convention. In the market I nearly wept with pain and weariness while waiting in the interminable checkout line. Outside the store I drank down the full quart of grape juice without stopping for a breath.

The road entered a busy urban neighborhood of old buildings and fading businesses. It didn't look very promising as a place to stay overnight, yet I was rapidly nearing the physical and mental end of my rope. I became frightened of the people around me and then had a new urgent problem; I needed to find a bathroom desperately. The foreign unfriendly neighborhood seemed devoid of any hope of bathrooms. Grimly, trancelike, I pressed on, a stranger in a strange land, withdrawn, oblivious to the figures around me. I raised my eyes from their downward cast and beheld a sign, PLANNED PARENTHOOD, across the street. Planned Parenthood! Bathroom galore! Nice people! With relief so close, my bathroom need increased alarmingly in urgency. I found the front door after some fumbling and approached the startled young woman behind the desk with my imploring eyes. She directed me to a bathroom where my intestines disgorged explosively. Pale and shaken, slowly I reentered the world of normal.

Back at the desk the eager questioning women gathered and gaped at me and my story in friendly amazement. One who was not so friendly told me flatly that I obviously didn't know anything about Kansas heat (she was right) and that I'd never make it (she was wrong).

A casual, unassuming young woman named Belle said, "Hey, why don't you come over to my place and crash for the night? You're welcome to my couch and my refrigerator, although it isn't much."

Isn't much? At that point it was the world to me and more. Safety, warmth, a haven. The Taj Mahal itself wouldn't have been more inviting. For the first time in my life I learned a deeper meaning to thankfulness, gratefulness. As if it were the most natural thing in the world, Belle bundled me and my pack into her tiny rattletrap car, picked up her five-year old daughter from a day-care center, and delivered us to the grand old house she rented in a deteriorated section of the city.

I met Stacy and Mary, two women who shared the rent and appreciation for the faded, elegant residence. Together we admired the richly carved woodwork and the exquisite stained glass windows. I was too crippled to make the climb to the upstairs, so Belle led me to the couch from which I never budged until morning.

I was demoralized, almost ashamed for being in such bad shape while still admitting to my dream of walking to California. Belle showed me a book about people who run across the United States, people who run through Death Valley, and people who run 100-mile races. She then looked straight into my eyes and said, "I think what you're doing is perfectly reasonable."

I clung to the memory of her voice and the miracle of that statement for many days afterward.

The next morning Belle and I sat around the breakfast table and communed in a spirit of sisterhood. We discussed a recent TV show about a mature woman who pursued her improbable dream to run in the Boston Marathon. There is a secret bond of empathy that binds together women who want more than is traditionally allotted us. I was to see it and feel it and share it again and again across this country, but never would it be stronger than in that Kansas City, Missouri kitchen. We shared blinked-back tears and cold chills of emotion, and then it was time to go our separate ways. Mary, a nurse, sent me off with some solid medical advice. "Walk with your head very straight to avoid pinching the nerve that runs close to the surface of that shoulder. Also, take two aspirins or even more every four hours until your body muscles toughen away from pain."

Belle dropped me off at the point I'd stopped walking yesterday, waved goodbye, and was gone.

An early morning thunderstorm had left the flowers and grasses bedecked with water droplet jewels. The air was freshly fragrant. I walked through high class Westport with its chic shops for the wealthy and then into an old exquisite residential area with heavenly grounds, parks, pools, fountains, statuary. Beyond this man-made heaven I emerged into a strip of highway with gas stations, dry cleaners, car lots and fast-food drive-ins. Beyond the strip was suburbia, which gradually gave way to farm lands. I crossed the border from Missouri to Kansas, walked in and out of a few new housing developments where in one I asked a young teenager for water. He refilled my water bottle and added ice, an extra little kindness that lifted my spirit.

I began searching for a camping spot, a hiding spot. The pain in my feet and hips had become excruciating. I had walked 26 miles in two days, but my general condition was deteriorating. Although I was in rural farmlands, camping spots were scarce. All lands were fenced or cultivated. Finally I hobbled over a slight hill and plunked down hidden in a tiny grove of trees near a stream. I would not even attempt to stand on my feet again until morning.

I felt like a frightened animal crouching in the brush, hiding. Because I couldn't stand on my sore feet, I felt vulnerable. Whenever a car or hot-rodding pickup careened by, I held my breath, threatened. I kept my bright blue sleeping bag cover rolled tightly and my bright yellow pack covered, although it made no sense unless I feared helicopter search. After a scrutinizing examination of my feet and downing a pack of sunflower seeds, I started to breath easier. And then, incredibly, my safe hiding place was invaded. A couple searching for mushrooms wandered within 10 feet of me. I don't know which of us was more startled. The woman was stepping cautiously, carrying a strange huge implement. "Is that for gathering mushrooms?" I asked.

"Oh no," she answered, "this is for snakes."

I gulped and looked around at my brushy hollow. "Oh well."

Just as I was dozing off in an exhausted stupor, a woman and her two children ambled by along the stream. Alerted, I remained motionless, and they didn't see me. I remained tense and watchful until darkness covered me. The dark thunder clouds that had been gathering released their first splatters. During the night it rained heavily with thunder and lightning. My bivy bag leaked again so that my sleeping bag was two-thirds saturated, but somehow I still felt warm. I thought I had solved the bag problem: zip everything shut except a tiny breathing hole out the side, but the water poured in anyway. Even my down jacket pillow was soaked.

In the morning I sat on my sodden equipment and indulged in an emotional outpouring as I confessed to my journal.

Miracles happen when I need them, but I'm in poor shape and under great (unconscious) stress, stress in the cities and urban areas. My mental state roller coasters rapidly during the day and often I do not realize how bad off I am physically. My shoulder simply MUST improve and I think it will. I love my family and cry when I think of them all. I feel relieved to have finally escaped the city, but still am on guard with hot rods and "trespassers." I go through cycles of exhilaration and peace to loneliness and despair. My feet last night were too sore to walk on so I felt vulnerable. I wistfully long to be a man so I could walk across the world without the ever-present background of fear. Then I get furious that the situation is so accepted (and promoted). If I were to be abused and murdered on some lonely road, virtually everyone would say, "oh, too bad, but she shouldn't have been out there alone anyway." So I must hide every night and walk the roads with my fear tightly pushed down. It's become obvious that the exact path of the Oregon Trail itself can't be followed across the many barnyards, cornfields and KEEP OUT signs, so I must now walk on the roads since the trail itself is off limits. I'm never more than half a mile from it, however. I can at least always see where it went, although really I couldn't care less when my physical torture and anxiety are so severe. Last night I noticed I was on a swale. I checked my map this morning and am stunned to conclude that I am probably right ON the trail as it came down to this little river. More significant things happen in each day than happen in a week of normal living. It's like a mental and physical crash course. It's always in the balance whether I can keep it together. I think I can, going on faith and conviction.

My third day on the trail was a repeat of the first morning's fresh beauty, but my boots became saturated in the tall, wet grass. My blisters got bad rapidly, and soon all I could do was concentrate on how and where I put my feet to angle off the pain. I was feeling futile and had gone only six miles. I could see the outskirts of a town ahead and a "Jack-in-the Box," so I plodded doggedly and painfully on.

Suddenly, ahead I saw two figures carrying packs, bent over. They were on the opposite side of the road and darkly tanned, a young couple and grinning broadly, so broadly, in fact, that it was startling. They were radiant, emanating health and happiness way beyond the ordinary. They waved hello and I shouted, "How far have you been?"

They called back, "Oh, thousands of miles. We've been on the road since August 1."

I said, "Really? I guess there's hope for me."

The man answered prophetically, "Just be sure to take good care of your feet, and you'll make it."

I limped into the "Jack-in-the-Box," and a young woman giving out cotton candy gave me as many as I could eat and talked in a very cheerful, optimistic way, mentioning that the other couple had been in and seemed so happy. I complained about my feet and she said, "I wonder if the wet weather makes it worse."

I stayed too long and when I got up, I could barely move forward. My legs, feet, and hips wouldn't go. The blisters had blown up, and I barely baby-stepped out the door, shuffling and sliding my feet. But my "spirits" weren't too bad. I baby-stepped six blocks to a motel, the faded letters "MOTEL" alluring and lending strength. There I was eyed suspiciously and greeted as if I were the scum of the earth. It wasn't until a few sleep hours later that I noticed what a horrid motel it was. I was the only guest. It was in a poor section of the "strip." There were no locks on the door or windows, and I vaguely recalled a frightening magazine article about women in un-lockable motel rooms as I barricaded myself in by lining up tables and chairs across the room to wedge the door shut and wedged objects into the window sashes. The room came to resemble the final siege of Mount Casino. Then I cringed to hear the hot rods blatting up and down the strip. I turned once again to my journal to pour out my heart.

Here I am in a motel room that smells like someone wet the bed. I realize that I MUST take care of my feet. EVERY book says, "Keep socks clean and dry, boots dry, tape BEFORE blisters come, etc." So WHY had I ignored this and figured I'd break in my feet by force? I'm absolutely helpless now and wasting money. The whole bottom of my left heel is a blister that I can't touch, let alone walk on. My right foot has the usual heel blister and a blood blister on my middle toe that is pushing out my nail (which later dropped off). The problem is that moleskin softens the skin, and I blister underneath it anyway. My boots are always wet from sweat. The double leather layer at the toe makes it worse. I wonder if water proofing would make it better or worse. I'm so damn crippled, I can't even go to the Safeway next door for food. This is learning the hard way. When I'm preoccupied with my physical and mental complaints, I couldn't care less about danger. I've lost so much stomach that my pack waist belt does not tighten enough anymore. I'm too exhausted and sore to have any appetite in the evening. Thoughts of my family fill me with unspeakable longing and love and self-reproach for the times I've ignored my kids when I should have been attentive. I was getting up tight about miles per day, but now I see that's futile. All the will power in the world won't dent the inevitable. I intend to get "trail toughened," feet, hip bones and shoulder and get to do 20 miles per day by week number three. We'll see ... (fool's paradise) Meantime, I must work up to it by cooperating with my body, not fighting it. One day at a time. After a long day with my pack, when I take it off, it feels like air under my body is pushing me upward, incredible sensation. I am more and more coming to believe that I'm being guided on this trip and am having less and less anxiety as to what to do about problems and decisions and more and more faith that if I hang loose, I'll somehow be guided. At these crucial times, the "answer" has popped up.

1. *Bumping into the Mormon at the Trail Restoration Society who mapped my route around the inner city area.*
2. *When at the absolute end of my endurance, coming upon the Planned Parenthood Center and the precious bathroom.*

3. *Bumping into Belle who saved me from self-doubt by showing me the book about cross-country runners.*
4. *Bumping into Mary who gave me the aspirin and head-holding advice.*
5. *Stopping at the swale where I had a strong impression of Sarah Keyes* (an older woman in the Donner Party who would be the first to die on the trail).
6. *Having the woman with the cotton candy mention wet boots and sore feet.*
7. *Having impulsively taken the road to Olathe instead of being crippled out in the middle of a soggy field God knows where.*

I believe my guide is my inner or greater self plus the "knowing" telepathy we have with others.

Tomorrow's problems:
1. *Getting physically going, if possible.*
2. *Laundry*
3. *Post Office*
4. *Dodging the dangers again.*

5

COPING

May 1 – May 6
(62 miles)

"You're going westward, woman. If you reach the Rockies, you'll have gained over a mile in elevation, but, don't worry. You'll never notice it. It's so gradual."   Man near Topeka.

He was right. Topeka, Kansas, elevation, 945 feet.
South Pass, Wyoming, elevation, 7,550 feet.

Like a child's drawing, everything sat boldly on the horizon line. 1979 ES

During the night in my barricaded motel room it had become apparent to me that my top priority for a while would have to be to baby myself physically even if it meant spending my precious money for motels and café foods. The little town of Gardner where the old Santa Fe Trail split south off the Oregon Trail was eight miles away. In the morning three people assured me that Gardner had a motel, "right across from the gas station just as you enter town." So I drove myself by sheer force of will toward that promise of rest and safety. At about 4 o'clock I tottered to the edge of town. I hadn't stopped for rest because stopping had seemed to make the blisters blow up worse the day before.

With disbelieving eyes and ears I learned that Gardner had no motel, hotel, nor guest house, and never had. It was my first encounter with the unreliability of people's knowledge of neighboring towns. I wanted to cry. I asked a few people where a motel was, hoping they'd take pity on me and invite me home. They didn't. Humbled and apologetic I crept to the porch of a laundromat where I lowered myself painfully onto a bench, frightened of being chased away.

During those fear-filled minutes a new attitude began to take shape inside me. Instead of relying on people's pity and charity, I felt the stirrings of assertion. "I am not a bad person," I said to myself. "I am not hurting any of these people. I should not need to apologize or grovel to find a yard to unroll my sleeping bag on." And with a wee bit of indignation I even thought, "Why, I even have the right to be treated decently!" But then the other half of the coin came into view, the most important lesson for many months: I would have to learn to <u>ask</u> directly for help. I would have to learn to ask without cringing, without resentfulness and with the assumption that I am a kind, reasonable person dealing with kind, reasonable people.

I took a deep breath and heaved myself after several tries onto my now full-blown blisters. "I've done nothing shameful. I don't have to feel guilty about my physical condition to anyone," I kept telling myself as people stared at me with embarrassed expressions. I decided to start my new regime by asking for help at the tiny library near the center of town. A faintly humane teenage girl directed me to it, and my unwanted belligerence began to melt.

The unflappable librarian maintained her controlled demeanor as she directed me to a possible camping place a few miles out of town. She turned away expecting to have efficiently dismissed me along with my problem. But I held my ground and leaned heavily on her good manners. "I could never make it that far," I said smiling. "Is there a place nearer by," I continued, "maybe a history buff who'd have a space in her yard," my voice trailed off open ended.

"I don't know of anyone," said the librarian in her polite voice.

"Well, what do you suggest I do?" I was only one sentence away from asking directly to sleep in her yard. With a sigh at this persistent problem who wouldn't leave, she turned to her assistant for help. This was a problem for the mayor, they decided, and placed a call to the town hall to which they directed me, down the street. They had been cordial enough, but the old me would have slunk away at the first hint, imaginary or not, that I was bothering someone. The new me, still limping, headed resolutely down the street determined to see it through.

The mayor was out of town, but a lively woman responded to my "deal with me" presence with resourcefulness. She called the Presbyterian minister, who said immediately, "Send her over." I had turned the corner! Things were going to be OK. I just knew it!

Reverend Ashmore   1979 ES

Reverend Ashmore greeted me with curiosity and eager-to-please generosity. He led me to a vacant house next to the church, which I was "welcome to." He began to give me a tour, faucets, etc., but I was too footsore to stand for another second, so I plunked down my pack and me in the center of a room, where I remained helpless to move until next morning. Rev. Ashmore left me alone with anxiety for my condition, finally deciding that what I needed was undisturbed rest. He checked back later to strongly urge me to see a doctor in the morning, offering to drive me there. I slept that night soothed and thankful for inspiring good-hearted people like Rev. Ashmore. Even the dry old wheat germ I carried in my pack tasted pretty good.

COPING

Next morning in the café, a line of smiling faces turned toward me. Word travels fast in small Kansas towns. I had been seen limping into town the day before, and now knowledge of my Oregon Trail attempt made me a bit of a celebrated person. (In the early days I used the more familiar name, Oregon Trail, which is the same route as the Donner Trail, California Trail, Mormon Trail, and even Santa Fe trail for many miles.) I basked happily in the good will. It was even more nourishing and needed than the good food. Gardner, Kansas, so unfriendly the day before, now extended its warmth and encouragement just as I was preparing to leave. In my short stay I had learned much here. Scratch a stranger and you'll find a friend, but don't be afraid to scratch.

The doctor at the hospital knew less about feet than I did, although my money was accepted cheerfully enough. The doctor suggested that I give up the trip as a sure foot cure. On the other hand, he murmured, my feet didn't look all that bad. It was true. Yesterday's bulging blister no longer stuck out one half inch, and the fiery red swelling was diminished. Only I could know that under that faintly discolored heel skin was a blister or an infection or some horrible sore that would turn my plodding into pure hell within a mile. But I was amazed then and throughout the trip at the rapid recovery rate of the human body. Feet and ankles that actually could not support me in the evening would be recovered sufficiently for a one-to-two mile walk by the next morning. Unfortunately, I would always try to extend that one or two miles to ten or twelve. After all, I was trying to keep up with the wagon train of the Donner Party, and day by day I was falling behind my eleven miles per day minimum.

Betty Turner   1979 ES

Betty Turner, a reporter for the local paper, found me at the hospital and in a very human, unreporter-like manner allowed herself to be amazed at my espoused trail attempt as she peered into my eyes. For an hour she played friend to me and took me under her wing. At the drugstore I bought an arsenal of Dr. Scholl weapons against foot problems. In the months ahead I was to support half the company, I'm sure. Few if any of the remedies helped except arch supports and athletic foot powder.

Later I said a quick goodbye to Rev. Ashmore. A few in the room expressed frightened doubts about safety, but the good minister said, "The Lord will keep her safe. She doesn't have to worry." We shook hands and I left with his optimistic benediction ringing comfortingly in my ears.

Betty drove me to my drop-off spot, and removing my jacket to the warming day, I waved goodbye and was off.

For the first time, for a few hours, I truly enjoyed the Kansas beauty. Kansas in May, could there be anything lovelier? "Kansas in May! Kansas in May!" I chanted rhythmically as I walked. The freshly plowed soil was the color of dark chocolate. The green hay shimmered like party ribbons. The sun was warm, the breeze fragrant, the horizon blue. I gazed around me in a full 360-degree circle. Like a child's kindergarten drawing, everything sat boldly on the horizon line. A fine red barn, a classic red tractor, a blue truck, a sturdy round-topped silo and shed. A white farm perched next to one perfect lollipop tree. Then my feet got bad again, and the grueling plodding began.

At one rest stop my shoulder nerves acted up like a dentist drill hitting nerves. I cried briefly, became enraged, and spoke between clenched teeth my desperate accusation: "Damn you, God, you're not helping me one bit, not one little speck." I'm not a member of any church, but even I was shocked at my blasphemy. I stopped. I tightened my strap, and miraculously the pain never returned for the rest of the day.

Toward the end of the day a husky young boy stopped to talk and brought me a luscious shiny red apple from his Grandmother's house. Nearby the kind woman directed me to her church, a tiny speck on the flat horizon, as a place to stay. She said, "It isn't far, only about one and a half miles." It seemed like a million miles to me, but it meant a place of quiet shelter, out of the rain, and I thought I could probably make it that far. I baby-stepped toward it. My blisters were growing rapidly.

A wonderful dog joined me the last mile. I wished he could stay with me the whole way. I'm not a dog lover, but this dog was so happy to be alive and delighted to walk with me that I found his presence very supportive. At the end of the walking I threw my arms around his smelly neck in a big emotional hug saying, "I love you. Oh, thank you. I wish you'd walk with me all the way."

Reunion with the wonderful dog. 1979

In the front hallway of the Little Friend's Church I collapsed and looked at the pleasant scene outside. A crippled man was walking around the ancient gravestones in an adjoining cemetery. Mile-square green fields stretched to the horizon. In the distance an abandoned homestead sagged sadly within its own clump of shade trees. My friendly dog waited patiently outside the door until the crippled man called him away, and they both left in a truck. Then I was all alone. It was spooky. There wasn't a person or farm in sight. I studied my maps and concluded with a surge of excitement that once again I was probably right on the old trail.

Sleeping in the church hallway that night was OK, but my blisters hurt in almost any position. While dozing off I heard, then felt, a faint patter and saw two little mice silhouetted as they scurried over my sleeping bag and

43

across my hand. With my feet wrecks, mice were easy to cope with, so I just moved my pack so my sunflower seeds were closer to defend and went back to sleep.

In the morning I again oriented and centered myself by writing in my journal:

Have no time for anything yet, except survival. Strange, no one offered to give me a ride yesterday although now I'm on very rural dirt roads. Earlier a woman stopped to say that lots of people were out packing in Colorado. It made me feel much better to hear that others are out walking the country and trails. I do not enjoy feeling like a freak. All this foot attention. I never really paid any attention to my feet before. Now suddenly they're very important and fascinating. My hip bones, which were excruciating, were OK yesterday although my body has developed thick pads over the bones, and my shoulder is infinitely better. (It still jolts pain sometimes though. Wow!) The pack is the killer. My feet feel bruised on the bottoms from the extra weight. All in all it was a good day, maybe because of the low mileage. I don't really look around much while walking. I have to concentrate too much on where I put my feet. If it's not a smooth level spot, it hurts worse.

I just looked up from my writing to see an older man, the minister, coming through the door. He handed me a church bulletin entitled, "Overcoming Evil with Good," along with a piece of banana bread. With unmistakable distaste and disapproval he said to me, "Do you realize that if everyone had as much energy to put into spreading God's word as you are putting into this ... trip, then just think how many more people would be saved." I was hurt. I'm oversensitive. It's a lifetime trait.

I taped around my bulging blisters and started painfully off. I hobbled for miles, the local older (and younger) farmers driving by, peering with mixed disapproval and fear. One man leaped off his tractor and peeked at me as he hid behind it. The more helpless and pitiful I look, the more negative the reactions. I guess I understand this. I tend to look at really down and out people, drunks, or starvation cases as less than human.

One bearded guy in a VW drove up gently and offered to drive me anywhere. I refused and he offered me water. His manner was so humane; he'll never know how much it meant to me. There's something Biblical comparing the minister and the bearded VW guy. It reminds me of the story of the Good Samaritan and the bum. In as much as ye have done it unto the least of these...

That evening in my journal I recorded the bare facts of that grueling day without acknowledging the tremendous, almost heartbreaking, physical and mental struggle that I had waged. There was no self-pity, and probably that's why my heart didn't break. It's amazing how a person can detach.

Somehow I got to Lawrence and no one else offered to give me a ride, incredible. Of course, I wouldn't have accepted one anyway. I baby-stepped the last 4 miles, barely moving. At one point the muscle in my left leg wasn't working. I'd been tiptoeing on that side for two days. I was near falling into a ditch and then something (quickly) told me to start squeezing my foot in a certain way, and, yup, that's what was needed to keep going. I'm in the Holiday Inn. Can't walk for food next door, crawled to the bathroom. I must say, despite the wreck I was all day, I feel triumphant and high. I "walked" 13 ½ miles and had a sense of victory all the way, plus a "new" for me, compassion for the dregs of society who I've always scorned. It's also a trip sleeping on the floor with mice one night and in a plush suite the next.

When I was dragging today I lost, for the interval, some of the vulnerable fear I had about being attacked. I figured if anyone bothered me, I'd let loose with an indignant blistering torrent of "what the hell's the matter with you bothering someone who's so helpless and suffering with such sore feet!"

Perhaps unfairly, Lawrence became a symbol of callous indifference to me. One tiny incident alleviates this memory. Along the busy strip I passed some road workers as my ordeal was full upon me. The Holiday Inn sign in the distance lent mental relief just as my physical predicament threatened to overwhelm. I searched the faces of the workers for the faintest sign of humanity, and one, a young black boy, paused and gulped and looked again. My eyes were pleading for some signal of understanding. He said softly, "Sore feet?" and I found the energy to whisper, "Awful." His small acknowledgment was enough to sustain me for the last half mile.

In the haven of my motel room I luxuriated in the sleep of perfect thankfulness. On awakening I faced two uncomfortable facts: first, that I would have to spend a second night and a large chunk of my vanishing money supply for the motel, and second, that my feet instead of toughening were showing definite signs of getting worse. Now I not only had surface blisters to contend with, but I was also developing deeper problems. Pains were coursing within my feet in more directions and places and varieties than one would believe possible. At one point when I managed to stand, I gazed down in utter amazement. My right foot would not, would absolutely not, flex upward. It was not a matter of pain but rather some kind of paralysis. Down from my brain would go the message "lift up," and absolutely nothing would move, not even a twitch. The sensation was one of amazement more than alarm.

COPING

My gray hiking boots stood beside my bed like a pair of medieval torture instruments. By the second day I could walk around my room barefoot, and I contemplated starting out on the road in thick socks only but decided to part with some more money and try flexible sneakers instead. I crammed my screaming feet back into the boots and hobbled, doubled over, to the nearest store. I hardly managed to open the door since the mere act of pulling on the door increased pressure on my feet. Inside the store the irony and hilarity of my transaction was lost on the shoe clerk, who never cracked a smile despite my explanations. I had minced into the store in my fancy expensive imported hiking boots. I bought a pair of cheap good old American (made in Korea) sneakers and presto! walked, not hobbled, out of the store a new person, head high, chin up, etc. To hell with those fancy expensive imported hiking boots.

That evening I tried again to come to grips with the fear theme: "I'm still disgusted with the effort spent in trying to play the odds at safety and avoiding kooks. I figure it's fairly safe on crowded highways because there's lots of people around and way out in the middle of nowhere because there's no one around (one car per hour). The chances of that one car per hour holding a primed criminal are small. I am more fearful of the bad guy who hears about me and comes after me when I'm alone. So in that sense, the less publicity the better, but on the other hand, a little publicity (grapevine or whatever) makes the good people more receptive, and meeting people is most wonderful. I think my fears of monster people will diminish daily, but EVERYONE says, "You're traveling ALONE??!!" gasp gasp. "You must be awfully brave. I'd NEVER do that... too many creeps out there running around." Gasp horror. So then all my self doubts get a new boost. No, I'm not brave, so maybe I shouldn't be doing this after all.

COPING

I guess people have always had fear on these trails. A thousand years ago the Indians feared the next tribe. Later the mountain men and fur traders feared the Indians. The wagon trains feared the Indians and I fear the psychos. We all fear the snakes and tornadoes a bit and sickness. We all worry about food supplies. The wagon trains and I are very, very concerned about getting in enough miles per day, pushing ourselves or oxen to limits but not too far.

I'm unhappy about wasting money.

For three days I have been obsessed with visions of a quart of milk and a box of Oreos. And so today I finally indulged, and it was a disappointment. Now I have a feeling of nausea, and a new craving - - for a hamburger.

After an extra day's rest I re-emerged from the warm soft womb of the Holiday Inn and re-entered the world of maps and miles and uncertainties and pain.

Today was very hard. Near the end I felt I couldn't go on and stopped by a pleasant house with an old man outside. I asked him for water and collapsed on his lawn. He was so very old, hard of hearing and barely walked. He scowled. I put on my sunglasses to hide the tears of weariness brimming. He said there was no motel at Big Springs. I asked if I could possibly unroll my sleeping bag in his back field. He said, "No. I'm alone here and it wouldn't look good." I didn't know whether to laugh or cry, so I laughed. What a tight old fart! The shock was so startling that I managed to walk again. I never expected to be considered a bad woman of the streets.

Assertively I asked for and was given permission to sleep behind the Methodist Church in Big Springs, Kansas. During the 17-mile day I had rotated hiking boots (for support) and jogging shoes (for relief from hiking boots) but I had overdone the mileage. I had six new blisters even

48

where there was no rubbing, but most alarming was the swelling. It ballooned out both feet to above the ankles like old ladies with edema.

During the night I crept into the basement Sunday school room when it started to rain. I had been invited to the 5:30 men's breakfast.

There were eight to ten farmers for the pancake feast, and they were "regular folk," coped easily with me, no fuss. They had a scripture reading, and, incredibly, I was in a time machine back to my childhood, same smell in the Sunday school room, same voices intoning the same incomprehensible scriptures, same groping for meaning as they all strained to discuss it. They were all good people, the salt of the earth. I'll never understand why they spend such seemingly fruitless effort and time on this Bible stuff.

One farmer stayed behind to talk, blue denim overalls and cowboy boots.

He gave me excellent advice for my trip. He said that I must not anticipate danger, live in fear, or expect fearful events because if I get really scared I'll end the trip. I must expect the best from people. He believes in the philosophy of expectations so never locks his house and always leaves his keys in his car. Also I must not be surprised if people see me as a bum because I am a bum. I must stop and talk with folks, tell them who I am and what I'm doing and give them a bit of time to adjust to me. All very sensible. I can see that I was unrealistic in expecting people to accept me so quickly. He said, "The world is full of good folks. Give them a chance." True, true. So as I enter the rural part of the trip, I'll have to be more assertive about presenting myself and asking for what I want and need. I think I will not be so shy about asking the churches for shelter. This man suggested I sleep in hay barns and sheds. I still feel better getting permission first.

COPING

Walked to Topeka in torment. This morning noticed my ankles black and blue after the swelling went down. I was very discouraged about my progress in general, my feet, my money situation and everything. The Ramada Inn is $21 which is really upsetting, but again, I could go no farther, and here I am stranded in bed again unable to walk. My muscles are getting into the act, too. If I stop for more than a few minutes, I cannot get going again. It takes all kinds of grotesque lurches to move again and then it's with a ludicrous limp. I really made quite a scene in the posh lobby here. It's strange how after a dozen or so yards the muscles can at least be directed again, but some of the pain remains. The phone call home was very encouraging, and I feel optimistic again.

I left the Ramada Inn and walked through Topeka to the far side of town. Some guy with a twangy voice approached me and asked if I had some drugs. Just what I need— to look like a drug dealer...

6

KANSAS

May 7 – 18
(119 miles)

"Do you have a gun?"   excited woman

"Where do you carry a gun?"   curious woman

"What? You don't even have a gun?"   incredulous man

In beauty may I walk, All day long may I walk, With head held high may I walk, On the trail marked with pollen may I walk, With grasshoppers all about my feet may I walk, With dew about my moccasins may I walk, With beauty before me may I walk, With beauty all around me may I walk.

       Navajo chant   1979 ES

It was only my 10th day and 97th mile on the trail.

The days and miles began to pile upon themselves

as my journal reflects the steady monotonous litany of pain. Incredibly, I kept going under the naive assumption that I would soon trail-toughen despite every objective indication that my feet were getting worse. Little did I dream then that it would be a full 400 miles before the condition of my tortured feet was not the dominant, unrelenting factor of my existence.

Despite the pain (and maybe even because of its effect of heightening my sensitivity) I found each day offered up adventures and experiences I would treasure forever. I write "each day" with careful awareness of its precise meaning. There was never a single day I would have done without. How different from my past life when whole weeks, even months passed at times without leaving a retrievable memory. When people have said, "How could you take the time out of your life to do this?" I respond that "so far this venture was not 'out of' my life but rather the heart and core of my life." But back then it was just the beginning. . .

Some of my journal entries are now humorous to me, some educational, some heart-warming, many tedious. I first encountered a snake theme even before the trip began. "My God! What are you going to do about snakes?" It hit me again only the second day out when the mushroom hunter lady crept fearfully with her snake weapon. In the Topeka motel I overheard a man outside my window, "I was cleaning out this hollow yesterday and found a cottonmouth." Another man answered "Yeah? Did you hear about Bill Marbey? He got bit by a copperhead last week." I was to venture forth the next day with every intention of camping out in this snake heaven. Oh well. . . I sighed again. But that was not to be the last of the snake theme. It would in fact plague and pursue me steadily across the entire country. There were times when it seemed to be the major preoccupation of the entire populus. Old men in cafes would invariably bring it up sooner or later among themselves. Tall tales would spin around my worried eavesdropping ears until I felt for all the world like David going out to meet Goliath the Snake.

But this day I was to cross the Kaw (Kansas River). It was an early milestone for the pioneers for whom it was often a terrifying experience. For me too it was not without its excitement. *I crossed the Kaw on a super highway bridge, and because there was no walkway I walked on the side ledge with the guard rail barely thigh high. The wind gusted, a big truck hit a bump, the bridge bounded wildly and I felt like the great Wallenda (famous tightrope walker), nearly, or so it felt, pitching into the muddy river far below. From there on I took my chances down on the pavement with the traffic. THAT'S what I probably should worry about anyway.*

In a motel I watched TV, "Elvis in Concert," his last one, which thankfully, got me out of my tiresome self-focus for a while.

It was a memorable day for Kansas beauty. The sky was blue with miles and miles of orderly fluffy white clouds. The rains had softened the ground to a perfect cushion. The shiny green ribbon grasses (wheat) shimmered and waved in the cool breeze, heaven, heaven, heaven. I was elated about life in general, and, of course, overdid it, walking 17 miles to Rossville.

I stopped for help in the local high school where some clear-eyed poised teenagers greeted me without suspicion. A young teacher, Steve Lewis, quickly invited me to his place for the night. Embarrassingly I was actually unable to lift my heavy pack into his pickup truck. We bounced along in the beat-up camper across the farm lands toward the old farmhouse that Steve and his wife Laurel were restoring. I could see it, a little dot across the fields as we approached. An old dream of mine was about to come true. Ever since my first trip out of the east in 1966, I'd been intrigued by farm houses which seem like little treed island oases in vast seas of crops stretching away in every direction. How often I had wondered what it would be like to be inside such a haven looking outward. My old wish was to be rewarded, and what a reward it would be!

On the way Steve said, "I often fantasize that this dirt road of mine was the old trail, and I can't tell you how many times I've marveled and wondered trying to imagine how the pioneers coped with the weather." He broke off wondering and swerved sharply to avoid a deep rut left over from the last rain storm. But today already the drying sun was starting to turn the old road into a dust hazard. Mud and dust—the pioneers were all too familiar with both conditions.

The Lewis' farm house was every inch a romantic, idyllic, old-fashioned movie set. Out comes the young plumping wife with baby to greet husband, long rows of flowers, iris, blooming in broad garden across the front yard, swing on a long rope from high on the shade tree limb, flock of chickens, red barn, freshly planted vegetable garden, endless flat plowed cornfields stretching away from the house on three sides, rolling pasture lands on the fourth side. Then a little girl runs up to her daddy and we go inside, boot rack on porch, flowers around back door, clothes line and bright clothes flapping in the breeze, tiny orchard, sand box, friendly dog running up with ball, bird houses. In the kitchen hard wood floor, old wood-burning stove with herbs hanging and drying about it, fresh cut flowers in center of round table, old-fashioned variety of chairs, old paddle butter churn, old tiffany lamp on the

54

table and on and on everywhere. Gingham curtains, cradle next to bed, freshly baked cookies brimming over in the cookie jar, bread loaves cooling on the wood stove, fragrant spices, coffee, flowers, and cookies. Every room with more dripping and unpretentious charm than the one before, needlework, patterned strawberry wallpaper.

Bread loaves cooling on the wood stove.   1979 ES

Steve, Laurel, kids, dog, cat, chickens… 1979 ES

In the midst of all this, Laurel was suffering a bit from an overdose of housewife syndrome, 24 hours a day mothering, farm isolation, etc. Steve was starting a chimney sweep business.

Steve and Laurel have had pigs, goats, bees, and chickens plus everything in the vegetable garden. Laurel has a ready market for everything in town because even though it's a farming area, the women who used to do gardening and barn chores for extra "pin money" now work in the towns at regular jobs.

For supper we had pancakes with sausage from their pigs and homemade elderberry syrup.

Next morning Laurel gave me a fragment of a china doll they had found while digging on their property. She said "Here, I want you to carry this. It came from the trail and was probably meant to go on." It stayed with me the whole way.

I left Rossville in the morning sunshine, bathed in the warmth and beauty of the people and farm and life I had shared for a few hours. Miles and hours of cornfields passed beneath my feet and eyes. I clung to the sweet memories all the harder as the unmistakable daily cycle of foot pain intensified. My yearnings for peace grew with every futile and desperate change of shoes and socks and back again. Finally I walked into the little village of St. Marys, and then after miles of empty fields and hostile heat, suddenly I was floating down tree-shaded streets with early-century houses gleamingly painted white, quaint, lovely architecture, small flowered, hedged yards, perfumed lilacs, neat sidewalks. An old Catholic mission, almost out of place in its grandeur and patient, quiet elegance, loomed graciously beside a tiny moss-walled brook which was bridged by a ferny walk. Vivid patches of sunshine dappled the cool, dark shade. I nearly wept with the beauty.

Two teenage girls approached and expressed friendly curiosity about "what are you doing?" Before they had the words out I had plunked down on the ground and peeled my socks and launched into a long explanation about each blister and bruise. Only later did I realize that my frantic explanations were hardly relevant to their question. Later that afternoon with St. Marys far behind, the two girls drove out to find me, with kindly concern to check on my *progress. I carry fine impressions of St. Marys.*

Toward evening, near tears with pain, I stopped for water at a farmhouse and was met by a very proper aproned grandmother and her two grandchildren. Before the first sentence was uttered, once again like a robot, there I was on the ground peeling off socks and pointing out blisters and swollen crooked toe nails in a compulsive mindless torrent of words. My left foot pinky was a pale white fluid balloon with a tiny dot indentation which was a toenail. On and on I rambled, utterly daffy. Only later was I to recall the startled puzzled expressions on the faces of the perfect strangers I accosted with my foot blather. The grandmother was moved to bring me some Mercurochrome and antibiotic salve from her medicine cabinet. She responded quickly as if an emergency had hit. Her concern, if not her salve, saved my day.

I limped on a final 2½ miles to an old Indian and pioneer cholera burial ground. A forlorn abandoned homestead was the only building within sight. A broken windmill leaned, screamed, whined, and moaned eerily as the wind gusted and the ancient fins tried to spin. An old man by the road glared at me. I hid in a scrub area behind the grave stones and camped numb with shock and worry. I was desperate with the fear that my feet wouldn't make it to Westmoreland (population 485) the next day. It was 16 miles away and I couldn't walk 16 feet! I slept fitfully, tormented by dive-bombing insects and howling packs of coyotes. In my journal I underlined, It would be such heaven not to be dominated by my pains.

In the morning I fell into a brief deep sleep, just as dawn was breaking. I awoke at 8:00 A.M. I popped my blisters with a sterile needle (a new procedure for me), applied Mercurochrome and salve, stretched my sneakers, took two penicillin pills, band-aided my feet, slipped into my thinnest socks and, with fear, slipped on my jogging shoes. I stood up, thinking that if my blisters were not a factor, I'd be the happiest person alive. I was incredulous: my feet DID NOT HURT! Step by step, no pain. I was dazed. Was my mind playing tricks on me? There was no time to waste. I felt I had to hurry.

I studied my maps and decided to set off cross country along the old trail. I could actually see the faint swale of the trace which emerged from the scrub and headed off over the pastures and hills to the northwest. I hit my high for the day, walking out of sight of roads or farms. I reveled in wild flowers, blue sky, birds, the softly rolling land stretching forever to the southern horizon, the hills to the north more pronounced. And then I lost my nerve. I headed east to a sure road, went down from the prairie hills to the scrub valleys, and in the process of avoiding thickets, I became totally lost, disoriented, wandering in every direction. Finally I dug deep into my pack for the compass and forgot whether it was the red side or the white side of the needle that pointed north. I followed the sound of distant machinery noises and eventually, shockingly, ended up stunned and back in the old burial ground where I had started hours earlier. I re-consulted my maps and headed west only to find the bridge over the Vermillion River was out. The current was too swift and deep for a wet crossing. My maps broke the deadening news: there would be a seven mile detour! I was dumbstruck. I had wasted precious feet and time wandering lost on the prairie and now a detour of seven miles struck as the final blow. Was I losing my mind? There was no choice but to go on.

I changed into shorts and a cool shirt, which was to be the final fatal mistake, and left the old pioneer burial ground for the third time that day. My journal best describes that long important day. *To make a long story short, blisters never once bothered me, but the arches and myriad muscles of my feet hurt with every single step. I cried a bit and paced off the miles one by one. Hours later, too late, I could feel my legs sun-burning but knew that if I ever stopped to put on pants, I'd be unable to get going again. I walked a total of 19 miles. I had underestimated the distance to town by a mile which meant 20 extra interminable minutes of agony. I stepped through town in a blur, went to the school with barely controlled hysteria, and sat down in the home economics room.*

Feeling like the biggest burden in the world, I was helpless to help myself. Somehow the fact that I had brought this condition upon myself by free choice made being a charity case all the more uncomfortable. The young student teacher coped by ignoring me, but a young girl staying after school broke the silence with a few questions. Eventually I was led to the principal's office under the premise, no doubt, that the buck stops there. Having stiffened alarmingly, my removal to that location was cause for comment around town for days. I proceeded up the hall inch by inch in a tight crouch.

Mr. Wilkerson eyed me with mild irritation as the unwanted burden that I was. Finding no one to take me off his hands, he reluctantly carried my pack to his truck and took me to his home where his wife, Nola, and their children viewed me with equanimity while keeping a discrete mental and physical distance.

I lowered myself awkwardly to the floor just inside their front door. For about an hour I actually could not move my legs or neck muscles. It was the worst I'd ever been. To change position I had to lift my legs with my hands. Finally I was able to crab walk to the bathroom. It was becoming apparent that my sunburn would be the worst problem; ankles and legs were swelling grotesquely, and the skin was turning a dark blotchy purple.

That night I lay in the basement and did some hard

thinking. I had not stopped to put on my pants because I would have been unable to move again and so had allowed my legs to turn to a crisp. *There are real questions in my mind about my own competence and sense,* I confided to my journal. *There's no excuse for allowing myself to get into such desperate physical condition. As a child I felt dominated by my body and at the mercy of my body-sickness, etc. As an adult, I decided to dominate my body with my head and so have said: "Body, you walk 20 miles," and have forced my body to do what my head dreams up. The time has come to listen to my body and incorporate it into me and to respect it and listen to its signals and warnings. I must stop driving myself from town to town and start having confidence in camping and stopping. There has to be some big changes in my head, or I'll never make it.*

By morning my leg muscles were better, but the severe sunburn made standing impossible, feet and legs swollen grotesquely. I wondered if they really would burst if I stood on them long. A nick with a paper edge brought forth a trickle of wetness from the tight edema.

I crawled about the house during the day and fixed lunch for five-year old Terry. We were alone, and I sat with Terry and ate what I estimated was a normal-sized portion. After we ate I gobbled what Terry had left on his plate. But my mind kept wandering back to the leftovers I had put in the refrigerator. Unable to stand it, I crawled back to the refrigerator and sneakily wolfed down the luncheon leftovers. But my eye had spotted another dish of leftovers from the night before. Within twenty tortured minutes, there I was crawling furtively back to the kitchen with an anxious eye on the front door as I prepared to click open the refrigerator door for yet another raid. I stopped momentarily thinking, "Dear God! Have I sunk this low? Stealing food from the people who I had forced to take me in?" But down went the food with nary a blink. It was my first but not to be my last experience with a runaway appetite. And my eating binge hadn't scratched its surface.

Later Nola returned home from school and recounted a conversation she'd had with a boy at school. The boy had warned, "I bet that when you get home that woman will have run off with half the stuff in your house." Nola and I roared with laughter as there I sat unable to stand let alone "run off" and carry anything else on my pack. But still, my mind WAS lingering longingly over a box of crackers I had spotted on the shelf ....

May 13 still at Wilkerson's I listened to my body which said, "not yet." I think I have not been a bad thing to happen to this family despite my uninvited arrival and over-long stay. Larry returned the money I had pressed on them. Maybe they're concluding that I'm not really such a weirdo after all and am actually human. So far all of my intrusions on people have, I think, been mutually rewarding. In every case I arrive bizarre and leave human and well tolerated. People respond to my terrific needs, and I respond with heartfelt appreciation (except when swiping food!). It's a situation that quickly fosters mutual love and appreciation.

The Wilkerson family   1979 ES

Doc   1979 ES

In the morning Nola took me to see "Doc," the local colorful character and editor of the town newspaper. "Doc" like the "Doc" in "Gunsmoke," the television show, had wrinkling squinty eyes, wore an old cowboy hat, and was surrounded with a wonderful aroma floating from his corncob pipe. Doc drove me back outside to a point out on the Oregon Trail ruts that had escaped my pain-blurred eyes days before. He pointed to the fields, and I strained with my full concentration.

"Now, do you see that hill coming down from the north?"

"Yes!"

"Now do you see the big slashes coming down the side?"

"Yes, oh yes!"

"Well, that's not the ruts."

"Oh."

"Those slashes are made by erosion, but the faint darker colored dips going at an angle are the real trail ruts. Do you see them?"

"Well, uh . . .yeah."

Not wanting to be a veteran Oregon Trail walker who couldn't even discern genuine ruts, I tried through sheer force of will to see the ruts, but my eyes were zipping frantically about without any real notion of where they were or what they looked like.

A year later on a revisit to Westmoreland, I confessed that I never really knew which darker shaded areas were the ruts. Nola sheepishly confided, "Honestly Barbara, I've gone out there with Doc too, and I'll be darned if I can find them either." We both finally laughed. It was a case of the Emperor and His New Clothes.

Westmoreland's pleasant green hollow traversed by a stream was a favorite camping spot for the wagon trains. I asked Doc for advice for my trip, and with a critical squinting eye on my purple bulging legs he said, "You know, those pioneer women knew more than anybody does today about what to wear on the trail. They had those long long skirts that kept off the sun yet still allowed ventilation. But the most important thing you already know," he continued tactfully, "and that is making friends along the way." I knew suddenly that he had spoken a truth. I would concentrate less on hiding and more on making friends. My mental set was changing importantly from one of defensiveness to one of assertive good will. Before I left,

Doc asked if he could snap a picture for the paper. It had begun to rain. As I hesitated to stand in the downpour, Doc cracked, "You were wet before you were dry, girl." And grinning through the deluge, I acquiesced.

I was grateful for shelter that day back with the Wilkersons. There were continual weather warnings on TV. The hail and windstorm became very powerful, frightening. The large white hailstones looked like popcorn popping all over the ground.

My forced physical recovery gave time for some more needed mental centering. I wrote in my journal: *Have been thinking of the mind-body business again. There's no doubt that I have been able to trance-like separate my consciousness from body torture and physical surroundings. I then plod on a rhythm for an hour, oblivious to everything but the random thoughts in my head. If someone interrupts with a ride offer, I'm amazed at how far away I was as I snap back to the present. In view of my body's revolt later, sunburn, blisters, etc., I think maybe this method is not good except in emergencies. My sunburned leg has been cooked about two inches deep. The pain is from the inside. I feel so very apologetic to my body for abusing it as a tool for my cerebral plans.*

Thinking more of the altered mental states while walking, I can have 2 or 3 definite mental activities, 1) my thoughts, 2) a definite yet not fully conscious singing of some song which spills through to consciousness only after quite a few verses and 3) subliminal awareness of where I'm putting my feet. The singing part is interesting. For a few miles before St. Marys, I was singing "The Bells of St. Marys" before I realized the song or what triggered it.

On my last day with the Wilkersons, Nola put aside her personal reticence and talked movingly of her grandmother, who immigrated from Germany at age four to western Kansas. She had remembered her father plowing (cutting) a furrow in the sod and the kids picking up the cut pieces and bringing them to make the sod house. Her grandmother recalled huddling on the deep windowsills set in the sod houses when it rained. It was the driest spot. She also was scared with the memories of snakes which often sought the sod house for their own. Nola talked of the windmills and pumps and her father "following the harvest." She talked of her own emergence as a person after finding that trying to be the perfect wife was not satisfying. Kansas or Boston, women follow similar patterns as we struggle to find an identity outside of unfulfilling prescribed roles. That evening with the Wilkersons, there was a warm feeling in the house. We were all happy to have found each other.

Sunday, May 14, on Mother's Day, the Wilkersons were more relaxed and happy than ever and solicitous of me. They sent me off without my pack, with promises to drive it to me later, which they did. They brought cookies and well wishes and warm, sincere pleadings to call collect if I ever needed help. As they left for the last time, Nola said, "We miss you already, and since you were here, we're seeing the countryside with whole new eyes." I blinked back a few tears and sighed as their car dipped out of sight. Why is it that everything seems to work out for the best? This interlude has been a rejuvenation, new body, new attitude. My mileage per day has been shot so there's nothing to do but calm down and go on. It was a sentimental Mother's Day as I thought of my own children and headed the last 2 ½ miles to Blaine.

KANSAS

... like a giant lazy roller coaster...   1979 ES

From Westmoreland to Blaine I followed the road like a giant lazy roller coaster. Each crest gave glimpses like the huge swells and rollers of the ocean. The pioneers thought so and said so too. The land is high and dry. At one crest I stopped and looked back and suddenly realized that I was leaving behind the Kansas River Valley forever. It was an uncanny awareness. That swell appeared no different from the rest, but it was the last possible glimpse of that land. I had labored 155 miles through it, the southern low hills, the fertile flat bottoms, and up and across the northern edge of the hills. The term "valley" is valley Kansas style. It appears to be incredibly subtle, hills 25 miles away and only a few dozen feet high, a vast flat land and more tiny hills, the Kaw River there somewhere, but invisibly tiny. Nevertheless, this barely perceptible valley was as vivid to me as Yosemite, and I'm sure I was tuning into pioneer awareness and emotion as I went over the crest of the hill and said "goodbye." Looking forward was thrilling. I felt the divide marked great progress. The day was a miracle, the breeze cooling, the pack riding effortlessly (for a change), my feet painless. A few more rollers and I gazed far, far ahead, toward Nebraska. It was like sensing the curvature of the earth by the ocean shore.

... like the helmets of crusaders   1979 ES

Then upon a modest crest to the left appeared the tips of a small army of cement crosses like the helmets of marching crusaders. What in the world were they? As I gained on the hill I discovered the crosses were the tips of tall Catholic Cemetery markers, plunked down there on the plains. Another scarcely believable sight arrested my attention: about two miles north on the crest of a long roller, gleaming red, strong red in the sun, rode a gothic-spired church, a three-story chunky brick schoolhouse, and a fat, square rectory. The blue sky formed a backdrop and the green-tan prairie the foreground setting. Surely I was about to witness a grand ethereal pageant. Closer inspection revealed a very few tiny white houses nestled in a trough near by, Blaine. But there were just a scant few houses with the empty prairie as far as the eye could see surrounding the tiny town. How and where did the people come from to fill the school and the cathedral?

A born and bred easterner finds it mindboggling to discover dirt roads stretching dozens and dozens of arrow-straight miles intersected at right angles rigidly every mile with identical dirt crossroads in a colossal grid-work pattern. But to top this off with a cathedral on the windswept prairie is inconceivable, but there it sits.

The huge cathedral in tiny Blaine 1979 ES

Later when I went into the church, I gasped. It was as elaborate and ornate with vaulted ceilings and gold statuary as in any big-city church. The stained glass window, robed figures, and Biblical scenes were as glorious as any I've ever seen. Astonished, I was told that there are two other similar cathedrals within ten miles, each representing the three tiny original ethnic settlements: Blaine was Irish Catholic; Wheaton, Dutch Catholic; and Fluch, German Catholic.

Scarcely believing my eyes, I walked past the bastion school (1928) and church and approached a Hispanic girl raking leaves. She invited me in. The Hernandez family, four teenage sisters and their mother, Benita, my age, incorporated me into their midst with total grace and naturalness. This Mexican family then fed me a most sumptuous meal. The enormous serving bowl of mashed potatoes drew me magnetically. Should I take lots of small helpings or a few tremendous ones? I couldn't stop. My body drove me despite my embarrassment and anxiety about my great cravings. As the meal wore on I consumed a half gallon of iced tea and the whole serving dish of mashed potatoes and gravy. First I craved the salty gravy and potatoes, then the sweet tea, then the potatoes and gravy, then the tea. I stared finally at the empty bowl and pitcher. I had eaten an enormous quantity of food, and I felt guilty about my gluttonous appetite, but my hunger had won, and I had eaten ravenously.

Benita and her girls.   1979 ES

Benita gave me a tour of her home, formerly the nuns' quarters for the cathedral and school next door. The sturdy old house was large, with carved newel posts, stained glass, and round windows in the entry and foyer. Years of neglect had cracked the plaster and darkened the carved woodwork, but when Benita told me she had bought it last year at an auction for $650, I knew I was in never-never land.

For the next four hours I lay on the library floor and listened to Benita's lilting Spanish accent as she led me through a Roots-type of narrative of her ancestors' migrations and struggles. It was a dreamlike recital as her cultural heritage met and diverged and re-met my WASP background. Although the temperature was warm, I shivered and felt very cold – sunburn? Sickness?

Benita had grown up in a family of 12 children. She was raised the old way, strict, no smoking, drinking, hanging around town. She was always required to dress properly.

Benita's winding recital hypnotized me as she led me entranced across the years. Her grandfather worked, slaved, in the mines. Her father farmed the land, "a little patch down by the Mexico-Texas border," clearing it acre by acre. Eventually the land was stolen from him in a shameful land swindle, but she had always yearned to buy it back since "his sweat and blood was in it." Her father, a proud and independent soul, was a rebel toward the Catholic Church. He pronounced the priests as corrupt; they took too much from the peasants.

Our dreamy reverie of the misty past was interrupted by a sharp knock on the door, and in strode "Pearl the Girl."

With "Pearl the Girl"   1979 ES

Pearl, a rawboned and large woman, had the presence of a giant, the appearance of a 40-year old, and the vitality of an adolescent. She was 60. She bowled me over with her thundering personality. Benita, Pearl and I talked far into the night, a coven of witches in a secret society. Benita and Pearl— two more alive and authentic souls I have never known. They talked about local history, and since the town of Blaine has declined rather than grown, all the old features are intact. It was as if the old days and the present moments were the same. The old nuns' quarters absorbed it patiently. Pearl said, "Since we'll never meet again, this is a good time to tell secrets," so with a devilish gleam she told me how 20 years ago when she was in her 40's, she . . . .

"My cup runneth over," said Pearl before she left. It expressed my feelings about the evening with these wonderful people.

I awoke to another glorious day and was on my way by 8:00 A.M. "My cup runneth over. My cup runneth over." That benediction from Pearl the night before overflowed from somewhere inside me, and I found myself chanting it as I walked. After a few miles I again perceived a basic landscape change. The Oregon Trail had followed the Kaw River Valley, had hauled up to the huge dry lands, keeping as usual to the high ridges. Now, I could see in the soft distance, it was headed toward another almost imperceptible but more heavily treed depression, the Valley of the Little Blue River, which I would follow deep into Nebraska.

I turned into a crude gravel road which was to take me many miles past abandoned farms. At the turn a hokey farm sprawled in disarray. Unlike a good or bad housekeeper, the farmer's mess or tidiness sits outside for all the world to see. A man and woman eyed me suspiciously, hands shading eyes. I called out assertively, "Good morning! I'm walking the Oregon Trail." The change was dramatic. There was an immediate relaxation and sigh of relief, and they repeated and called to each other, "She's walking the Oregon Trail. She's walking the Oregon Trail," in a vivid hillbilly twang of amazement.

I pushed on in a state of peace and grace, at one point even forcing myself to stop just to soak in the heady beauty. By mid-afternoon, I was deep into the stupor of pain and heat once again as I sat on the steps of an 1881 one-room school house to change my shoes in a futile attempt to make things nice like they had been earlier. I then ate 1 can of tuna, ½ cup of peanut butter, ⅓ cup of honey, ⅓ cup of wheat germ, ¼ cup of bran, ¼ cup of sunflower seeds, and drank a pint of water. There seemed to be no limit to the quantity I could consume once I got started.

Finally, hours later, the rarely used road dipped from the sweltering fields into a cool hollow. I passed an ancient stone hog barn, saw a windmill sticking up and the jumble of sheds and small barns. Then the small, very very old house showed through the trees. A colorful, profuse flower bed nestled around the house in the tight little hollow, and I thought hopefully, "People who like flowers this much must be good people." I could feel my sunburned face throbbing; my back and pack were soaked with sweat. I opened the ancient gate— "the Smiths" it said, and I crossed the tiny stepping-stone yard, passed a red water pump and lots of kittens, and knocked on the door. The reassuring grin of an old healthy farmer greeted me. "My cup runneth over." Now almost a year later, I can still feel the nervous, anxious anticipation and the flood of grateful relief when that unforgettable smiling face appeared.

Clarence and Lillian Smith have farmed this tiny shady farm in the hollow since 1931. They are both 77 and look and act 60. Clarence is topped with an up-swinging overgrown brush cut, of all things! When they first came, half a century ago, they routinely found Indian arrowheads, and artifacts by their creek, but not knowing their value, covered them to expand the fields. The farm was built by homesteaders who worked it till 1931 when the Smiths bought it. It is a vivid contrast to most western farms in that it's cozy and tightly treed in its protective hollow. That's probably why the Indians and first homesteaders chose that spot. The chicken yard provides an incessant cackling background hum. Lillian showed me the historic stone barn, stone hen house, and two half stone red barns similar to a root cellar, entered by cellar type doors. Inside are shelves lined with canned goods from the vegetable garden, crocks, etc. Sometimes the crocks are built into the floor for sauerkraut.

KANSAS

Occasionally on my journey a person would make a simple gesture or statement that would be such an appropriate expression of support or approval for me that indeed it seemed made in heaven. Lillian never did do much talking, but soon after I arrived, hot and bone-weary and footsore, she eyed my sweat-soaked pack with curiosity. Then in an endearing gesture she accepted my suggestion to try it on. Clarence and I hoisted the wet sweaty 38-pound monster onto her 77-year old petite back, and she teetered about the tiny living room exclaiming, "Ohhhhh, it feels like it's pulling me backwards." In her own way she said she was impressed that I was carrying such a heavy thing and thereby endeared herself to me.

There was a poignant shadow hanging over the Smiths. Their little farm so pulsating with sentimentality was to be sold that fall. They were living their last spring, their last summer, their last months and weeks and days there. After half a century of plowing and gathering fresh eggs and weeding the flowerbeds, the Smiths were leaving, moving into town. Clarence said that sometimes this made him feel so sad that his heart hurt, "but," he said bravely, "there comes a time when you just have to let go." Somehow I felt that the old farm would hate to let go of them too.

The Smiths gently and unknowingly forced me to make a big policy decision about my trip. The Benton Farm, a commune, was nearby. The Smiths had a special relationship with these people and wanted to take me there for a visit. Spending an extra day would set me another day behind the Donner Party timetable, yet surely it would be foolish to wear tight blinders in pursuit of my Donner goal. The trip had a way of unfolding to unforeseen opportunities so far. To hell with my schedule; I would visit the commune with the Smiths. This flexibility became a part of my

76

philosophy and was to serve me well in the future. Through it, however, my ultimate goal never wavered, as the man on the bus to St. Louis had suggested.

Thomas Hart Benton, the famous painter and friend of President Harry Truman (who called him the "best damn painter in America") started a commune near the Smiths. Previous to the Kansas purchase, the commune had two branches, one in Boston and one in Los Angeles. I was told that when a farming branch was needed the planners drew a line between Boston and Los Angeles, circled an area halfway between, and bought land within that area.

Communes (throughout the country and especially to conservative mid-plains people) connote images of drugged hippies, free love, and bare breasted women behind plows. I assumed these images to be incorrect... and yet, well, I was curious. There was something about the way old Clarence lauded and defended his commune friends that impressed me. There was courage and independence in the way he stood up for them. I wondered if he had endured criticism from the local Kansas folk for his association. "They're just grand, fine people," Clarence earnestly declared of the commune community. "Why, whenever I need some help here on the farm, they just come right over and never ask for a cent, and that's the way it works when they need a hand or advice from me. Aw heck, they're just the nicest people, I just can't find anything bad to say about them. Now they do have babies there, there's no doubt about that, and I don't know that any are married, but where and how those babies come from, well, I just figure that's their business. I'll tell you one thing, I just can't get over how nice those people are. Why I have no complaints at all."

Clarence drove the long mud-rutted road to the Benton Farm, someday hopefully big enough to be named

Bentonville. He pointed to some high hills along the way that are topped with Indian burial mounds, but I strained ahead to catch the first glimpse of the larger-than-life people I expected to see.

We pulled up to a collection of buildings set among some rare Kansas hills. Not only was there no beehive of activity, there was no one around. I took a minute to give my eye a critical inspection tour. There were neat fields of crops, a few barnyard animals grazing here and there, a couple of saggy barns, a nice enough old house, and a new structure, a large building constructed high and against a hill. Finally a tall, lanky guy unwound himself awkwardly from some farm machinery he was repairing and shyly suggested we try the old house to find someone.

In the old house we found a young woman squeezing bags of dripping stuff making cheese. She said that she had tried something new with it and that the cheese was good. UMMmm... She didn't have to tell me; I could smell it and felt nearly frantic wanting some. Instead, she offered us coffee. A few more adults wandered in and we all sat around the table. We could have been any collection of ordinary people anywhere. The commune people drank coffee by the gallon and smoked like chimneys. So much for the health image!

Another man came into the kitchen and lounged next to the stove where the coffee was brewing. Divora, the woman sitting next to me, stood up and went through considerable inconvenience climbing over people and chairs to fetch and serve him the coffee he stood six inches from. So much for the image of new roles for women!

I was interested to hear that they went to great effort to avoid sending their children to the public schools. "Aahaaaa," I thought, "here comes the wild, free school scene!" But in fact they were about as old-fashioned and strict as possible: copy books, drilling, writing misspelled words 100 times each, etc. The children are in school from 8:00 to 12:00 and again from 1:00 to 4:00 with homework until 9:30 P.M.   So much for the free school scene!

Divora graciously took time from her million chores to give a tour of the farm. At the moment there were 13 adults and 15 children living there. The number of adults is variable since they travel freely between the three sections across the country.   Their goal is to be self-sufficient eventually, with the farm the major food supplier for the three.   As I listened to their worthy and ambitious goals and looked around the tiny conclave, I paled at the thought of the work ahead and silently rooted for them as one would for a favorite team way behind in a lopsided score. The current crisis was the broken farm machine, but it wouldn't be long before the sagging barn would threaten collapse, and the approach road would become impassable through the swamp and ... and ... So much work and so few people! But the big house on the hill was their pride and joy, as indeed it merited. They cut and cured and stained their own lumber from their own land. They hand-carved their own banisters and drew and designed their own plans. Antique furniture from Europe purportedly used by the Three Musketeers, tables and ancient chairs, reposed in settings worthy of their importance. The house was creative and impressive.

After two hours of imposition on these people struggling against heavy odds to do so much work, we turned to leave. I wished I could have talked with Divora longer, but my real questions were too impertinent for a mere two-hour acquaintance. With our thoughts on history, Divora showed me an old child's school slate with a little girl's name scratched on it which had been turned over unexpectedly by a plow in the field. Thoughtfully, she said. "Did you ever think that you might be one of the Donner Party reincarnated?"

"Not really," I said. Such a thought seemed too presumptuous.

Later as I prepared to leave, Clarence Smith gave me a buckeye to carry for health and luck. I carry it still. I waved goodbye as the old road dipped down past the enormous elm tree.

The commune kitchen.   1979 ES

Late in the day I passed the townsite of Bigelow. No buildings remain in the area where the town once flourished. Virtually every speck of evidence was removed in case of flooding, by the detested Army Corps of Engineers to build a "damn dam" downstream. Along the road, however, bloom patches of day lilies and iris planted by an old woman, Mary Carpenter, fifty years ago. She planted flowers on her daily walk to the post office. It's all that remains of Bigelow.

In parts of Kansas there are miles and miles of stone fence posts. I am told they are limestone. When first removed from the earth and cut, they are soft. After years of air and weather exposure, they become very hard.

After walking an hour, a wizened farmer drove up and stopped his pickup truck. He smelled of alcohol, red shiny face, and my prejudices flared up. I got ready to smash him with my water bottle if necessary. He asked me the usual questions and seemed impressed. He contributed a few trail rut stories and blearily studied the map. Later (hour) he drove up again and pulled in front of me, blocking my way. Again I got ready to smash him, but I was in for a surprise. He had gone home and his wife had baked some cookies which he then gave me in a brown paper bag with a big bottle of Pepsi Cola. I was humbled.

Walked 12 miles in four hours. Right in the middle I was overcome and overwhelmed unexplicably with a desperate longing for my family. Did Paula need me? I was nearly frantic with the conviction that they wanted me to call. Marysville was too far away and I started to cry. Now here's a secret. When I'm out in nowhere without a house visible for miles, I indulge in unrepressed, uninhibited crying. I make a face like little crying kids. I make noises like little kids, and then I make up my own most (to me) heart rendering wails, like a little kid getting a shot, etc. Then I decide to send my peace vibes to the family telepathically, and I felt better. I can only guess the whole thing was a hormone swing. But I remained shaky for the rest of the night.

Before approaching farms to inquire about camping on their property, I go through my quick routine to make me look harmless and friendly: off with the sunglasses and bonnet, neaten my hair, straighten my bowed back, relax and brighten my face. I do have a cynical streak.

After I introduce myself, name, where I'm from, what I'm doing, etc., I say "My husband and kids are joining me on the trail as soon as school's out." That's always the softener. "Ahhh ... She's a MOTHER ... and her family is going to WALK together." Pause ... "Would it be OK with you if I unrolled my sleeping bag somewhere on your property for the night?" smile. . .

Once I was dumbstruck. "No, I think not. I don't know you and I don't trust you." I was a woman alone, at night, in the middle of nowhere, crippled with sore feet, exhausted. Me? Dangerous? After a tear quivered threateningly on my eyelash, they relented. I hobbled to the yard and dropped and kept wiping the now flooding tears with my sweaty sleeves. I must have looked as forlorn as I felt because the people were nice to me after that with kind offers of inside shelter for sleep. But I stayed outside.

One morning a farm family invited me in for a chat which lasted two hours. Their final conclusion was that a city child could benefit much from a visit to a farm, but a visit to a city by a farm child would be worthless.

On the table was half a grapefruit, uneaten. Later on the road I was mad at myself for not asking for the grapefruit.   Mile after mile I was obsessed with mouthwatering thoughts of that damned grapefruit.

I was approaching an important landmark on the Donner Trail. I put aside my 20th century preoccupations for a while and pondered the 1846 scene. Prominent among the Donner Party was the Reed family. James Reed, the father, was a dynamic and impetuous co-leader of the wagon train. His wealth and arrogant manner often separated him from the rest of the party who, in the frontier code of the day, respected wealth but resented its conspicuous display. His wife, Margaret, a frail 32-year old woman, had borne four children and, we are told, suffered from migraine and various other complaints. Traveling with James, Margaret, and the four children was Sarah Keyes, Margaret's mother. Having raised her own family, Sarah was well on in years and failing but stubbornly refused to be separated from Margaret, her beloved and only daughter. One blinks and rereads this passage. An old woman near the end of her years leaves behind grown sons and a comfortable life to follow her married daughter into the wilderness. Sarah's devotion was firm, so firm that James Reed had a special wagon built, oversized and with a springy feather bed, just to ease the journey for his mother-in-law. It is a story with a Victorian sentiment oddly startling to 20th century senses accustomed to 20th century love stories.

During the last week in May 1846, barely as the journey had begun, Sarah Keyes died. Her granddaughter clipped a lock of her hair which she would carry through to California. Sarah was buried in an achingly beautiful little valley that was named Alcove Spring. Here a small streamlet spills over a rock ledge into a ferny glen, and the grass grows green and lush in the natural meadow. James F. Reed carved his name and the date on a boulder within the natural enclave.

Alcove Spring   1979 ES

     Late in May 1978, I climbed over the fence through beer cans and walked back to the half-forgotten little spring. The stream bed is a jungle of tossed boulders. My eye wandered across the lumpy landscape as I began to climb across. Without any strain or search, I looked down and there it was: J.F. R(eed) worn away, 26 May 1846. I sat next to it resting my hand on the bumpy surface for a while, and then I got up and limped on.

1846, faintly visible   The Reed boulder   1979 ES

The day I stopped at Alcove Springs was also a big day for dogs. Throughout the journey I was to be an object of thundering excitement for thousands of dogs patrolling thousands of farmhouses. Time and again they would spot me coming and either wait lazily until I came abreast of their property or zealously rush for the confrontation on first sight. In either case we came to immediate agreement: I would not alter my route or pace one iota, and they were free to put on an impressive pyrotechnic show of noisy defense. I perceived a sense of mutual amusement in that arrangement.

But on the day of Alcove Spring, I found myself out of water in addition to the other tediously familiar complaints of fatigue, overheating, and mind-dulling foot pain. I turned into the circular drive of an old house with the intention of asking for a refill of my water bottle. Half way to the front door the peaceful scene electrically erupted into a bedlam of a dozen (or more) snarling, snapping, growling, barking dogs, all sizes but of similar rotten dispositions. They leaped from under the shrubbery and dashed out from under the cars. Crossing in front of their house would have been provocative enough but to actually walk ON their territory! This surely was a declaration of war to them. Such audacity! Unforgiveable.

During those hours of the day when my physical agony weighed heavily with every step, my spirit and will followed unusual priorities. In this case even mad dogs were not enough to induce me to take one extra or unnecessary torturous step backward. My goal was to get some water from this house. To turn back then would have made the painful 30-foot trudge in vain. So I continued on through the astonished dogs up to the porch and knocked. It didn't occur to me until later that the woman's shocked expression on seeing me was the realization that her dog defenses had been pierced, but she gave me the water, and I continued around and out the circular drive with the dogs snarling in impotent fury. I'll never know why those dogs didn't bite. I think that my abnormal attitude of determination and preoccupation with other things beyond fear threw them off. Later I looked back on that interlude in amazement. Once again, "Fools rush in where angels fear to tread." Maybe naivety does have advantages now and then.

I checked into an old Gunsmoke-TV-show-type hotel, old men sitting in the paneled lobby, ancient elevator, cracked Spartan plaster rooms. The little booth-filled restaurant downstairs serves luscious food, cheap and lots and wonderful 24 hours a day. My room is $7 per night. I'm on the third floor and, surprise... right over the railroad tracks, DING DING DONG whoooooo whooooo and the windows rattle mightily, and the bed shakes punctually *every 30 minutes. The hot water tub faucet is so mineral-encrusted that the water comes out as if through a hypodermic needle. It took 20 minutes of fierce running before it got hot and 45 minutes to fill the tub. I love it.* (A year later this venerable old hotel had closed. I peered through the windows into a sad and empty lobby, the marble floors already in deep layers of aging dust, so sad…)

My interactions with people are very emotional and draining, and staying alone in this hotel is very much needed. It restores and rejuvenates me. Today walked 14 ½ miles, 2 new blisters, toe and heel.

The term "limp" connotes an image of walking out of balance to favor an injured foot or leg or hip, but when both feet and legs are exuding pain with every step, then the whole gait becomes peculiar. To keep the pack from bouncing, to land as softly as possible on the heel, to avoid bending the feet too far, to place the foot on whatever angle of surface would take pressure off the sorest parts, to keep the stride short enough to minimize pain but long enough to keep moving, to put full weight on each foot as short a time as possible; these were the delicate factors to be gauged and adjusted with exquisite precision. The tension of walking on egg shells or thin ice must be similar. Each hour of walking in a day accelerated this accumulation of tensions until my whole being felt embattled and a touch of dementia would set in.

Small and large instances of kindness from strangers again and again would bring me back to rationality. The unexpected gentle concern of farmers, "Whaddar ya doin?. . . I sure do admire ya for it, Madam." "Thad house up thar is empty and yer sure welcome to it if ya need a place to spend the night." "I sure would be happy to drive you up the road a piece, but I understand your decision to walk it all the way." In one section the farmers plowing for miles and miles somehow passed word along about what I was doing and my pitiful-looking condition. Each would come to the edge of the field to offer water and encouragement and concern as I passed his section. Once a tractor pulled up on the road behind me. I was too pained and stiff to turn to look, but the soft and gentle way he decelerated and stopped said as much as his kind words.

Emil and Lula with pump cover and artifacts.   1979 ES

One man passed me not saying a word but beamed the most radiant smile I have ever seen. I turned into the lane leading to the loveliest farmhouse and barns and flowerbeds and vegetable gardens and lawns imaginable. It reminded me of the Country Morning cereal boxes. It was owned by a German family, the Heistermans, who kept things in a state of perfect German tidiness. Mr. Heisterman was the man who had beamed the silent smile. He hadn't spoken verbally because a laryngectomy had taken his voice box. But I learned something about communicating in that house. Perhaps because he couldn't talk, he was vividly expressive with his eyes and manner, radiant with emotion and eagerness and encouragement, bursting with things unsaid. Occasionally he used a pencil and pad on which he wrote with great care and neatness; no quick scribbling for him.

Mr. Heisterman had a lifetime of interest in the Oregon Trail, which traversed his crop fields. Since he was unable to communicate freely, the situation was poignant but bridged somewhat, I think, by our mutual appreciation. He disappeared and reappeared with his arrowhead collection carefully mounted and framed, at least 50 perfect various sized arrowheads, all found on property he'd farmed. He had spent many hours searching plowed fields after rains. He also showed me a pony shoe, a mule shoe, and an oxen shoe he'd found on the Oregon Trail across his land.

That night I slept on their land. Mrs. Heisterman the night before had viewed me with some suspicion and distrust that I had not fully dispelled. In the morning Lula Heisterman said that she knew I wasn't bad because she'd been able to sleep during the night, and if I'd been a bad person, she wouldn't have been able to sleep. It was her acid test, and I passed it.

As I was packing to leave, I heard a shy knock, and in came Emil Heisterman who sweetly presented me with a little four-leaf clover for luck. He disappeared and after a while came back with two more, real thank-you good-luck offerings. I placed them deep in my map pile by Utah and California for a surprise when I got that far. It didn't seem possible then. Mrs. Heisterman and I had also become friends at last, and I left with unexpected emotion.

One year later when I drove the route, Mr. Heisterman emerged carrying a flat stone originally turned up by his plow 14 years before and since then having served as a filter cover for his water pump. A few months after my visit he had walked past the innocent looking stone just as he had a thousand times before, but he stopped and looked again. The angle of the sun had thrown into shadowed relief what appeared to be faint lettering. The year "1842" was visible, and after hours of searching the weathered slab, the words "Rest in Peace" appeared. A tantalizing puzzle, the pioneer grave marker yields its secrets slowly. The letters "Edna" and "18__" have been deciphered, traced as the tenuous connection of human beings therein to bridge the gap of over 100 years. Mr. Heisterman has a new pump cover, although surely not as exotic as the first.

A few hours later I suddenly realized I was on my last Kansas mile. In a burst of emotion I turned and looked back. Goodbye, Kansas. I wept tears of thankfulness that I had reached the border and that I had left behind a successful struggle, thereby part of me.

7

NEBRASKA
May 19 – June 1
(172 miles)

Even more
because of being alone
the moon is a friend.
Buson

Asleep under the prairie skies.   1979 ES

Nebraska looked flatter immediately, more open and less settled. Now and then I got a knock-out whiff of hog manure. *"Why is it that the wind always blows my way just as I pass the hog farms! Whew!"* I grumbled into my journal. I took a primitive farm road and inched my way through two miles of thick marijuana along the ruts. Farmers are supposed to use weed control to eliminate the marijuana. It's a common joke among the farmers after still another bad year for crop prices that "we'd be a heck of a lot richer if we'd herbicide sprayed the corn and harvested the marijuana instead."

The ironclad old-fashioned rules of morality are alive and well in the rural mid-plains. The attitude toward marijuana reflected this stability. Nowhere did I ever discern even the faintest curiosity about trying it; in fact, there was a widely propagated and subscribed myth among adults and children alike that "this stuff that grows around here ain't the smoking kind anyhow." The hippies, occasionally sighted picking it along the roads, were dismissed quickly as so many alien vermin best handled with a quick call to the sheriff. The notion that any ordinary human being like you or me would ever smoke the stuff was incomprehensible.

I listened in quiet horror one evening to the editor of a small town paper who told approvingly of a local vigilante group who "knew" of a man pushing drugs to young school children. Impatient with the slow "due process of law," the group took the "pusher" for a ride to an empty stretch of road with a ditch and "put a bullet through his head." I gasped, speechless, dumbfounded. "Sometimes that's the only way to do it," the editor stated with an air of self-satisfied finality.

I reeled in disbelief. The world was suddenly out of whack. This was 1978, not 1900, and this was rural mid-plains farming country, not the deep south, and these farming people were the most loving and generous and cordial I had ever met anywhere. And yet at that very minute some of my friends back east were probably smoking pot as easily as the farmer lights up a Marlboro cigarette now and then. Then somehow my innocent friendships in the east made me feel vulnerable. Would I be judged guilty by my associations? I shivered, but the editor and farmer were soon talking of other things, and their faces and manner were as normal as my own father's. That night the katydids sang me to sleep, and by morning with the world fresh and sunny, the previous night's conversation seemed a fragment of a disjointed (!) bad dream.

But daily I was falling deeper and deeper in love with the Kansas and Nebraska farm country, the people, the land. Like a Grant Wood painting, life on the farm was straightforward and clear.

One day I was in a race with my feet again, no panic, just the familiar daily tension of wondering if I'd find a camping place before they gave out completely. I spotted a farm. No other was in sight for miles. My feet were done. It HAD to be this one. I took a deep breath, tense. Then, thank God, I saw a young woman weeding with a baby carriage nearby. It knew it would be OK, and it was.

With Jan I helped "deliver lunch" to her husband in the fields. It wasn't my idea of women's lib, but somehow it seemed right. We bounced along the lane in the pickup truck (what else?) until we spotted the tractor far across the field. Lloyd was preparing the earth for planting corn. The tractor slowly made its way down the furrows toward us. He joined us and wolfed down his "lunch." It was 5:30 P.M., but he would remain in the fields until dark before returning home for his fourth and last meal of the day.

We were sitting next to an abandoned one-room school house. Lloyd's neatly plowed furrows diverged and encircled it. "I went to school there as a kid," he stated simply. It was fitting and perfect that he was so intimately rooted to this land patch on this face of the earth. Swept away with the romanticism of it all, I asked Lloyd if the planting was the best time of the year for him. "Naw," he chuckled, "I think I like the harvest best. When I'm planting, I get pretty tense trying to hold that tractor steady to make the rows straight."

"He does have the straightest rows of all the farmers around here," Jan added proudly.

Lloyd in front of his old school house. 1979 ES

It was easy to be proud of Lloyd, a big ox of a man, sturdy, simple, honest, and good. He rarely spoke but his silence was the silence of content. He openly adored their new baby, especially thrilled that it was a boy... (No women's lib there.) His devotion was beautiful, his manner calm and sure.

Lloyd's worry about straight rows was one I found amusing. What did it matter, I thought, with greater problems like hail storms and droughts and farm prices so much more logical and worthy of worry. But the straight-row fetish surfaced again and again crossing the plains. It was right up there comparable to crabgrass and dandelion shame in the east. One farmer went so far as to hire another man to plant the rows visible from the road so the neighbors wouldn't see and laugh at his wavy ones farther in.

A farmer outside Ogallala sat gazing out his window from the breakfast table. The corduroy ridges of last year's wheat crop stretched in a straight-ribbed pattern to the horizon. "Thank heaven my brother-in-law planted those rows straight," he sighed. "Imagine having to look at crooked rows for two whole years!" (Wheat is planted every other year with fallow years alternating with the crop years.)

A man in Cozad praised a particularly attractive farm on the basis of its crop rows. "Just look at those straight rows!" he beamed even as I was more admiring the handsome barn and flowerbeds. To each his own.

But apparently there was more to this crop row pride than I had first assumed. Farmers preferred flat land partly because they could make the rows straighter. In the endless Nebraska farmlands, a Sunday afternoon ride in the family car became an outing, especially for townspeople, to inspect the local farmers' rows. One farmer joked about old Jim, who, I was told with a twinkle, "planted his corn in wavy rows to make the rows longer and thereby get a bigger crop!" I laughed heartily but secretly scratched my head for a while trying to figure out why that wouldn't work.

Judy   1979 ES

Not all Nebraska was as predictable as the seasons. One sparkling surprise stands out as a sunflower among daisies. In a typical forgettable cozy village, Endicott, population 167, I doubled back to a tiny cottage where a woman about my age had given me a nice smile. She met me at the door and without preliminaries invited me to stay overnight. Our rapport was total and instantaneous. We both love butter, were 37, played the flute, read the same books, have thirteen-year-old sons and hate cooking. As we sat munching snacks in her charming cottage, Judy spun a tale of her adventures 14 years before that seemed all the more incongruous in the peaceful conservative Nebraska setting. She had run off with a German poet to Mexico where, totally broke, they visited ancient ruins, lived with peasants, begged rides and food, walked a lot, and barely survived. She contracted malaria, and tests revealed she had 10 tropical diseases. After having a baby, she divorced her vagabond husband, whose violent streaks were becoming too hard to live with.

But the revelations of that Nebraska afternoon were not over. Judy confided that she, alone in the endless conservative farm country, she, all by herself, is a practicing Hindu. She receives instructions from her guru in Hawaii by mail, meditates daily early in the morning. Very early next morning I awoke to the faint, exotic aroma of oriental incense. I foolishly found myself strangely unnerved and tried to get back to sleep. It wasn't exactly that her practices were secret, but somehow, recalling the violent anti-marijuana reactions, I felt it was a private thing, very fragile in Nebraska. How different in Boston where the Hare Krishna people and Black Panthers rub elbows with everyone else on the subways.

Reincarnation is not a scary word to a Hindu, and Judy stated flatly that I was probably a reincarnated member of the Donner Party, one who didn't make it the first try in 1846. The notion was romantic enough to entice me to spend a few moments wondering just who I might have been in the cast of characters. I was amused to find myself selecting only the noble ones as possibilities. "Let's see now, was I Margaret or Tamsen or..."

My close rapport with Judy faded a bit before we parted. I was sad to feel this happening. For a while I thought I had found a rare soul mate to share mutual understanding (if not religions). But as we talked I found a disturbing and basic difference between us. Perhaps because of Oriental beliefs, perhaps simply because no two people are alike, Judy and I disagreed about women's paths in life. She felt that there was a natural harmony in male as leader, female as follower, or a man as dominant, a woman as submissive. But, I left with the image of that sunflower growing and thriving in the patch of pretty daises.

On Judy's wall hangs a framed Hindu saying:

A kindness done in the hour of need

may itself be small,

But in worth, it exceeds the world.

As I walked away from her house, I thought of all the small gestures of humanity that people had offered on my journey: the free cotton candy, the foot massages, the band-aids and fresh cookies, the four-leaf clovers and the buckeye, the extra ice in my water jug and warm words of encouragement, the waves and smiles and small gestures of caring that defy description. Even the smallest good wishes took on extraordinary power to fuel me, to anesthetize pain, to buoy my sagging optimism. Judy's adopted Hindu culture knew about such things and expressed the truth which I repeated many times that day:

> A kindness done in the hour of need may itself be small, But in worth it exceeds the world. (Sometimes I changed it to "in weight it exceeds the world." I liked both ways.)

In Fairbury, Nebraska, an encouraging woman named Barbara summoned reporters from three newspapers to interview me. So far the unexpected interest in papers along the way had been fun, but a familiar pattern was emerging that was starting to irritate me. It was the reporters' version of the common first comments of many.

"But what does your husband think of you doing this?"

"I can't believe your husband let you do this."

"Hello," said the reporter. "Where are you from?"

"Boston area."

"Are you married?"

"Yes."

"What's your husband's name?"

"Howard Maat."

"What does he do?"

"He's a college professor."

"What does he teach?"

"Philosophy and English."

"Oh," heavy laden, "What college?"

"North Country Community College."

"Where's that? What does he think of all this? Do you have any children? How old? Boy or girl? What are their names?"

Then, after I had been thoroughly defined by my husband and children, the reporter asked, "What is your name?"

It wasn't that this information was not important, because some of it was, or that people weren't interested in this, because they were. It was just the priority and order of things that annoyed me. Somehow I couldn't imagine a reverse situation, a reporter interviewing a man hiking the Oregon Trail. "Hello, are you married? What's your wife's name? What does she do? Where does she work? What does she teach?" And then, "Oh yes, what's your name again? Howard?"

A few times I said, "I'd just as soon not talk about my husband because this trip is mine." This was usually accepted although one reporter in the Nebraska panhandle became belligerent. (Interestingly, he went on to write a very nice article.)

In Fairbury, the interview continued. I was learning to hold my breath for the question sure to pop up that I never could answer satisfactorily. "Why are you doing this?" There it was. "Well, I aaah, because I want to." A glance at the reporter told me as usual that this was not enough. "I want to see what it was like for the pioneers." That sounded silly and juvenile. Besides, one reporter pointed out with contempt, the pioneers didn't have roads with restaurants along the way. "Well, I aaah, uh. I just felt it was something I had to do." Whoops. There I was painting myself as the compulsive, obsessive neurotic and a weird one at that.

"What made you do this? Are you just trying to prove you can do it?" the reporter helpfully coached.

Truthfully and honestly the answer was no, but my paranoia made me bristle. And so it went, week after week, fumbling, groping for an answer that would be truthful and play well, but it never came. It still hasn't.

But the Fairbury reporter probed more deeply than many. After initial skepticism, he continued the questioning. Ever the naive optimist, I said that I saw signs that things were getting better with my feet because I hadn't cried for four whole days. "But if it's been that bad," he said leaning forward earnestly, "why in the world haven't you given it up and gone back home? No one could say you didn't give it a good try."

That questions made perfect logical sense, but from my side it was ludicrous. I felt a great gulf between the two of us—and probably just about everyone. My difficulties had been severe, mentally and physically. A quick hop on a bus would have ended all the fear and pain honorably. But my problems were of no consequence next to the personal rewards the trip dished up every day. I never even remotely considered giving it up.

I would have missed too much. I would have missed a little bird roosting resolutely in her favorite bush two feet from my head for the overrated comfort of my own soft bed at home. I would have sacrificed the electric tingling of trying to outrace a thunderstorm for the bland experience of watching it safely from inside my real estate office. The little scraps of paper with names and addresses lodged in the corners of my pack served as testimony to the new friendships that bloomed daily. To continue was no big deal; anyone would have done the same. The trip fed on itself, but I fear I was not successful in conveying this.

The reporter ended the interview and asked for a picture of me changing my socks. As I stooped to comply, I unceremoniously rolled backward off my feet because of the unbalancing weight of my backpack. There I lay momentarily like a turtle on its back, arms and legs waving feebly in the air. Now THAT would have been a picture for the front page, but the humane man waited tactfully for me to right myself before he clicked.

Right or wrong, fair or not, there's no doubt that publicity helped my journey by making people more receptive to me. There was nothing like a newspaper story to make me legitimate, to turn people from ordinary skeptical frowners to smiling encouragers. A few days after Fairbury, the heat and foot agony became almost unbearable. I turned into a shaded drive that led to a pleasant farmhouse. Sheltered from the driving ferocity of the blazing sun, I slowed my pace to a snail's on the approach to the door. After lots of knocking a gracious but startled woman opened her door for me. My story about walking the pioneer trail sounded unlikely and preposterous to her, but she tried to hide her confusion as she escalated her hostess gestures. "Well, come in ... Sit down... Here's

some water... Would you like ice? I'll put some ice in ...
Come out here in the kitchen... Would you like iced tea?
Are you hungry? Maybe you'd like a piece of rhubarb pie.
Would you like a piece of rhubarb pie?"

Dear God, would I ever! But I said discreetly, "I'd
love some." As I was about to leave, I glanced down on a
chair and saw the *Lincoln Star* paper. We both saw it at the
same time, and on the front page was the picture of me
changing my socks. Instantly the good woman's
nervousness vanished and her human curiosity took over.
"But, but... well, my goodness, where do you go to the
bathroom?" she blurted.

"If it's number one, I go in the woods, and so far
I've otherwise waited to get to a proper toilet."

I bit my tongue as I noticed her startled expression.
I left relieved that the newspaper article had allayed her
nervousness, and I was renewed beyond logic by the
heavenly rhubarb pie.

That article was the first that preceded me. People
who read it watched for me or recognized me as I trudged
by. I became concerned that people would feel obligated by
the publicity to fuss over me. I began to feel like a pain in
the neck when I had to ask for a yard to bed down in. But all
in all people were wonderful and some of the things that
happened were not without humor. Many farm houses had
"sun tea" brewing on their sunny porches, glass gallon jugs
with tea bags hanging in the water and held by the screw
tops.

I had really begun to drag. No cars passed. The
heat had become intense, the worst of the trip. Then
suddenly, two more houses and one car gave me iced tea,
and I felt like a celebrity again. And then I had a new
problem; I could never refuse so kind an offer as someone
taking the trouble to bring out a glass with ice and tea, so I

gulped down all these generous offers and sloshed on, my body awash with fluids. Never mind that my legs would twitch all night from the caffeine, what about a toilet, now! I didn't dare go in the ditch because I foolishly felt people in distant farms might be watching for or looking at me.

A few days after the article in the *Lincoln Star* appeared, I was lying in the grass behind a hedgerow too weary and sore to move despite the gnats and ticks around me. I heard a voice say, "Hello, Barbara," and I jumped. It was the reporter who had interviewed me in Fairbury for the *Star*.

He had written in the article that I had been in tears daily from my blisters and sore feet. A Lincoln, Nebraska podiatrist had been so touched by the story that he called the reporter. The podiatrist had said, "This woman needs help. She shouldn't be having all this trouble. Is there any way you could locate her? I have the day off tomorrow and will gladly go to wherever she is to examine her feet and see what I can do for her. Of course, there would be no charge." That was the first part of the nice story. The second part was that the reporter had traveled up, down, and sideways over the grid-work of farm roads and had by some miracle found me lying out of sight behind the hedgerow.

Later in my journal I wrote, *"Unbelievable. Incredible. I guess I never will find nicer people than right here in Nebraska."* But as I sat listening to the story, my emotions were more complicated. I felt silly inconveniencing people about a condition I'd brought upon myself. After the earlier doctor fiasco, I was wary of doctors and preferred to rely on myself, thereby feeling less vulnerable emotionally. But the hope for a magic cure from a doctor began to seduce me. I took the podiatrist's phone number. Common decency demanded I at least call him. Indeed, the reporter had said that if this story had a happy ending, it would make even better reading than his original one. By evening I was feeling less resigned and stoical about my feet and had succumbed to the hope that the podiatrist would be my savior.

Later that night I finally reached the doctor by phone. I could hear my voice quiver. It took only a few seconds to dash my hopes. Apparently the doctor's initial burst of altruism had faded during the day. The offer to come check my feet was withdrawn under a veil of kind-sounding words and voice. Seeking to cover my hurt disappointment, I spoke with a clinical voice trying to salvage what I could in the way of information and advice. "Why, after 250 miles of walking, am I getting new blisters in new places?"

"Because your gait keeps changing as the body adjusts to compensate for the soreness."

"Well, what can I do?"

"I can't really tell much without examining your feet. Is there some way you could get here to Lincoln?"

"No. I have no car."

"Well, there's a product out called Skin Toughener."

"Nope, I already tried that and it was worthless."

"It sounds like you need arch supports, but I'd have to fit you for them."

"What about the kind you buy off the rack in the store?"

"Well, if they don't fit properly, they do more harm than good, but you could try them. You really should have seen a foot doctor before you started the trip. If your boot doesn't have a soft sole, you could try a new product called the Spenco innersole."

The doctor went on to say that if I did see a doctor somewhere eventually, I should be sure he was a marathon walking specialist, "Otherwise he'll be of no use. This is a special field." He said that he knew one in Hastings if that was on my route. It wasn't on my route.

The conversation came to an end with me, the goody-goody, gushing thank-yous. I hung up and tried not to cry. The man had been nice enough and concerned, but because I had allowed my hopes and emotions to be raised so high, the fall was all the harder. Now all that I had from the good doctor was a new worry that maybe my arches were falling.

The next morning I walked to a new chant, "My arches are falling, my arches are falling, my arches are falling... "

The Currays with their farm hands   1979 ES

After a few miles a pickup truck pulled along
side. A handsome farmer and his Betty Crocker wife
extended their arms through the window to shake my hand
and say congratulations. Their frank, unclouded smiles
wiped away my foot preoccupation. They said, "We'd love
to have you stay with us," but I had many miles to go yet
before my day was over, so we said goodbye and parted. An
hour later the familiar truck appeared again with Mrs.
Curray, who rescued me with a pitcher of iced tea and
cookies and an invitation to pick me up at the end of the
day. We examined the maps and decided on a time and
place for the pickup.

During the next few hours the heat became intense.
It was blowing in scorching blasts, even smelling like
smoke. I kept turning around expecting to see a fire nearby.
Something had gone awry within my body. My hands and
legs were swelling. I limped on toward the rendezvous
point, worried that my eyes had bitten off more than my
legs could chew. I didn't know it then, but including deserts
a thousand miles ahead, that Nebraska heat would be the
most horrifying I'd experience. Somehow I made it.

Mrs. Curray, solicitous and competent, drove me the
miles back to the old homestead, her husband's boyhood
home. Later as I stood barefoot on the cool tile floor of the
bathroom, I noticed that something felt peculiar. I looked
down and saw that my toes were not touching the floor. My
feet had swollen so much that it felt like I was standing on
fleshy cushions. I crawled to the living room and lay flat on
the carpet for a while. I wondered if I was crazy. I said to
Mrs. Curray, "Do you think I'm crazy?"

And she answered, "Why no! If you have a dream
to follow, then you should follow it." She seemed like a
mother to me as she stood in her cotton print housedress

silhouetted in front of the window. I could see the long straight rows of corn and the barn through the window behind her. A Nebraska woman. I almost cried because she, above all others, seemed to be touched by my physical hardships. That night I found myself humming, "You've got to have a dream. If you don't have a dream..."

The next day Mrs. Curray dropped me off under threatening skies with a hint of tears in her eyes. The ominous weather was thrilling to me. The sky was an all-engulfing movie, changing rapidly, action, contrast, dynamic. There is no way an easterner can picture it because the sky looks so much bigger here. Part was blue with white clouds and slants of sunshine bouncing off distant silver barns. Part was the deepest, darkest storm, purple-gray with jagged lightning streaking down. Part was sort of a smoky marbleized cloud business. I've never seen such webby, pretty texture in the east. And part was a smoky, scary, greenish color with shafts of filtered light. Another section was a blurry vertical gray streak, the spot where it was raining. Off to the side was a rainbow. We had driven through a few seconds of torrential downpour and out into sunshine again.

I donned my massive rain regalia, garbage bag over pack, rain pants and parka, and walked away; but after all that, only a few drops got me as I walked out from under the dark, clouded rain front and into blue sky and sunshine. The whole sky seems higher here as well as wider. A few people stopped. One man and his son returned with a gift. His wife sent fresh breakfast rolls and the clipping from the newspaper. Another son rode out on a horse to meet me. They were such handsome people.

My new great hope, the arch supports, aren't working, pain in arches increasing.

For the next few days my journal depicts rapid mental deterioration although I didn't know it at the time. I was enmeshed in an unfamiliar world of contrasts, overwhelming kindness from outsiders (eliciting an exhausting gratefulness from me) and unremitting physical stress. Any little thing could have pushed me into hysteria, and two things finally did. My emotional vulnerability became extreme.

One dynamic semi-retired farm couple took me home and pampered me like the critical case I was. My attraction to them was intense so that every little nuance in their treatment of me assumed extreme significance in my perception of myself. Understandably they were extremely solicitous to the point of actually feeling sorry for me. Margaret shook her head sadly. "But what are you going to do farther west in Nebraska where there is no shade, and it'll be getting much, much hotter? With the pains you're having in your feet, they aren't going to get better. They will only get worse. Oh, I wish there were some way we could gather you in every night and take care of you."

The sorrier they felt for me, the sorrier I felt for myself until my self-image dissolved into one of a valiant little loser struggling hopelessly. Poor, poor me... what a pathetic girl... I napped in a darkened room. The house was hushed as if for a seriously ill person, which in a way, I was.

In the morning Margaret drove me toward my drop-off spot, coaxing me persuasively to let her take me an extra 15 miles or so. "No," I protested, feeling a bit unbalanced for my show of stubbornness. But in flat Nebraska all the corn fields looked about the same, and before I knew it she had sped two miles past my drop off point. I pulled out my maps. "Whoops! We passed it," I said apologetically.

She sneaked in a few more hundred yards of road and turned to me saying incredulously, "Do you want me to go back?"

Sweet little me responded meekly, "Oh no, you don't have to." We parted, and I dissolved into tears over my perceived inadequacy.

My journal reveals my irrational crack-up.

Away I went and about two miles later I suddenly was shocked and horrified and appalled with the full realization that I'd RIDDEN two miles of my route. What a bitter, cruel realization. I had struggled 297 miles with blisters and pain and had steadfastly turned down all ride offers, even in my darkest pain, and to have ridden the two miles almost unknowingly in the fresh morning seemed like a cruel happening. I had somehow placed the integrity of the trip at an unbroken line of my footsteps the whole way, and now to have that two-mile gap made almost unconsciously and certainly unnecessarily was unbearable. I was sick. I felt worse than I could remember, a horrid futile sinking feeling. I cried for two or three hours, throwing out my whole supply of Kleenex tissue one by one. I never littered before but now I became a veritable Johnny Appleseed strewing the little white tissue papers across the countryside. To go back and retrace was too far, much too far.

Today I reread that section with embarrassment. It is the height of egotism.

The pressures of that day mounted. I misread the map and found no bridge where I expected one. I tried to take a short cut by following a railroad track. It turned into a bridge over the turbulent Little Blue River. I started across. There would be no room on the bridge for a train plus me. There were big spaces between the ties. The motion of the current glimpsed through the spaces made me dizzy. My heavy pack and sore feet made me totter unbalanced. I kept glancing back for a train and stopped to listen for a roar. Despite the hot day, I broke into a cold sweat of fear, and my breaths came in panicky jerks and gasps. I made it, but the tension was all for naught. I later learned that the next train was due in five days.

I was heading for a town where I hoped to find a churchyard to bed down in. My journal describes problems leading to my second breakdown. My perceptions were distorted, overly personalized, and exaggerated.

Approaching the town was a sinking disappointment. It was as if a disaster had swept through it. Not a person was in sight. Row after row of tiny, empty, or unkempt houses lined the dirt streets. Far away in a trailer, a woman yelled at her kids. It was the most horrible, poisonous town I ever saw or felt; not a ghost town (they at least are quaint) but a death-like place, decayed, depressed, really indescribable. I saw a church and a huge brick school. The school on closer inspection proved to be a hollow shell, empty, a rotten tooth. The church was the same way, the steeple half gone.

Across the street one white neatly kept trailer stood in stark contrast to the hovels around. I knocked, and a very suspicious, proper, chunky woman appeared. At a glance I could see that not a hair escaped from her gray hairnet nor a smile from her pursed lips. She opened the door, and I started to hold it for her, and she yanked it back with fear, revulsion, and hostility. I'm sure she thought I was a Charles Manson hatchet woman. Peeking through the crack, she said that no one in town would let me unroll my bag on their property. The tears spilled over my face, and I began to sob, a terrible error, whereupon she slammed both doors shut and peered at me from behind the curtains. I walked aimlessly and in a daze of tears, reversing direction every few steps while the woman still gaped from the shadows. I walked through that godforsaken town crying openly and hopelessly. Once I started crying, I could hardly expect anyone to take me in. I walked through the rotten place and out the other side. Later I learned that lots of people had watched, peeping from behind their curtains, as I went through town.

I heard someone yelling at me. Police? A white haired old man waving a cane was gesturing for me, and I walked back to him. Startled, he said, "Well, what are you crying for?" As I sobbed he led me back to his tiny house to meet his wife, Rose.

As I learned later, Rose had read about me in the paper, had been hoping I'd go through Deweese, and had been watching for me. She just happened to glimpse me in the split second I passed between her window and a bush. She had cried, "Everett! Come! Look! I think it's that lady from Boston who's walking the Oregon Trail. Go around to the side window. Oh, Everett, go ask her if she wants some coffee or food."

So Everett, hobbling with his cane, chased me cross-lots while Rose ran the sweeper over the floor. Everett brought me back, a sobbing heap. They invited me in.

"Here now, you sit right down in our special rocking chair. How about a root beer float? I'm going to make you a root beer float. How about a nice foot soak? I'll bet you'd like a foot soak. I'll make a foot soak for you."

Everett kept saying, "Why, it's all right to cry. Even our Lord Jesus wept." At that point I was even into those convulsive things where you can't even catch your breath, alarming.

I had hit bottom.

I am resting here for a day after my worst day of the trip, yesterday. I diagnosed my crying last night from exhaustion that I hadn't even realized.

Rose and Everett restored my mind and body with their solicitous ministrations.

Living in poverty, they had, for example, babied their stopped-up sewer for years, flushing the toilet but once a day (which is why I didn't defecate there for two days) and throwing all wash water and dish water out the back door. The town's un-neighborly poisonous paranoia meant for them an expensive eight mile drive to reach a phone, which they insisted on doing so that I could call home to reach my family. When I finally left them early the second morning, they called loudly and proudly to me, "Goodbye, Barbara" to show off to their neighbor who had been sitting on her porch since before dawn just to see me go by. Word had spread that I was there. The rare courage of Rose's and Everett's kindness within that sad town made me love and admire them all the more. And then, once again, I was on my way.

Through it all, my aesthetic sensitivity was heightened and remained so for days afterward. The next day I wrote:

The wind waves the wheat heads making the fields a soft feathery green instead of the shiny rustling bright ribbons of a few weeks ago. The gray sky or the blue sky, each gives a totally different atmosphere as a backdrop to the farmland scene, both beautiful.

But my stability was still shaky.

Through all these 340 miles, I've stumbled upon the knack of living close to the surface, childlike (or baby-like). I've walked over the crest of a rise and spontaneously said,

"Oh boy!" at the view. I find myself grinning and laughing at my thoughts or suddenly dripping tears at the sight of a dead rabbit or bird. When talking to reporters, I can barely catch myself from bursting into tears describing the Donner disaster or my hurt at being turned away at farms. I have a prediction: Some day there will be an unrepressed person in the public eye, such as a politician, with enough status and stature to be able to burst into tears. The thing is, if tears are spontaneous enough, they may last only a few seconds, unlike the common situation where tears mean a bottled-up breaking point and are frightening to all involved.

As I followed the orange crayon line on my maps northwest toward the Platte River, I became aware of Hastings hovering off my route to the east. The Lincoln podiatrist had mentioned a foot doctor there. I knew I was deluding myself when I felt my feet were getting better. As truly a last-ditch effort, I went off the trail and headed toward Hastings. In the back of my mind I was toying with the possibility of having to switch to a bike, or getting a donkey, or something. It would probably be possible to do the trip on sheer grit, but what was the point if I could only half-see through the haze of pain? I went to see the doctor.

Strike three for doctors. After a skin softening treatment in a whirlpool, he ridiculously gave me a lecture on toughening my skin. He showed no interest in my footwear. He pulled out a formidable roll of tape, announcing he was going to tape up my arches. I said, "Teach me how to do this in case it works."

"Oh no, Madam, you could never learn. See a doctor."

"But if it works and I'm in the middle of Wyoming 50 miles from a town, I'll have to know how to do it myself."

"You couldn't learn how. You'd end up taping your foot in some crazy position."

I should have told him to go to hell, but instead I laughed sweetly. Meanwhile, I carefully watched what he did. Any dope could have learned it. But he did allay one worry: "If you ever get to California, you'll have the strongest arches in the world."

I left with the sinking feeling that I'd wasted two days and another $15. I also bought some more worthless junk at the foot section of the drug store.

Within two miles, I had to acknowledge that something felt suspiciously peculiar about my feet. The tape hurt for sure, but it seemed more than that. I sat in the front yard of a house in the Hastings suburb and peeled off my shoes and socks. As I bared the skin, a very fine fountain of fluid was actually squirting two inches into the air from a tight blister. The skin had stuck to my sock and peeled off where the doctor had sprayed adhesive to hold the tape. I was faced with a bloody half-inch band of blisters and open sores from the edge of the tape across the entire top of my foot from the big toe to pinky, and blisters rose on the knuckles of each toe. In one quick visit the doc had managed to ruin my feet for walking by creating open sores, the one condition I had solemnly guarded against all these hundreds of miles. I cut back the tape with my knife and used up my entire supply of band-aids. The woman working there in her yard gave me another whole box of them. I went on with the realization slowly dawning that something had to change drastically.

But there was to be no time for self-pity that day. I became oppressed by stultifying heat, humid, hard to breathe. I scooted along as best I could. I was straining and heading for a dot on the map, the farm of a friend of some folks I'd stayed with a week before.

I went on, aiming for the Jordans' farm, the name and place suggested. The heat suddenly became awesome. Sweat ran down my face and neck in streams. Three more miles to go and no farm in sight. I became nervous that the Jordans would be on a different road. Then I saw a farm and hoped that the mailbox would say "Jordan." Two more miles to go. Sky began to blacken ahead; tornado? The mailbox DID say "Jordan!" I straightened my shirt, removed my glasses and hat, and knocked. After a long while an old lady appeared, scared and scowling. Her disapproving looks and manner made my heart sink, but I played my smiling friendly role, and her husband came up and was nice, but she made it clear that she wanted no part of me. So I waved and turned and dissolved in sobs and limped away into a gathering storm.

Then began a startling exploration into myself. Her attitude of suspicion, fear, and revulsion had infuriated a deep part of me previously untouched. Behind my tears a new sensation stirred, at first vaguely but then powerfully. I felt a strong urge toward violence and would have taken great pleasure in living up to her fearful image of me by swearing obscenities at her, pushing her so she would stumble and fall, and just generally scaring the life out of her. The image of violence became actually sensuous. Her attitude and expectations had stimulated this in me, ordinarily so meek and civilized. Later I wondered if her fear posture was similar to the goads that set off criminals' acts of violence against their victims. For me the lesson from her behavior? Never, never show fear. Never.

The atmosphere that had been so oppressive had been the low-pressure front preceding a storm. With shocking rapidity the wind picked up. The thunderheads blackened the sky, and I had suddenly a minor emergency on my hands: evening, gathering bad storm, no plans. I spied a mailbox one mile ahead as lightening flashed. I was the tallest thing on a flat field, but I just walked faster and faster until I was running, trying not to bounce the pack, ignoring my screaming feet. I felt something hit me and noticed a fragment of ice, then another ahead, hail. The pieces were not round but jagged, ½-inch wide. Finally, I reached the house and rang the bell. In the distance, four miles, I could hear sirens and bells; tornado warnings in Kenesaw? No one answered at the house. Were they all in the storm cellar?

While leaning under the eve, I put on all my rain stuff and pack cover. At that moment I suddenly had a great surge of confidence. I was taking charge of events instead of being battered by them. I decided to walk on toward Kenesaw to find a church. Hail and rain splattered and stopped as the storm passed to the north. Finally I spotted a pleasant brick house and limped up the drive.

A older smiling man (thank God) came out. Later he confessed that he'd thought I was an old crippled bum, "bent over, limping, and moving so slowly with such small steps."

Mrs. Miller emerged and gasped when she tried to hoist my pack. She said with complete seriousness, "Why, you need a little red wagon to pull." The image that flashed in my mind is unforgettable and dear.

My turning point was with the Millers   1979 ES

I stayed with the Millers, Hannah and Fred, a few days until the oozing sores scabbed over enough to continue. Although I wasn't aware of it at the time, this was the turning point of the trip, for here I took the weight of my pack off my back and feet once and for all and put it on wheels, a golf cart.

Fred Miller seemed healthy, happy, even serene, but I learned that he actually had a blood disease, arthritis, cancer, and more. He had started life with no money but worked as a mechanic for years and had invested his money in farm land until now his wealth was "more than I know what to do with." "See those (metal) barns? I don't need them, but the government pays me so much not to grow crops that I built them anyway." The Millers, however, still live simply, still shop at thrift stores where Hannah took me to buy a white cotton blouse.

I liked the Millers' attitude. Mr. Miller, a practical man, didn't sit around bemoaning my sorry condition; he set about wracking his brain for solutions. Mrs. Miller had

117

started the process when she blurted out the little red wagon idea. We finally settled on the golf cart.

The Pratts, the Millers' daughter and son-in-law, gave me their golf cart. Mr. Miller welded a brace to it, and we tied on my pack. It seemed like such an ignominious comedown to see my beloved pack tied to a golf cart. I actually had come to like the feel of my pack on my back. It was only my feet that objected.

The golf cart became a new adjustment; my self-image was suddenly radically altered, no more chance for the elite backpacker image. Now I would be a strange woman pulling a cart, an oddity.

Thursday morning, Fred gave me a can of oil for the cart's wheels. Hannah packed six sandwiches, (three fried egg and three peanut butter and jelly), four bananas, and a roll. I ate them all a mile beyond her house. Hope and optimism and new beginnings were my feelings as I left. I walked for an hour on back roads with the wind rustling the maturing wheat around me.

And then two sturdy matrons drove up and stopped. They were from the Kenesaw Nursing Home and had received a call from a citizen saying that one of their patients had escaped—me! Gee, did I look that old?

Three times I passed an oldish man running a road grater. He was vaguely Mexican with leathered brown skin. His teeth were rotten or missing, his eyes slightly crossed. Oily hair hung limply over his ears. He was dirty, disreputable looking. Early in the day I had firmly answered his questioning look by calling out, "I'm walking the Oregon Trail."

Toward the end of the day he stopped far ahead, parked his road grater across the road, blocking it, and waited for me. In flat treeless Nebraska, there was no place to run, no place to hide. He crept behind his machine and watched as I approached. I took a deep breath, tried to maintain an attitude of fearless calm, and walked toward the machine, careful not to slow my pace. He edged hesitantly toward me, his hand nervously reaching in his pocket. "Hello," I said.

He pulled his hand out of his pocket. In his palm was a little scrap of paper and the stub of a pencil. "Would you write your name down here for me?" he pleaded gently. "You sure are one magnificent woman. It is an honor meeting you." Then he confided shyly, "I like history too."

"Happy trails to you" is what I wrote for him and signed my name.

It was a wonderful walk. I could look around (no backpack to hinder me) and savor the scene. I got my first glimpse of Nebraska's famous sand hills, round undulating hills of sand, dry, covered with sparse grass for grazing. (I would come to love them.)

With my golf cart I walked 23 miles, way too far for my still tender wounds, but it gave me a big confidence boost. I reoriented myself to my pilgrimage, stopping reverently beside the lone pioneer grave of Susan Hall, who died on the trail at age 34.

The lonely prairie grave of Susan Hall.   1979 ES

Susan Hall's story brings a pang of emotion to the otherwise impersonal landscape. It is said that her husband, grief-stricken at her death camp, was unable to tear himself away to continue westward with his wagon train. Instead, he placed a temporary marker on her burial site and returned alone on foot to St. Joseph, Missouri, to procure a proper grave stone. He then retraced his route, carrying the little monument in a wheelbarrow, back to the prairie. Out of the thousands who died on the trail, Susan Hall is one of only a rare few whose name and burial place is known today.

I renewed pioneer identification as the sight of the Platte River in the distance brought a surge of anticipation and a big grin. I reached historic Fort Kearney, and my spirits soared. Incredibly, I fell asleep on the lookout next to the ancient parade grounds. Reaching the Platte was the completion of my first big goal, and I snoozed in the sun in the delicious rest of satisfied exhaustion.

———

The Platte River is important and special. One can sense that with a quick glance at any Nebraska map. Its lazy, colossal meander undulates in easy disregard and defiance of the rigid right angles of section lines and highways. Historically it was the dominant great road for east-west travel migrations for thousands of years. Ancient Indians were following its course for centuries before white people dreamed of the new world. Later, explorers and fur trappers and mountain men traced its path across the plains. For the pioneers traveling with their herds of thirsty stock, the rivers became their lifelines as they inched their way across the vast "featureless" plains. The Platte was the Granddaddy of them all. In the old days the weary emigrants followed it hundreds of miles without seeing even a single tree to break the horizon line. Pioneer diaries chortle and chuckle in the astonishment at its peculiar characteristics. "Too thick to drink and too thin to plow" was the familiar muddy refrain. "A mile wide and an inch deep," "a river without banks to hold it in," a joke that turned exasperating when it softened the lowlands making the laboring oxen strain through the mud.

Today's Interstate-80 follows its shores as surely as yesterday's wagon train, but there the resemblance stops. The mighty river has been tamed beyond recognition. Dams and irrigation diversions have reduced the "mile wide" to a mere trickle and extracted its silt to a crystal-clear sparkle. Its once treeless banks smoothed by prairie fires or buffalo grazing are now a veritable tangle of cottonwoods and jungle growth. The old oceans of grass have disappeared along with the brown carpets of buffalo. Today's skyline is broken with pivot irrigators, silver silos, fields of corn and wheat and verdant clumps of trees cuddling peaceful farmhouses.

Everything has changed since 1846—everything, that is, except the weariness and the thrill of reaching, finally, an important landmark.

Friday evening Fort Kearney
I have a feeling that this marks the end of one phase of the trip, a completion. The end has come abruptly, but things will never be the same.
Whatever happens in the future, I'm no longer committed totally to backpacking. The golf cart may wear out, but wheels are now part of my image, quite an adjustment for my ego. (Later on, I would come to feel proud of it.)

Reaching the Platte is a milestone. Now after 380 miles, I feel legitimate. Now, following the Platte, I hardly need a map. I feel I've been tested and passed, barely.

My relatively populated, civilized farming area is nearing an end and will never reappear to this extent throughout the journey.

Until now the great physical rigors have been internal, my own foot problems, etc. So far the weather has given me a break. In the future I expect more external rigors, heat, terrain, water scarcity, lack of shade, and God only knows what else.

My intuition proved accurate. The inward focus of my attention would be steadily turned outward, at last, with the slow process of my feet healing and confidence growing. My adventures ahead would focus on outside events. I had grown and matured in the soft benevolent womb of the farmland. I emerged into the more rigorous western world, ready.

Fort Kearney

Looking back, I'm amazed. Today's reporter and others have asked me to report any great adventures (meaning near abduction), and I have none to tell, but to me my own mental adventures are just as interesting

No person is an island. If pressed, I know now I can carry on somehow on my own but quite numbly and not very effectively or efficiently. The real sensitivity, elation, or despair, the real color of living comes in interaction with other people. Simple little gestures of kindness or friendliness (ride offers) at crucial (or even any) times can mean the difference between living and merely existing.

1) Kindness from others breeds optimism, the fuel for really living.

2) Weather and luck also greatly influence mental set, sense of well-being, and confidence. When storms brew, I feel threatened, a sense of urgency, grim. I am NOT in total control of my emotions. I am not totally objective, or even objective at all.

3) There are two parts to me. One is very immediate and dealing actively with the current physical situation. I eat; I cry; I hurt; I search; I interact with others. There is another part of me. It is detached. It is a constant. It is a observer and, when necessary, a guide. Sometimes I'm aware of it, other times not. It is the "real me." It is on the side of and rooting for the immediate me. It is my friend. It rescues the immediate me if I go off the deep end. It regulates the intensity of what the immediate me experiences. IT steps in to help. Now, I know this all sounds like the ravings of an insane person, but there is a difference. I sense the real me. Some may call it God or guardian angel or instinct or intuition or "the force" or what-not. I call it part of me, my greater self.

Here's how this other side of me has been most evident. My feet, ahhhh yes, back to my feet, what else. My feet have been to the point where outsiders have thought me a crippled old bum while watching me, actually doubled over, slow five-inch steps, limping and lurching, and this has gone on for miles. Then where was my head? When the chips were down, I could be really quite detached, not feel sorry for myself. Anyway, the mind is strange in what it can take bodily, depending on attitude and set. It works both ways, tolerating a lot or going to pieces with very little. The thing that pushes me over the brink is other people, meanness or kindness. Meanness stiffens my resolve (tears not-withstanding). Kindness cures me. Indifference from others demoralizes me. Pity demoralizes too.

4) I can respond to and sense two different parts in other people, the immediate physical presentation or the less physical, enduring, real person. I'm still learning to shed my preconceptions of the immediate physical personality. When the inner me and the inner them communicate, it's deeply satisfying.

5) I've learned another thing about me. I am a very restless, driven, exploring kind of person. I can clearly see that the pace of life here in the Midwest is harmonious, peaceful, and works like a smooth-running machine compared to the frantic, busy scramble of life in the east. The farmers have a way of life that is ordered and familiar. They have time to cope with a woman walking the Oregon Trail who drops in out of nowhere on them. In the east, such an unexpected drop-in, I think, would be very disruptive and burdensome. Perhaps I'm confusing the east with merely my own personal lifestyle. Anyway, I see the peaceful life of rural America, and I appreciate its value, but for me it would be a personal challenge. I thrive on the cultural clashes and stimulation and complexities and big problems of life in Boston. On the trail, I long for a rest, and now that I've had two days, I'm frantic to read something, anything. I feel I'm wasting time. I want to get going or doing. And yet it was just yesterday morning that I was so tired I fell asleep on the lookout platform of the Fort Kearney stockade.

8

ALONG THE PLATTE

"The journey is all: the end, nothing."   Sign in a Nebraska cafe

June 2-15
(184 miles)

everywhere beautiful remains from olden times   1979 ES

I recuperated for three days at Fort Kearney while waiting for Ken, an old friend, to join me from Iowa. He would walk with me for three days. What I feared at first would be an intrusion turned out to be a wonderful break from the tension of being alone as well as a new point of view, another set of senses to perceive the world around us.

The effect of the three-day walk in Ken was startling. He arrived with the tensions of normal daily life assaulting him fearfully. After every snack along the way, out came his toothbrush; after all, weren't the bacteria there just waiting for a stray food particle to attack his teeth? At every rest stop, down would go the plastic ground cloth; didn't I know that the smallest dirt smudge would irritate his skin? And so it went, hour after hour. But by the end of his last day I knew that the trail had worked a miracle on both of us. Ken actually forgot to brush his teeth the whole day, and I had come to wait eagerly for the ground cloth to come out before sitting down.

I reread my journal entries for those three days with amazement. So much happened. So much variety. A few examples:

I'll say this for Ken, he appreciated all the beauty all the time, even the most subtle beauty: the soft mist hovering low over the fields and cottonwoods in the distance along the Platte, the medley of fragrances we enjoyed for three days, the bountiful variety of grasses that I had not ever taken time to specifically examine. Ken collected seeds from them and then I looked, really looked, at the prairie grasses closely for the first time and beheld their microcosm of loveliness.

We watched a large number of huge fish (apparently spawning) in irrigation ditches. They roiled and flipped and charged about in determined circles. The water was so shallow that their top fins were completely out of the water.

We stopped to rest a long time by an old barn. Only later did we notice the avalanche of ticks that had descended upon us and the poison ivy that carpeted the old barnyard.

One night we camped in a very active barnyard. Chickens, turkeys, cats, kittens and dogs ran around together all over the place. I put my sleeping bag down over some hollowed dirt that the chickens had rounded out for their dust baths. It was perfect for fitting hips and shoulder into, a kind of barnyard contour chair. Only later did Ken let on that he was horrified with my chosen spot. The

126

barnyard din and the harvester in the next field that ran all
night, reminiscent of New England snow plows, kept Ken
awake. I slept like a log in my chicken hollows.

    The second morning after an early start, a pickup
pulled up next to us and a farm family offered us a breakfast
of fresh fruit: strawberries, oranges, and bananas. They had
seen us walk by and had gathered the fruit and come
looking for us. I had been raving like a pollyanna to Ken
about the Nebraska farm hospitality, and it bloomed for the
two of us just as it had for me as a woman alone.

Ken   1970's SS

    Our third day turned rainy and dreary. We trudged
on endlessly past fields, the rain penetrating every wettable
fabric, the sweat and condensation under our rainwear
soaking us from the inside. Ken had sprouted blisters, and
my feet were sore. The whole drudging walk had become an
ordeal. Ken spotted the tongue of an old wagon for sitting
down. We both sat there under rain, in the middle of
nowhere, heads in hands, despair. There was not even the
drama of danger to spark us. This was a slow, endless
drizzle, without even the hint of lightning. I found
throughout the trip that sometimes the most ordinary times

were really the hardest. No heroism, no danger, no great obstacles, just patient enduring.

The road was straight as a ruled line. There appeared to be a house in the distance miles away. Ken declared with awe, "It's the longest looking road I ever saw." Finally, because there was nothing else to do, we got up and toiled on toward the distant house. We passed it and lay down by the side of the road in the grass. I immediately fell asleep and awoke an hour later to... clearing skies, sunshine. Such are the small gifts on the trail.

We camped in a tiny graveyard, the site of the Plum Creek massacre. We used the last of our precious water trying unsuccessfully to prime the ancient water pump. Just as we were getting annoyingly thirsty, a tiny speck appeared on the line that was a road. A farmer in a pickup truck who'd passed us earlier was coming to check on us, talk, and bring extra water. The overalled farmer in his pickup rode to the rescue, a modern day Lone Ranger.

At dusk that same farmer, Roy, returned a third time with the local newspaperman, who interviewed me with a long monologue of his own. Darkness fell, and the reporter remembered he'd forgotten to take my picture. Roy groped his way through the darkness to his truck and returned with a weak flashlight which he shined on me while the man focused his camera. "OK, I've got it now," said the photographer. Off clicked the flashlight, and I sat in pitch blackness waiting as if blindfolded before a firing squad. Then, FLASH! Out of the darkness exploded the flashbulb, and the act was done. Months later I saw that funny picture, me ghostly white and startled in a field of blackness. As they were leaving, Roy reminded the reporter that he hadn't asked my name. "Oh yeah. What's your name?" he asked pulling out pencil and paper for the first time that evening. I heard a brief crinkle and scratch as he wrote in the dark night.

Next day a tame deer, wearing a red ribbon around its neck, daintily tripped across a cornfield to greet us and then stayed and walked with us for a way. I trembled before his aura of exquisite fragility.

Ken was lame; there was no doubt about that, so we crossed to the north side of the Platte to Lexington where Ken planned to get a ride back the 35 miles to Fort Kearney. We both spotted a Kentucky Fried Chicken store and lusted for it. When we finished our meal, we tried to rise, but our muscles had stiffened during the feast. Lurching and thrusting our bodies, we finally managed to get onto our feet before the startled eyes of the other customers. With my first bizarre step, Ken burst into hysterical laughter at my grotesque appearance, and seeing myself through his eyes, I joined him. Totally out of control, we doubled over with hysterical laughter at ourselves. It was hopeless; convulsed and gagging, we couldn't stop. It was the second time in three days we had found our physical predicament ludicrous enough to incapacitate us with laughter. Finally we pulled ourselves together and staggered out of the store, two crazy limping ghouls. I felt freer to laugh at my predicament because Ken was with me. In the past, alone, I would have surely been carted off to a psychiatric ward. With Ken, all the stored laughter came out in a wonderful orgy of comic relief.

With propriety we shared a motel room in Lexington. The receptionist eyed me with distaste but treated Ken respectfully. Her double standard annoyed me. The next morning, we parted and I was on my own again.

The Oregon Trail followed the south side of the Platte and the Mormon Trail the north side. I followed Highway 30 up the north side for a few towns. It was my first experience on a major highway, and it was a rude awakening. Right away there sprang up a mutual tension between me and the fast, heavy traffic. We were competing for the same skimpy strip of concrete on which to roll our wheels. There was no shoulder on the road side, only a three-inch drop and stiff weeds. I tried dragging my cart off the little ledge for every car that passed but my progress slowed nearly to a stop.

Still under the influence of benevolence around rural farming roads, I glimpsed the flash of a waving hand and waved back with a big smile. As the car came abreast of me I realized that the hand was a fist being shaken at me in anger. I was ashamed and embarrassed by my naivety. I gave those uncomfortable feelings careful thought for many miles and decided that the naivety of expecting friendliness from people was nothing to be ashamed of. Later, hostility toward me made me feel hurt and angry but never again ashamed.

Day by day I inched my way from town to town upstream alongside the Platte River. From Lexington to Cozad I bent double as I battled into a steady headwind. The sensation of pressing so hard against such a resistant wall of air was unfamiliar to me. Finally, I sought rest and shade in a rare clump of trees and learned something about wind on the Great Plains. The valiant little band of trees arched and twisted grotesquely under the windy onslaught. The silvered leaves turned belly up as the branches streamed forth in a spasmodic tension. Accompanying all the visual motion was the crescendo sound of swishing and moaning leaves. This was the wind I knew in the east, noisy and visual, gusty and unpredictable among the foliage. The alien sensation of wind I had experienced earlier on the road had lacked the old familiar wind accompaniments of sound and waving branches. The western wind from my eastern point of view was spooky, silent, and invisible, a steady, mute wall of resistant air to be pushed against. It sapped my strength quietly and masked the sun's heating effect as it coolly dehydrated me. I gained a new respect for the wind that day.

That night, as I lay limply in Cozad, the wind subsided and the dew settled heavily on my sleeping bag, so heavily that it saturated through the bag and my clothes to my skin. Not a drop of rain had fallen, but I might as well have slept through a cloudburst.

To Gothenburg 11 miles. It was a glorious day, but my legs ached from yesterday's battle with the wind. Arrived in town, and the heat hit.

As with the wind, my eastern background did not prepare me for the western sun. I was learning how quickly the sun could do its insidious damage. In June, when the sun's rays are most direct yet the temperature and humidity fairly comfortable, I dressed as an easterner would, shorts and bare arms. Yet by the time (noon) that the heat suddenly descended like a sledgehammer, the damage was done. The last mile before reaching town should have been a simple 20-minute walk, but it became an anxiety-laden race with a nameless urgency. The last hundred yards became an almost impossible obstacle of distance.

In a near panic I obtained directions to the nearest supermarket, a Jack and Jill, and fled into its air conditioned interior. From inside the darkened store I peered fearfully through a side window into the blazing sunlight. I was paranoid with my sudden fear of the sun. As in a horror film, its power and omniscience seemed relentless and inescapable. My personal sense of isolation increased as I was surrounded with dozens of people oblivious to the menace I perceived. They went about their normal shopping and even walked relaxed and smiling outside into the glare. "How dare they be so stupid," I marveled. "Didn't they know any better?!"

I walked up and down the aisles cooling down and calming down. I sensed that I needed help but was too confused to know what I needed or how to ask. I decided to pretend I was normal, and my fumbling inquiries among store personnel brought casual directions to a KOA campground, "just a few miles across town." "Just a few miles?" It might as well have been the other side of hell to me. After a few more failed communications, I turned myself and my golf cart toward the door and walked bleakly out into the sun with vague intentions of heading toward a campground.

With extreme effort of will I tried to remain calm. People on the sidewalks around me were going about their business normally. I felt invisible and out of touch with them. I felt I had to keep moving, and then disaster struck; a traffic light turned red. I had to stop and wait. What a stroke of frightful luck! There was no shade. The sun bore into me, pressing me downward. My tight control screamed on the edge of panic. Then finally the light changed, and I bounced my cart over some railroad tracks and headed aimlessly away. After a few blocks I turned back and pointlessly retraced my steps only to turn down another street. After a few blocks I changed my mind again and headed in a new direction. In a daze I passed an empty newspaper office, at some point wandered in and out of the Jack and Jill again, headed toward a park, and reversed direction once again. Some shred of rationality that remained within me said sternly, "Barbara, stop this foolishness and take care of yourself NOW!"

In the end I stumbled into an old motel where I lay in the hot but soothing darkness and shivered violently while drifting in and out of a stuporous sleep for many hours. I ate six sugary donuts that I had bought sometime during the day.

Late that night I awoke and finally "came to," realizing fully for the first time how irrational and dazed I'd been since just before I'd arrived in Gothenburg. It was a sobering realization, alarming. I wrote in my journal:

My mind was not right when I got here. Was I tetched from the sun? I feel afraid, uneasy, weary. My mind is off. Yesterday I had a high and today I'm in a low. I'm worried about my eating and my health and the desolate areas ahead. Why am I so unstable today? Things are infinitely easier than when I had the pack but still not as easy as I'd hoped. I'm tense about spending money, am down to $160. I think this bed has bugs. (Sleeping outside with bugs all around was fine with me, but having bugs inside a motel room seemed degrading.)

About a week later when approaching Ogallala I experienced my first bona fide "hot dry wind," as the natives refer to it. I again had walked many hours in reasonable comfort because of the cooling effect of the "dry wind." There was a vague sense of being assaulted by a dangerous sun rather than acute physical torture that the muggy east serves up. Toward mid-afternoon I felt queasy nausea and a vague but persistent urgency. I was wearing long pants and a sun hat, but my forearms were exposed to the sun. I ripped out the hem of the sleeve to cover another inch of skin, but even so small an area as my lower forearms exposed to the direct sun tormented. It wasn't just the hot sensation; it was a feeling of sickness and poisoning that is hard to describe. The old Gothenburg sensation of mental confusion descended. I misread my map, took a wrong turn, and followed a dirt lane a futile two miles to a dead end and had to back track, swearing profusely as I shed a few tears of frustration and rage. Later that night, safely encamped in the shade of a farmhouse, I soberly pondered the sun factor while anticipating the months and deserts ahead.

133

I tried to make it 24 miles but the sun was scalding and the wind blowing a dry blast that even seemed to make the wheat rattle. After a while I almost panicked. I felt confused, sick, swollen, burned. The sun was my enemy. It bore through my bonnet, through my Desitin-smeared nose, and actually burned through my shirt.

A few days later the brutal sun forced a halt at 10:30 in the morning. I sought refuge in an empty bathroom in an empty campground. I pressed my legs against the cool cement floor. I drifted into a confused stupor, repeatedly falling asleep sitting up. A pile of broken ceramic tile lay on the floor in the corner where I longed to lay my head. I remained upright fearing that if I were asleep in a public bathroom with my head on a pile of broken tiles, I'd be taken as a drugged vagrant, which, of course, was not far from the truth. As the long day wore on I wrote in my journal as my mind cleared:

The heat stopped me before Brule. I saw migrant workers wearing long pants and shirts. Maybe the sun is a bigger enemy than the heat. My face is burned despite my bonnet, and the skin is swollen, not to mention my dementia. A hot dry wind can make it reasonably comfortable, but the sun's effects continue. Now I'm hiding from the sun in a campground bathroom absolutely terrified of the heat outside, and as I look out I see people going about quite normally, a man cleaning his car, two motorcycle people (with jackets!) and long pants. Someone is nuts and I fear it is I. Something has to give with this sun phobia of mine. So I go out and it's like stepping into a blinding blast furnace, and I turn and flee back inside again. When the sun set that evening, I felt like I was coming out of the effects of general anesthesia as my head cleared and I rejoined the world of the human race.

My sun-fighting policy took shape during those brutal Nebraska June days. Taking a tip from the Arabs, I put on a search for white, cotton, loose-flowing clothes. They were surprisingly hard to find even in the sun-baked west. Finally, later in Wyoming, I got it all together: white baggy cotton long pants shortened to "high waters" for ventilation, white cotton loose shirt with the sleeve arms slashed for more ventilation, wide brimmed light straw hat (or loose peaked bonnet in case of wind), sunglasses, sunscreen lotion (I used opaque Desitin on my nose with a clown effect). During the hot months I started walking before dawn (4:30 A.M.) to be able to get my 20-mile allotment in before noon if necessary. I drank gallons and gallons of water routinely even when not especially thirsty. I'd let the cooling water spill all over my clothes as I drank. The dry western air evaporates sweat before it collects on the skin, giving the sensation that one isn't sweating much. Dehydration can occur quickly without steady fluid replacement, and I believe it, considering how little I peed on those days.

The importance of white clothes was dramatically demonstrated by the difference between my white shirt and my checked shirt, the dark checks absorbing the radiating heat onto my back like an oven. My cotton pants were so superior in absorption and cooling to my part-synthetics that I mailed home the non-cotton, as they are useless in the summer. By mid-summer coping with heat and sun was well under control. I was always meticulous about clean socks and underwear; otherwise I was unconcerned about the "clean dirt" from sun-sterilized soils.

Another possible cause of my heat stupors might have been "sugar comas:"

It suddenly occurred to me that my problem was not only the heat but my old enemy, sugar. I had been steadily increasing my sugar intake under the heading "carbo loading" (a marathoner's gimmick), the rationale being that I need more carbohydrates for energy, but it had gotten out of hand. In towns I'd head like an addict for the nearest store where I'd buy a half gallon of milk and a big bag of cookies (like double-stuffed Oreos or French Vanilla creams). Then I'd go somewhere and devour the whole bag and milk, after which I'd drift inexorably and irresistibly into my stupor, falling in and out of sleep for hours.

Those times when I tried to keep walking, the desire to lie down and sleep was so strong that I could hardly remain upright. I would fight the urge to lie on the shoulder of the road by closing my eyes for three or four steps over and over. This phenomenon lessened as I cut down on my sugar binges, but my cravings for sugar assumed astronomical proportions whenever I walked past the cookie aisle.

Coincidentally, about the same time I was thinking of my great sugar connection, I wandered into a macabre family situation while stopping at a farm for water and rest. The old woman of the house had developed severe diabetes with periodic frightening symptoms of blindness, diabetic coma, retinal hemorrhaging, leg ulcers, and crippling. She seemed somewhat confused and childlike, senile. She confessed that she wasn't supposed to eat any sugar but that often she couldn't resist it so ate it anyway. While we were chatting, her grown son, a teacher, came home with a bag of a dozen of the most sugary, creamy, chocolaty assorted donuts I've ever seen. He offered me one, left the open bag on the table next to his mother, and departed. Giggling childishly the old woman grabbed two donuts saying, "I think I'll still be able to see a little bit if I eat only two." I was appalled at her self-destruction and her son's acquiescence. I left with a shudder, eager to get away from the sinister household. Outside an old man was pushing wood shingles into the soil behind every garden plant in a futile attempt to shield the wilting plants from the hot wind and sun.

The little towns along the Platte are as unique and vivid as different children. In Brady, I camped in a tiny, pleasant town park. In the evening I joined the townsfolk and farmers as they gathered casually for the girls' softball team practice, surely a slice of pure Americana. After everyone had gone home I unrolled my bag and prepared for a peaceful night's sleep. *It was quite a feat getting sleep here. The tennis court spotlight, the street lights, railroad lights, motel lights, and feed factory lights were blazing in my eyes from every direction all night. The trains ran faithfully all night and whistled (screeched) their codes, long long short long, continually as they approached town or stopped at the feed factory. When the trains left, the all-night machinery from the factory ground on in a steady, grating throb. I'm sure it was noisier than downtown Manhattan. Brady, population 257.*

Along a short stretch of road near Brady I saw a long, bright plastic peach-colored flower on the shoulder of the dry barren road. I spied another about a hundred feet later and soon a third. "How strange" I thought as I bent and examined the long series of petals more closely. "Perhaps a box broke loose from a truck." In the distance I spotted another bright peachy dash of color on the dry gravel. I bent to pick it up and gasped, puzzled. The waxy looking, gaudy "plastic" flowers were alive, growing from a root. Within a mile they disappeared; I never saw them again on the trip. Such were the pleasant and unpredictable surprises I found along the trail.

I learned that money (alas, mostly pennies) was found on the roads within the half mile outside towns. Once in Utah on the desert I found a huge bag of cookie cutters. There must have been a hundred different kinds. Already loaded with water and equipment, I had no choice but to leave them behind, regretfully. I was always puzzled by the great assortment of clothes along the road: men's, women's, children's, all kinds.

In one spunky little town I was directed to an old hotel. It was a nondescript white building with a small neon sign saying simply "Hotel." I entered the lobby and was struck with the atmosphere, the smell of squeaky clean Nebraska, unpretentious and practical. So what if the wallpaper was a "not-yet-quaint" 25 years old. If it still did the job, why change it? I rang the silver-button bell on the simple desk in front of the "ring for clerk" sign. From the back wall emerged a serene woman walking with a dignified carriage. She looked directly at me and said pleasantly, "May I help you?" Growing forth from the left side of this woman's head was a tumor that rivaled in size her original head. Its lumpy contours were marbleized with the delicate blue tracings of blood vessels beneath the soft skin. "Yes, I'd like to rent a single for tonight if you have any." The little hotel was overflowing with construction workers, she replied, but one would leave later, and a room would be ready in the afternoon. With respectful deference, I asked for permission to sit a while in one of the ancient chairs in the lobby. I didn't know it then, but I sensed that this was no ordinary hotel clerk. In fact, this women presided over the old hotel like a queen; it was her domain from cleaning to policing, and she did it all with an air of unquestionable royal authority.

The old hinges on the front screen door squealed nostalgically, and a man wobbled in sheepishly carrying a brown paper bag. "Shame on you," said the woman with pleasant aplomb. "You know I don't allow drunks here."

"Why, I'm not drunk," said the man with an earnest smile. He sat on the old leather couch respectfully.

Thereupon followed one of the most astounding exchanges I have ever heard. The woman stood before him with confident dignity while her gleaming tumor wobbled massively. The man sat as a pupil before a teacher, listening.

Didn't he know that drink would never solve problems, that it just made them worse? Didn't he know that the Lord would give him strength to bear any problem without drink? On and on they went with references to family problems rebutted with exhortations to heed the Lord. Finally, offering herself as an example the woman said, "Look at me. I'm a perfect example. Because I'm close to the Lord, I'm in good health!" ... Well, I had to admit that there was some truth in that statement. It took a person of extraordinary mental health to meet the public daily, run and clean a hotel full of construction workers, and command an instant respect while sporting a gigantic grotesque tumor on the side of one's head.

A few people I saw and heard in that hotel were each more peculiar than the last until I pictured the whole scenario as a Fellini film. What was I, a 37-year old suburbanite, wife, and mother, doing there unknown and alone? I reveled in a most delicious feeling of escape from conventionality.

In this hotel with all these kooks, I have left my cart and everything I own in a downstairs hall. I must be crazy, but the place is Nebraska immaculate, and for some unfathomable reason I'm not afraid. Have to share bathroom and shower down the hall (so that night I became daring and inventive and peed in the sink in the room.) (May the woman with the tumor and God forgive me.) But even the alcoholic and the double-headed woman simply seem like plain ole human beings, not really so different from you and me. It's another side of American society we proper people seldom see. Meantime I will jam the chair against the door (just to keep it shut and block the big crack) and ponder how crazy this world is. People have assured me that long before now I'd run into the impossible: heat, terrain, desolation, snakes, no water, no shade, murder, etc. They've been proven wrong. What more can I do than to feel my instincts and judge by what I see for myself? So far I'm scared by other people's stories more than by what I've experienced.

Last night at the hotel was novel. I guess it's the mid-plains version of a flop house. Off and on during the night I was aware of the drunk down the hall having DTs, moaning and jabbering wildly. I stole out of there at dawn, my cart creaking deafeningly. Later I heard that a murder had occurred on the next block that night: wife shot husband. I ate at the trucker's café at 5:30 A.M., me and 40 men. I ate and left, set out dodging trucks and pickups, friendly and hostile, and tried to get into my rhythm, which was hard in coming.

I began to seek out old hotels as interesting and affordable. In one town along the Platte a fine old hotel was on its last legs. There was no construction boom nearby, and as far as I could tell there were only four people in it the night I stayed: the desk clerk (who waitressed nearby and ran back when a rare customer like me showed up), a lost and lonely man who had one whole hall to himself, old Jake, and me. The lonely man said to me, "If you smell something down the hall, that'll be old Jake." I never did whiff old Jake, but that was just as well; being almost alone in a big old hotel at night was plenty spooky enough.

It was a perfect setting for a heavy, gothic murder mystery with lots of suspense and horror. It's amazing how one's own head creates the atmosphere. Later when I phoned home in the lobby, suddenly it all seemed safe and friendly, the maroon carpet and dark paneled walls cozy instead of funereal. (Skipping far ahead, the best accommodations for the price were in Bridgeport, Nebraska, where a huge room with two double beds can be had on the third floor for $6 a night.)

Sat in the lobby chewing the fat with old men and feeling very much at home. One, a cook, brought me a sandwich. The sandwich gives me goosebumps knowing the old man who made it, but my philosophy is anything given in love or thoughtfulness or kindness won't make me sick, so down it goes. Not bad ... ham, cheese, lettuce and mayo on white.

An important incident occurred early Sunday morning on a lonely stretch of road east of North Platte. This is how I wrote of it in my journal:

I awoke at 5:00 A.M. as I told myself to do and it was still dark. It sure is a lonely wistful feeling to be waking up while it's still dark so far from home in an unfriendly town. I decided I wasn't going to walk on that damned Highway 30 in the pitch dark, so I waited till 5:40, about 20 minutes before dawn. The sunrise was super over the darkly etched, barren sand hills. My left foot was very sore. I was alarmed at the unsavory characters on the road, many more than usual. Then a souped-up car (big tires, shiny new custom Mach painted with stripes) pulled ahead, stopped and backed up to me. In it were four long-haired, rock-band-looking young men. The car was aswirl with pot smoke, the occupants heavy-lidded, slow-speaking, stupid jerks. Two started combing their hair when they stopped. Then came the stupid, slow-witted remarks, to which I responded with all the firm and direct neutrality I could muster. "What's your name?" "Come in here with us, Barbara. You could take off your boots." "Do you know my name?" "Who did you sleep with last night?" "Here's

141

*room for you right in here. We'll give you a place to sleep."
"Do you want to sleep with us? Come on in here." This
continued pointlessly until I said an assertive "goodbye"
and strode away with them still babbling. They finally left
with squealing tires, and I had to admit that I was afraid,
full of revulsion, furious and immediately converted to an
anti-long-hair, anti-marijuana, anti-punk-rock zealot. I was
afraid because I was alone and vulnerable, few cars on the
road at that hour, no farms for nine miles, etc. Because of
their mind-altered state, I felt I was not communicating with
rational, real people. I tried to hang on to my fury and
dissipate my fear in case they returned. I breathed easier as
an hour passed... and then they returned. They alternately
accelerated and braked and zig-zagged all over the highway
as they sped directly toward me. Then they swerved off the
pavement and headed straight at me. At the last second they
steered back onto the highway, laughing stupidly, and went
on. In 480 miles of walking those are the first mean, bad,
hostile, people. Others have acted heartlessly, but it has
been out of fear toward me, not meanness. These jackasses
were simply rich (car), horrid, drugged scum.*

At that point I was scared and furious. Today I
could easily embellish the story to suggest a narrow escape
from rape or a premeditated hit and run. Since the incident I
have spent considerable time trying to evaluate its actual
danger, and in total honesty I cannot paint it as a close call.
There is a vast difference between being coaxed or
threatened and actually being raped or hit by a car. I can
only rely on my own honest assessment, which is that I was
not in any great danger.

Almost all media reporters asked somewhat
hopefully if I'd had any "trouble," the code word for rape,
and have sighed with mixed feelings when I report a firm
NO. There goes a possible juicy story... A few times when

pressed hard by incredulous reporters, I mentioned this North Platte incident, and it was seized upon as the major thrust of the story. Although I never knew what lay ahead, I felt that the greatest and most important news of my trip so far was the vast reservoir of kindness in the American people so easily tapped by a lone traveler like me. A woman <u>was</u> walking alone on the public highways day after day unharmed.

At Ash Hollow, Nebraska, a vibrant family from Ohio on their way to an Alaskan adventure were absolutely exultant by the safety of my trip thus far. "Why, that's wonderful news!" they exclaimed. "That's not only great news, it's very important and deserves banner attention."

But reporters print what sells, and there was a definite palpable interest from many people for a gory anecdote from me. One woman a thousand miles later leaned forward toward me and asked conspiratorially, "Tell me, have you had any... uh... you know... trouble?"

"No, not really," I answered cheerfully, "and I think that's probably the vital lesson from my trip, that a woman CAN do what I'm doing and have great adventures without being molested."

"But," she pressed on undaunted, "surely there must have been times when you had some very bad moments."

"Oh, I've had some very bad moments all right, but they weren't from anyone trying to assault me."

"Really now," she coaxed, "there must have been SOMETHING along those lines that scared you?"

"Scared me. Oh, well, yes, but that was months ago and I don't really think it even deserves to be told."

Pressed further, I told the story briefly about the North Platte encounter without any dramatic flair, but apparently that was enough. A few hours later this woman's husband came home to meet me, and he had no sooner opened the front door when this woman rushed forward breathlessly saying. "Oh, Walter, this is Barbara, and my God, did she ever have a bad scare!!"

I remember the town of North Platte itself pleasantly enough. I splurged on a safe motel room and fell asleep only to be awakened later by a friendly newspaper reporter who had been called by the motel owners. We went outside for pictures and resumed the interview in the room. Only after she left did I sit down and notice with a startle that my pants were fully unzipped. I smiled ruefully trying to imagine the picture that would appear in the next day's paper. After the trip many months later I did see that picture which, of course, gave no indication of my pants situation.

I took a good look at myself today and have to conclude that after nearly 500 miles of walking, my body has not changed one bit. Now that my sunburn swelling is gone, my leg muscles are just as they always were. Ken said I hadn't changed, and the reason is probably genetic. This is a whole new concept for me to adjust to, but on second thought, I rather like it. It means that in truth I am really a very ordinary physical specimen, just like many pioneers were. It means that to struggle 500 miles does not require any great musculature or even undeveloped muscle potential. Even a very, very ordinary person can (and did) do it if one wants to. Mind and desire can make up for a lot of absent muscle. Of course, most people wouldn't want to do this, and that's OK too.

Also, I'm getting a new perspective on people and what types seem to get the most out of life (and what characteristics are deadeners). In every type of case I see, I used to be the wrong way. It sounds simple-minded but the most important traits are trust, optimism, openness, eagerness, and kindness. Suspicion, fear, timidity and

144

hostility are the deadeners. Unfortunately, in the past I was too often more like the latter.

The farmers and men on the road who give an approving smile, a healthy wave, and aren't afraid to pull out to give me more room are a big contrast to the many (too many) frozen-faced women who are afraid to leave the lane and see my strangeness as danger. Some of the women, however, are paragons of plain heartfelt kindness in bringing and packing extra food, showing genuine sympathy for physical weariness, etc. The healthy, happy people take chances, extend themselves, find delight in newness, and have a reserve of trust. The unhappy people are very careful, very self-protective, cautious with fear and suspicion of strangeness. I have not found any common pattern. Both types are found in small towns and cities, men and women, young and old, rich and poor.

I crossed back to the south side of the Platte glad to have reentered the farmlands and put Highway 30 behind me. Some friendly, eager children rode bikes out from the distant clump of trees that was their farm, expressing a healthy curiosity as to who or what I was. With effusive hospitality they invited me to camp on their farmland for the night. Later when I pulled my cart into the drive, the parents were as warm and casual as the children.

I had arrived on a special day. That evening there was to be a community 4-H meeting for teaching hog judging, to be followed by an old fashioned barbeque. "My cup runneth over," I sighed as I lay dreamily in the shade resting and waiting for evening. I heard a stir and looked up to see a peacock stepping daintily less than two feet from my head. The strains from "Saturday Night Fever" wafted across the farm becoming forever the theme song for my joyful journey. Later I described that evening in my journal:

145

There was a healthy acceptance. Before I knew it, I was swept into this farm community group and driven in the big pickup with the women up to the hog pens where we were all given rating cards and had a talk on how to judge hogs. The farmers are very masculine and picturesque. Mystique hovers around them, blue jeans or overalls, and hats and cowboy boots and belts, etc. I could hardly believe that I was sitting on the fence of the hog pen with a judge's card in my hand while peering intently at these squealing pigs while trying to decide if all that bulk was muscle (good) or fat (bad). "Muscle ripples; fat shakes. Muscle is round; fat is square." The ground in the showing pen was a swirling pig manure pulverized powder that we breathed and walked in and settled all over us. In another hog barn the manure is hosed out, and it stands like pale brown sludge a foot thick as it oozes down a slope day by day. Two kids stepped in it half way to their knees. The stench is overpowering to a naive eastern nose so that the air actually feels thick with it. And when the breeze is right (or wrong) a whole house can be permeated with it; even the food tastes like it. But back to the hog judging.

I kept thinking of the kids. The farm way of life is as harmonious and satisfying a family role style as anything I've seen, but it is only one style and woe unto the person it doesn't suit, because there is no other style handy to observe. I was dismayed at the way the pigs are treated, the old callous attitude so shocking to a Humane Society educated easterner. The pigs are kicked to move them. If the panic-stricken lustily squealing pig wanders out of the area, kick it back. If you want it to turn around or walk, kick it. The pig squeals louder with every kick. At one point a panicked pig was blindly running down the pen, and nearly everyone got into the act so that it was being kicked from every side, at every side, head, belly, etc. Back to the kids: some were obviously not cut out for the role. They wore frightened, worried, upset, distasteful expressions as they tried to become good farmers— i.e., kick the pigs. One boy would run out and kick the pig viciously for no reason, wearing the excited, fearful yet satisfied expression of a hunter. Perhaps this is similar in function to the Masai killing a lion or the old Apache learning to torture, part of becoming a MAN, learning to be callous. We went to a pen with sows and piglets and the kids, again tense, seemed to get a charge out of chasing the mothers (showing off) and getting the animals into a bellowing turmoil. One sow was lying motionless. "Ma, there's a dead one here. It must be that crippled one." "Is it dead?" "Wait, I'll see." Poke, poke, pig moves slightly and flaps ears. Kid backs up and kicks it repeatedly as hard as possible. Pig responds feebly.

Later back at the barbeque, I mentioned it was great, but I felt sorry for the pigs. There was a roar of amusement. "I can see you've never tried to load them into a truck. They're the most ornery creatures on earth. I'd give you one day at them and you'd change your mind quickly." I laughed. It was probably true...well, maybe...

Jane, my hostess, related what must be a common lament of hog farm wives. A few years after she was married, she longed for a proper green grassy front yard. After weeks of careful seeding and watering and nurturing, her yard began to look respectable. She hovered protectively over it daily. While away shopping one day, the hogs broke through the fence and headed straight for her precious lawn. By the time she returned, the smooth green had been transformed to a brown rutted mess. She sat down in the middle of her ravaged dream and sobbed inconsolably. She told her husband that she couldn't stand to live like that. A green grassy lawn was important to her. Her husband, pushing other matters aside, then immediately went to considerable time and expense to construct a sturdy hog-proof fence, and on that luscious green grass is where we had the neighborhood barbeque that warm Nebraska evening.

I woke up before dawn and torturously forced myself up and out and on my way. The agony turns to exhilaration the second I hit the road. It is very cold. I shiver and walk faster, crunching along the gravel road. The pale bluish light gives a shadowy black and white TV look to everything. Then in the east a faint pink glow at the cloud-smeared horizon. Dew is on the wheat and corn. The pink becomes a bright peach and spreads pink and peach and touches the fields which seem to be sleeping. I walk on in this exquisite dramatic yet subtly changing beauty for a mile, two miles, an hour. The sun slips a sliver edge above the dark horizon and then quickly comes up, a gleaming ball, and wakes up the fields with its quickening shafts of gold, orange, and yellow light stabbing out. My shadow is 200 yards long over the alfalfa. Another hour and the greens are fragrant and bright before giving up their dewdrops jewels. Clear and crisp and suddenly I'm a little girl long ago on the first day of school, startled by the unaccustomed earliness of the hour and the unexpected cool crispness of the air. Yellow school busses and yellow pencils and new crayons seem close and real. Then I'm changed and a young woman in the high Sierras or the Rocky Mountains, breathing gulps of the cold air which seems so contradictory to the vivid colors bathed by the bright sun. The wheat had become the soft feathery green of a thick new blanket. How can I describe how it lay in gentle strips over the dirt. Red-winged blackbirds hovered over me chirping in dismay as I passed through their territory. A white husky malamute joined me reveling in the new day as much as I. He would plunge into a wheat field and his plume tail would be all that showed as it bobbed jauntily through the parting wheat heads. I saw a deer in the early morning. It stood in the road, antlers and all, and watched me approach. When a dog barked it took off faster than the wind in light springy kangaroo leaps across the fields so so far.

The killdeers nest in the moist ditches by the road, and as I approach they "lead" me away by cheeing and running, keeping a few steps ahead of me.

The constant inspiration was the vastness and scope of the earth that a single glance could encompass. I could see the rolling pasture land stretching invitingly forever. I was seeing it briefly through the wondering eyes of a pioneer on a wagon train. The sun touched my back and warmed it, and later I peeled off my extra shirts.

An old graveyard sat triumphantly at the top of a perfectly rounded hill facing the sun. The green pasture beside it was brushed vividly with a wide stroke of yellow wild flowers. Walked through fields with freshly stacked green alfalfa and hay, giant green loaves of bread, each one high as a shed, here and there on the gentle hills.

Then a car pulled up and out hopped an old lady, the editor of a small local paper. She had farmed for forty years and suddenly lost her husband. So at age 59 she went to college, taught high school, and then started a new career in journalism. As editor of the paper she was working 12 hours a day, age 72. She took a quick photo, asked a few questions, popped back in her car, and was gone.

Later that day the heat descended. A dog followed, both of us getting tired and thirsty. We were joined by another funny looking dog, small, virtually no hair, bright pink (sunburned?) skin showing through, ugly brilliant pink block nose. Heat. Saw some hippies camped. One guy naked, scrambling into his trousers. Ate lunch and on to a highway. Prevailed upon two young guys to drive the dogs home. The dogs were bewildered by the traffic on the paved road. They'd never seen a paved road before. Good miles and big heat. Land changes to up and down hills, advancing waves.

I think about box turtles and think about the beauty of Nebraska now basking in the heat, and over the next hill, unmistakable with its rockety gait, my turtle, handsome and dark, with its yellow and black inkblot shell designs and its bright orange eyes (male) and beaklike overbite. He pulls in momentarily as I lift him and almost immediately comes out again. I am overjoyed and talking to him and carry him off the road to the top of the hill where he was headed. And I put him down and off he goes with determination. "Good-bye, you little traveler, and good luck to you forever." I've become quite nature sensitive, avoiding even running over beetles and bugs. Onward in the heat.......

Way ahead, is that a newly shingled, old-fashioned barn? Is someone actually repairing one of those old gems? Forty-five minutes later..., it IS a newly wood-shingled old HUGE barn. My heart accelerates and I breathe rapidly as I approach the neat flowered grounds and the happy old house.

The most crucial part of every day, the time that always found me tense with hope of acceptance yet fear of rejection was the afternoon or evening when my energy allotment for the day was depleted, and I desperately needed a spot to camp for the night. I would search farms and houses yearningly for clues indicating nice people. Somehow I would emotionally attach a great symbolic significance to things such as profuse flowerbeds, friendly dogs, children's sandboxes, red tricycles or, as in this case, a big old barn newly shingled... Knock, knock... an older

150

woman answers. (She said later that she thought I was a Jehovah's Witness.) Thank God! She smiled! Things go well. The tension dissolves in floods of relief. She's a widow, has survived two husbands, is in her 70s (looks 50), calls me "kid." "You can stay here with me tonight, kid, and we'll have a ball." She talks with vibrant animation and tells the tale of her life.

Ella Jorgenson Miller's parents came from Oklahoma to the sandhills to homestead, an awesome undertaking which partially failed. The sandhills wouldn't grow crops, so they moved to Paxton. My body relaxed as my mind gave itself completely to the marvel of Ella's remarkable love story.

"When I was 17 years old, I met a 17-year old boy, Ray, on a train trip. We were together about two hours, and you know how young kids are, well, we wrote and exchanged pictures for a few months. Then we just kind of lost touch. Years later my daughter found his picture up in the attic; I had almost forgotten who it was."

Ella and Ray had gone on, each with their separate lives, each marrying, each raising a family and living in different states. After 40 years on the farm, Ella's husband was killed in a tractor accident. Meantime, Ray lost his wife to lung cancer.

One day Ray, a retired railroad man, was traveling through Paxton and faintly remembered that Paxton was where that 17-year old girl from more than 40 years ago had lived. He stopped and inquired about her at Ole's Big Game Bar and was directed to widow Ella's farm just outside of town. Ella wasn't home so Ray left a note in her mailbox. They exchanged letters and arranged a meeting.

"Well, you can imagine I did have butterflies in my stomach," Ella continued. "I mean after 43 years we sure didn't look the same. Well, he drove up, and do you know how I broke the ice? I just went right up to him and said, "Remember how we used to sign our letters, 'love and kisses'? Well, I'm finally going to give you a kiss right now." And I gave him a big kiss, and that broke the ice and we hit it right off. He had such a good sense of humor. When we went into the house I went to the attic and brought down that same picture he'd given me 43 years ago and he just couldn't believe I still had it."

After 43 years of separation Ella and Ray were reunited and married. They had a joyous eight years together... and then Ray died. Irrepressible, upbeat Ella allowed the only shadow I ever saw cloud her face when she said, "I only wish we'd had more time together. I just don't understand why we couldn't have had more time together." After a pause Ella turned to me with an infectious grin and said, "Well come on, kid, let's go out and see the barn!" I unlimbered my stiff legs and followed.

On the way to the barn we walked past her exquisite flowerbeds and vegetable garden and through the chicken yard. The chickens, happy to see Ella, strutted around us in a happy cackle. Ella, like many of the farm women I met, thoroughly enjoys her chickens. We paused in the hen house to gather a few warm brown eggs.

Ella   1979

Ella upstairs in her cathedral barn.   1979 ES

But the barn, the pride of the property, dominated the scene. It stands empty now and would be gone but for Ella's fine and stubborn appreciation of its historic and aesthetic worth. Her friends and even the roofers urged her to tear it down. She had a hard time finding a contractor who would even attempt re-shingling its high arching roof. Sadly, three large cupolas were removed from the top to make shingling easier, but otherwise it stands pretty much as it did in 1911 when erected. It is a Sears precut, hauled beam by beam to the farm site. We stepped reverently and quietly from the hot, bright sun into the cool, dark interior. Shafts of light beamed through the darkness to illuminate the brick pattern of end-sawed blocks of the wood flooring in the horse stalls. Ella stood and gazed, saying, "I can see it as clear as yesterday, all the horses here, and back there are the stanchions where we milked the cows." We climbed the stairs to the loft where I nearly fell over backwards. Up, up soar the majestic curving beams to … to … way up there, the peak, a vaulted cathedral, awesome.

Vivacious Ella kept up a lively chatter, bustling about as she led me back to the house where like a mother hen she set me in a reclining chair and put on some soft music (Tijuana Brass) for relaxing. At one point Ella looked me over and stated, "Why you have no bosom at all to speak of. It's better that way. No sense going through life like me carrying all this extra weight around."

I dozed lazily until Ella announced that she was taking me on a tour of the sandhills around Paxton. We picked up Grace in town, "a widow lady like me," and we were off.

Grace, a spunky 80-year old, looked 55 and acted 35. If my trip was laid out in heaven, surely this was the day entitled "Life Begins with Widowhood: Great Old Women of Nebraska". Grace, the third super-senior of the day, had her own remarkable story. She too survived two husbands. Her first died young leaving her with five small children whom she raised alone and well in Paxton by working 40 years in the local food market. The children are all grown, college educated, and scattered about the country. Then at about the same time that Ella was marrying Ray, Grace had a chance meeting on a bus trip, a man who had gone to her high school in Paxton "about a zillion years ago." They too were married... and he died within five weeks. Grace chuckled and laughed as she told this, as if life were too ridiculous to fathom. Earlier Ella had showed me the local cemetery and mused, "Look at all these names on these stones; every single one is familiar to me. I can see every one of those people just like yesterday with all the memories ..." All the death talk was done with a kind of matter-of-fact enjoyment, a celebration for life back then as well as now. It was a whole new concept for me.

In the car through the sandhills the reminiscences flew between the two old friends. "Here's the house where there were those two sisters who did the suicide and murder," "Oh, remember when that house and the one next door were built! The pride of Paxton!" The house was on the edge of town, shabby now but Victorian in flavor and once obviously graceful and beautiful. "Oh, there's the old swimming spot the Lion's Club fixed," which to me now looked like a mud hole. "My my, here's Wind Bluff Hill. When I was a kid, my brother and I used to have to go up there to get the cattle, and we thought it was higher than a mountain. Look at it! It's really nothing, but how we felt like really something when we got to the top. I can't tell you the hours we spent climbing there." Both women roared with healthy laughter.

I listened with rapt attention to the remarks about the sandhills as we drove deeper into the now empty stretches. I have never felt quite so inexplicably drawn to an area. As far as the eye could see, under the pale blue-wash sky were the gentle, treeless undulations of dry, wispy grasslands. To my unaccustomed eyes every little hill appeared identical to every one beyond it or behind it or beside it, and yet I felt an insatiable desire to go over the next one and the next one farther and farther, deeper into the sandhills. To lose one's bearings here would be disastrous. To live here would be unthinkable, and yet these were the very hills that the pioneers so bravely tried to homestead in their tiny little soddies. Grace and Ella recalled how the now empty, lonely road once had homesteads and sod houses dotting its edges. All evidence of their existence was now gone except for a rare clump of trees a hopeful pioneer had once planted. The soil had been too dry and sandy to make a go of it. Once the prairie sod was broken, it was vulnerable to wind even in the wet years. Ella turned the car back toward Paxton. Near the town where the land was moist Grace smiled and said, "To you it probably sounds silly, but to us, seeing the cows with their calves knee deep in grass, well, to us it's a kind of beauty." I vowed to come back someday.

For dinner and breakfast next morning, Ella fed me and fed me from her vast store of home-canned foods from her garden. After a warm hug from Ella, "Goodbye, kid," I walked down and out her long drive with a last look at the big barn and the wooden windmill, past the little cemetery where Ella buried two husbands, and on to the west.

Ogallala, the next town, sported a newspaper that invited and got participation from its readers. Within a few hours after my arriving, the paper had received four calls from citizens tipping it off to my presence. The reporter later said that when the phone rang again he was tempted to simply pick it up and say, "I know, I know, I'll get to her as soon as I can."

9

THE NORTH PLATTE AND THE NEBRASKA PANHANDLE

June 16 – 25
(148 Miles)

"...'tho your dreams be tossed and blown, walk on, walk on..."
Oscar Hammerstein, II

Heartland America...   1979 ES

The pioneer emigrants had been following the mighty Platte upstream across much of Nebraska. They had come to its two feeder rivers, the North Platte and South Platte, which forked. It was imperative to cross the south fork to rejoin the northwesterly route that the north fork of the Platte would trace deep into Wyoming. Near the present town of Brule, the emigrants took the plunge, crossing the fearful river at California Crossing (now tame as a mill pond), pulling hard up California Hill to the high plateau that separates the forks and heading toward the North Platte. It was near Brule by the California Crossing where I had lain in the bathroom, demoralized by the heat and my pitiful six-mile day.

But the next day I arose before dawn and experienced an ecstatic 27-mile day. I climbed and crossed the high flat plateau separating the two Plattes which brought me to Ash Hollow, the most feared landform yet to the emigrants on the trail.

The wheat is waist high and now turning golden. I have watched it since Kansas go from brilliant green shiny ribbon grass to head up in a feathery bluish green to now a chartreuse yellow-green. Next it will be golden, I'm told. With the wind stiff, the wheat was in dazzling motion. Not only does the wind race across it in rapidly advancing undulating waves, but each tiny bunch of wheat moves in a circular motion so that the whole world is swirling and zig-zagging and beating up and down. An occasional tumbleweed bumped me.

It was quickly turning into another fantastic super day. I was enraptured. I felt the same excited anticipation the pioneers must have felt knowing a radical land form change was about to unfold after an eternity of flats.

At the edge of the plateau the emigrants had the problem of descending a steep hill to rejoin the North Platte far below. This frightening descent, known then and now as Ash Hollow, is today a state park where the series of ruts which plummet down Windlass Hill are carefully acknowledged and preserved. The hill so terrified the pioneers that one described it as "a bit past the perpendicular." The terror was not for the people, who would walk down the hill, but for the danger to the animals and equipment. Everyone would be enlisted to slow the descent with ropes and brakes. Truly, the hill is nothing to scoff at, and many a wagon and animal lay smashed in accidents at the bottom in the old days. However, it was nothing, absolutely nothing, compared to the terrain and mountains that lay on the emigrant trails farther west.

Ash Hollow was a sudden plunge into a taste of the old west, dry baked ledges and cactus and a spicy aroma and bluffs and defiles and washouts and erosion and scrubby evergreens. Inadvertently I chased a loose calf and startled lots of speedy lizards and cruised happily down the canyon while hawks circled above.

This day alone makes everything precious.

In the evening I walked up to the Visitor's Center alone and felt a surge of deep-toned self-satisfaction. I was utterly at peace and felt secure in my aloneness, so far from home yet totally at home here, or wherever I am.

At a nearby campground, when night came so did the mosquitoes. They sat on my head-net by the dozens and whined and bit through my clothes, a horror show. I moved my bag to an enormous field, but then late-night campers driving in nearly ran over me because my sleeping bag was not as tall as the surrounding grasses. Oh well, the bugs were bad there too anyway.

Later the wind came up. Branches crashed around me. In the distance, lightning (40 to 50 miles away) lit up the sky like a flickering light bulb. When I say "flickering light bulb," I mean like no eastern thunderstorm ever dreamed of being. None of this waiting between flashes. It's more like a steady flare with short "off" flickers. The sense of natural power with the terrific wind and the far-off electrical storm was exciting but not unsettling enough to keep me awake more than two minutes. Thank heaven, at least the mosquitoes were gone. Then I awoke to the first drops of pelting rain so I ran to a neighboring trailer (as agreed earlier if it rained), pounded on the door, and they let me in, where I fell asleep within seconds on the floor. A man next door, whom I had passed in his underwear, was outside tying things down and was terrified. The thunder sounded odd to him and he feared a tornado. I mentioned this to the aroused neighbors who in turn were scared. I sensed that we were only getting the edge of the storm and wasn't in the least concerned and fell asleep, but it was a new and novel situation to be so unaffected while the adults around me were quite agitated. I recall being hysterically afraid of tornadoes and thunderstorms on a return trip from California 15 years ago. The emigrants? Most surely they too faced these fears.

Goodbye Ash Hollow.

This morning on the way to Oshkosh the sky was still unsettled, dynamic and dramatic, black with stormy clouds on one side and pale blue with brilliant sun on the other. The sun touched the cottonwoods along the Platte, turning them bright green against the stormy purple backdrop. On with my turtleneck, off with my turtleneck, on with my turtleneck, off, etc. Finally, toward noon the sun blazed fresh and fierce. Meantime the barren western hills across the Platte went from looking stormy, black, and wintery to fresh, tame, and mellow green, inviting and then to a forbidding sun-scorched hell. These same hills that I watched all morning took on such a willfull dynamic personality.

Saw my first rattlesnake, dead, a very small one, cute baby, triangular head, brown diamond pattern on beige, tiny rattle at tip of tail. Saw hundreds of snakes, dead, along the road. When I walk at dawn, they will be stirring, and that's one reason I hesitate to leap in the weeds every time a car comes.

161

People have various ways of reacting to me. Here in the west, "I admire you for doing it" is the most common. I react to "I think you're crazy" by saying nicely and honestly, "Please don't say that." And my pet peeve is "Whadda ya think you're trying to prove?" Me sweetly: "I'm sure it doesn't prove anything, does it."

Every so often I hear the music from Saturday Night Fever and it sounds so alive, like the travelin'-on theme for my trip.

Some early mornings I have the dread feeling that I'm going to be killed.

Yesterday morning left Oshkosh before sun-up and walked into the beauty of the awakening North Platte. I crossed the bridge in the eerie light just as the sky was pinkening, the cattails and bullrushes murmuring with marsh birds. Ethereal ghostly mists clung around the water surface and defined the outlines of every lush island in variegated shades of cool dark grays and greens. The swallows around the bridge darted and cheed in crazy circular patterns. There are so many scenes of perfect beauty on this trip, harmony, balance, and a throbbing life.

After turning down a dirt road, I came to my first of many hundreds of cow guards, a grate across the road of shiny, slippery bars about four inches in diameter, slippery and real leg breakers. That's why the cows avoid them, and it eliminates the need for gates across the road. After teetering a bit, I finally worked out a way to get me and the cart across; the cart bounces fearfully, but...

My second surprise was that suddenly there I was in the midst of a herd of Hereford cattle, and they didn't stampede away from me like those behind fences; they started loping toward me and stopped and retreated, then came at me again, stopped and followed me, then ran over the hill in a modest thunder. It's true; the ground does tremble.

Then I had my third surprise. The road turned to soft sand and suddenly the pioneer and Mormon hand cart complaints about the agony of soft sand became agonizingly real. My God! It was worse than dragging a 100-pound bag of potatoes the length of Jones Beach. Two hands on the handle, body sideways, doubled over, side-stepping, foot by foot up and down (really down!) hills, over flats. What a nightmare! Happiness is a stretch of hard-packed gravel after a haul through sand. It was different from the toil and struggle of sore feet. Now I had no pain, only intense effort, preferable. I wonder if the infinitely harder struggle for the toiling oxen was fully realized by the pioneers.

Suddenly and all day I was on the range, no trees, no houses, only softly rolling prairie, sage brush (mmmm... fragrant), terrific heat, tumbleweeds, grasshoppers, big big sky. I could nearly see Indians watching me from the distant bluffs. Yucca and prickly pear, cactus and hidden rattle snakes. After intense effort, I stopped and lay down in the skimpy shade of a lonely prairie cemetery in the hot, fierce wind. I had gone 20 miles, amazing considering the body-breaking struggle along the sandy stretches.

As I started out again, an old man (cowboy hat country now) stopped his pickup truck and reminisced for an hour (while my feet swelled) about his life on the range, his early years in a soddie, his mother's fear of Indians and how she kept a loaded Winchester rifle by the door, how his family arrived with only a map and needed help finding their Kincaide on the vast, featureless (only to us) plain and how once every section had a soddie homestead and there were 40 kids in the now-gone school house, and now it's all gone, gone back to wild prairie again. He gave me a rattle from a rattler he'd just killed. He suggested that I go another two miles and stay with Nellie, a famous painter who "paints so a horse looks like a horse, not like those types that make a picture that looks like nothing, and you don't even know what you're looking at."

Those last two miles were the worst of the day. They did more damage to me in the heat than all the rest. I fairly staggered into Nellie's ranch. The old rancher had described Nellie to me as 80 years old, never married, manages the big ranch herself, and "smart as a whip." "You probably won't get her to talk much." "Wow," I thought, "a real eccentric tough old shrewd pioneer woman." I knocked on the door, and after a long wait a little wispy frightened-looking woman uncertainly came to the door. She had a vulnerable, soft, doe-eyed shy gaze and a naive childlike smile that never left her face. She looked 60, not 80 (here we go again). This delicate creature was Nellie. She seemed nervous and shy the whole time but hungry for relating to me.

When most people hear that I'm walking the pioneer trail, they inquire into my motivations with the quiet, delicate finesse of a Mack truck, "Well, whadda ya doing THAT fer?" The curiosity is honest and sincere, but I always wince at the harsh quality of the blunt question. Gentle, sweet Nellie's curiosity was no less active, but she softened her already soft voice and asked delicately, "Why are you doing this... just trying to get the swing of the Oregon Trail?" I felt myself smiling with love for her gentle coaching and answered, "Why yes. That's as good a way to put it as any." And then there was perfect understanding between us.

Here is her story: Nellie Hannah's grandmother grew up in Pennsylvania and moved to Illinois, married and had eight children. Her husband died. She left two children, one of the oldest and one of the youngest with a childless relative and piled everything else into a box car and set off to homestead in Nebraska with six children ages 2 to 16 and no husband. This was 1883. They arrived at Sidney, staked a claim but could not find water, and were forced to move 46 miles north where they, women and children, put down a soddie and homestead. She had to drive a horse and buckboard wagon 46 miles for groceries, got caught in a blizzard once and had to stay in an abandoned shack half way, the only structure the whole 46 miles. Nellie's mother was the 13- year old daughter. Nellie's mother married at age 19 and had three children. When Nellie was 3 months old, her father was killed in a well digging accident, so Nellie's mother raised the kids alone. Nellie and her two brothers lived all their lives in the original soddie or in the stone house her father built. Neither Nellie nor her brothers ever married. Her two cousins, "old maid" and bachelor, lived in the next section and also never married. Nellie's brothers both died, one in a helicopter accident while checking the windmill watering tanks. "I miss them so bad," Nellie whispered with an ache as fresh as yesterday.

They built the ranch into vast acreage, over 1,000 head of cattle, minimum 12 acres to each animal plus vast acreage for hay and alfalfa. Nellie's land went as far as the eye could see, out to the little dark dots which were "pine trees on those hills that the pioneers used to get logs for the roofs of the soddies." Nellie's greatest pleasure had been riding horseback with her brothers out on the range checking the cattle. She rode till age 77 but stopped because she didn't want to go riding "with no hired man. Besides I need a nice tame horse. They don't break them in good any more the way we used to."

As a child Nellie loved to draw, and "the half hour drawing hour on Friday afternoons in school was not enough for me." Her mother encouraged her. She showed me her first oil painting, horses, and lovely (just like the

165

man said). She gets $100 per painting, has a back order now for 18, has won numerous awards, and her paintings hang all over the U.S. She does mostly waterfowl and wildlife....Nellie Hannah.

Like all farm women I'd met (except one), Nellie would rather be outdoors than do housework, and unlike others, her house showed this. Unlike others too, she's all thumbs in the kitchen, but she made a wonderful supper and breakfast for me. She loves her chickens and animals and enjoys the coons, coyotes, and colts, etc. There is a minor grasshopper plague on. They've stripped her garden and hop all over me as I walk, like the staccato keys of a typewriter. This morning as I left, Nellie walked ½ mile with me. As we passed two cows with their calves I said, "Now, which is the better cow?" For a few seconds Nellie's childlike innocent face changed as she intensely and coolly appraised the two animals. "I like that one," she said pointing. "Why?" I asked. "Because it's got a shorter face and you can tell the other's an older animal because its nostrils are farther apart." The shrewd rancher had shown through for a minute. She likes to go to the cattle sales to bid on and buy the best bulls. "I like 'um chunky but not too short. My steer has three times brought the highest prices on the market." Nellie gripped my shoulder briefly the morning I left, and I was honored. We said goodbye, and I left a complex person. She's never been east of North Platte, she, unsure of herself in social ways, yet an established artist, successful rancher, now without any family left.

After returning home to Massachusetts the following November, I found this letter waiting for me.

Dear Barbara,

Congratulations on your successful journey.

Sorry to have to inform you of this, but Nellie passed away June 28, a little over a week after you were there. Although I never met you personally, I feel like I've known you a long time with what Nellie told me and the cards you sent her. She would have appreciated them. I will always remember the little tire tracks from your golf cart, coming down the road and thru my yard, as I live 4 miles west of Nellie.

I and the community will miss her greatly.

Sincerely,
Soren Hansen

A year later while in Nebraska, I stopped at the lonely prairie cemetery where I had taken shelter from the sun and hot wind a year before. On the way out, I glanced at a fresh- looking grave and stopped. It said, NELLIE HANNAH.

Left Nellie Hannah and within a few miles walked into another herd of cattle. Nellie had been surprised when I said I wasn't afraid of them. "Should I be?"
She said, "Lots of people hereabouts are." The man at Cozad had said that the black ones tended to be mean and hard to handle. Well, here I was right in with the herd, a mixture of colors. This time I knew enough to be a bit afraid, mean bulls, black Angus, cow with calf, all potentially mean types, and I'll be damned but the whole herd started toward me and cut in front of me. "Whew!" I thought, "now they're beyond me." And then they stopped, turned and came at me again, and again padded in front of me. This was repeated until I was finally ahead of them, and then they started to charge me from behind, led by an all black one! I shouted (even though it had had no effect before) and all but this one turned reluctantly and clambered faster and faster up and over the hill... finally followed by the black one. Whew. Thunder ... earth shake.

Do I have a million mosquito bites or poison ivy? I enjoy the itching and scratching as usual.

Walked impatiently. I hate the highway.

The sunrise was hot pink yarn over a bed of lavender gray smoke. How can one describe a sunrise? On the opposite horizon the moon was leaving. A luminous creamy plate, flat and enormous, slipped behind the blue horizon clouds and disappeared. The sunrise meanwhile became a garish contrast to the cool moon. The hot pink yarn and purple smoke was dripped all over with rivulets of gleaming liquid gold. I really didn't like it, too garish. My mood was with the departed creamy moon.

I knew from my maps that I was almost within sight of Courthouse Rock, the first great landmark of the Emigrant Trail. The sky was providing an appropriate backdrop for so important a meeting; it was a dynamic stormy blue-gray with shafts of sun breaking through here and there as clouds jockeyed for position. And then there it was… Off to the south, a good 20 miles away yet, but unmistakable, a boxy mesa rising defiantly out of the smooth horizon. Jail Rock sat appropriately next to Courthouse Rock like the little sister it is. For my meeting with the rock there was no mistaking the appropriateness of its name. The sun miraculously broke through the fathomless gray and illuminated the courthouse to a gleaming ivory white. A satisfied grin welled up from deep in me. "So there," I mumbled, fairly sniffing at the historians, "it really <u>does</u> look like a courthouse." I felt I was evening up a score. The pioneer diaries one after another chortled their delight and amazement at the white marble courthouse, but later historians have often written patronizingly about how the travel-weary pioneers sure did stretch their imaginations to call that a Courthouse. Then I saw why. As the clouds shifted, the great landmark was suddenly shrouded in shadow, turning it a flat, dirty brown. Indeed the pioneers probably saw it both ways since it

168

would have been within their sight for days and nights, mornings, evenings, storms and moonlight before their dots of wagons inched past and out of sight. Those who found it especially alluring would set out on a jaunt to its base when their wagons drew the closest along the route. The short jaunt would soon turn into a long haul when the adventurers found out that what looked four miles away was in fact more like twelve.

Helen   1979 ES

Helen and Paul Henderson, a retired railroad family, live in Bridgeport, Nebraska. They have devoted a lifetime studying the Oregon Trail, not the study of academic and esoteric classroom lectures but the study from days on the trail fighting buffalo flies and rattlesnakes to locate the precise spring or campsite mentioned in an emigrant's diary.

Within minutes of my arrival Paul told me with obvious disgust, "You have no idea what you're in for when those buffalo flies are out. They can even kill an animal, drive 'em crazy."

Within a few more minutes I learned that Paul had just that morning received a grave medical report. I suggested to his daughter that surely this was not a time for me to intrude. But she said that this "would be the best thing in the world for him: to be out on the trail." We would all go out to a pioneer stop at Courthouse Rock for the afternoon.

Helen, Paul, and their daughter drove me to the base of Courthouse Rock. The Hendersons came alive and talked with absolute authority and love of the trail, rich with knowledge, total knowledge. We gathered buffalo bones and flint chips and bits of charcoal. The Indians for thousands of years gathered at the high site and scraped marrow from the buffalo bones and chipped their arrowheads and made their campfires in the circles of stones, and we found bits of pottery, lots and lots of all this at the base of Courthouse Rock. We saw eagles nesting on Jail Rock. At one point I gazed into the distant west and saw Chimney Rock unexpectedly. A ripple of thrill and excitement ran through my very bones.

Chimney Rock   1979 ES

In my journal I wrote prophetically: *I foresee the truly great loss approaching when the Hendersons are sick or gone; no books could be long enough to capture all the stuff of knowledge that they fairly ooze.* Seven months after I wrote those words, I received notice that Paul Henderson had died. In retrospect my afternoon with them spent wandering at the base of Courthouse Rock seems all the more rare and privileged.

Feeling a bit like a trail veteran, I left Bridgeport and headed toward the most famous landmark on the trail west, Chimney Rock.

I kept looking back at distant Courthouse Rock. This angle enhanced its dramatic rise out of the featureless plain. I tried to see it through jaded yet grateful pioneer eyes. Then the land gave way to long, gradual hills, and I toiled to the top of one and gasped. Ahead of me stretched a flat valley with a pencil line road fading off into the distant mists. No trees, no towns, no houses. A line of buttes and bluffs bordered to the south and way ahead was the pictured familiar silhouette of Chimney Rock, the whole scene virtually unchanged since pioneer eyes beheld it. Its immensity propelled me to the faint stirrings of panic. The road looked so long in the pitiless sun, and my cart and I felt so small. But reality prevailed. (I never again felt this degree of apprehension, although later desert stretches were far more difficult.) *The air was still cool and the beauty exhilarating so I breathed deeply and soaked in the scene. A carpet of sunflowers filled the grasslands, all faces seeking the rising sun at my back. Here and there the perpetual motion of oil wells caught my eye. Yucca and sagebrush, jackrabbits and adventure carried me.*

While walking I ruminated about periodic discussions on the sandhills and got quite worked up. The Nebraskans who live in or near them love and appreciate them but see no danger to their disappearance. A corporation last month bought 20 square miles of the sandhills, leveled and irrigated, yet the Nebraska natives say they're not threatened. "Nature won't permit their cultivation" or "the large land holders will never sell." The tall grass prairie is gone, all gone, under cultivation. The buffalo are gone. The west coast redwoods are virtually gone. Yet they cannot see that, clearly, the very moment the economy makes more farming yields profitable, the sandhills will be gone. Nature will be conquered. The old land holders will die and their grandchildren will collect the corporate dollar. The hills will be leveled and cultivated and be only a memory. (Pessimistic me.)

The sun heated me as my mind heated me and I took off my heavy shirt and three miles later had lost my map. It must have been dropped when I peeled off my turtleneck. I have some kind of quirk that needles me unmercifully when I lose something. When I describe the pioneers dumping valuables to lighten loads, I invariably choke up. Now the loss of the map sent me into torment. Did the pioneers suffer like this when something was inadvertently left behind? The pack of cards explorer John Fremont saw lying on the ground? The shirt left hanging on the sagebrush? It tortured me for miles and miles. But the sight of Chimney Rock pulled me like a magnet. It lured me onward.

As I came abreast of Chimney Rock, I somehow had no desire to make the side trip to its base. It not only would have meant two extra hours of painful walking on the baking, shadeless plain, but I was repeatedly warned of severe rattlesnake infestation at its base. Passing Chimney Rock gave me a taste for success and accomplishment and whet my appetite to move on toward the western horizons faster and farther. So I did.

I was still pushing myself to my physical limits, daily depleting the last ounce of strength, my energy, tolerance for heat, and feet and leg endurance. After stopping at the end of my long daily hauls, I knew and expected my muscles to tighten and lameness to set in for hours. This became part of my daily routine and I came to tolerate it without fright or alarm, confident that by next morning my body would rejuvenate.

On the day I stopped at Albert and Margaret Hickey's, I was near tears with exhaustion and heat fatigue. The little adobe ranch cottage seemed to be hanging by a thread for its very existence — an artist's dream. It beckoned from every corner with its picturesque weathered corrals, sagging sheds, and weed choked yards. I knocked on the old door as an assortment of dogs and cats darted around me. A pleasant faced, strong and calm woman answered, and I was thus guided to these heaven-sent proud people who kept me and shared themselves with me for two days.

Prairie dog   1979 ES

In this age of ruthless animal husbandry they seemed to be out of another era, another world. They are not merely close to nature; they are part of nature. Because they won't kill the prairie dogs, their cattle pasture is pock-marked with their dirt mounds. They won't kill the coyotes. They won't even kill the snakes unless they are first sure of seeing rattles. Mr. Hickey eats whatever the cows eat when out on the range, Snatch! He swoops down and stuffs a handful of grass into his mouth, and Swipe! In goes a mouthful of cottonwood leaves. Chomp... Chomp... Their beef cattle are not merely an animal crop to them; they are a family of living things that require all the care and personal concern of any aware beings. In these scientific days when cows are artificially inseminated from bulls who might have died five years before and when cows are culled for slaughter if found "clear" (not pregnant), Margaret Hickey

174

related a heart-rending story through her tears of a mother cow with cancer of the eye who bawled for hours after her calf was taken from her and another story of their old bull who was allowed the run of the ranch far into useless old age because the Hickeys couldn't bear to send him to the competitive agony of a feed lot. Albert confided later with a fond smile, "Margaret likes the animals; sometimes she likes them too much."

Albert, age 72, was raised in a soddie in South Dakota among the Indians. He has a full head of white hair, dark skin, weathered piercing eyes, aquiline nose, high cheekbones. He speaks incredibly slowly, softly with distinct resonance and laughs mysteriously as I listen entranced to the stories of Indians that crowd his memories. He walks with deliberate, stealthy, natural movements, and the air around him is thick with powerful vibrations that I can't understand.

Albert   1979 ES

In the evening Albert quietly and persistently insisted I check his cattle with him, so we climbed in the wobbly pickup and set out, slowly opening the rickety wire gate and creeping out across his two-mile cattle range. Castle Rock Butte was looming picturesquely to the east with other mesas and bluffs rising dramatically in the background. The evening cooled. The sun slipped low behind the western clouds. The old wooden windmill leaned crookedly, and we drank the cold water running from the old pipe. Prairie dogs yipped all around us. Cottontails hopped in fearful flight, and tiny owls stood by the prairie dog holes. The sagebrush perfumed the air. A big owl sat at the entrance to a coyote den, originally a badger's hole. Every half mile or so Alfred would stop the rocking pickup and step out and call his cattle in his low hypnotic voice, "c'm boss, c'm boss" or "skip... skip..." and the cattle would move slowly toward him from far away. He was leading them to fresher range away from the overgrazed area by the windmill and water tank. Finally, deep in the range he dropped alfalfa bales and corn, and the cattle appeared from over the hills and milled tamely around us slowly and massively. It was like a dreamy ritual through eons of time, man and cattle, knowing and trusting. Slowly we rolled rockingly back home across hogsback hills as the sun set lavender and the full moon glowed for those moments.

Next morning at dawn Albert gripped my arm briefly and movingly, and Margaret walked to the end of her lane, stood, and watched me go. I pulled the cart down the road and turned for a last look, and Margaret was still there watching, a tiny tiny speck so far away. A few steps more, I turned a corner, and she was gone from view. I can see her still, watching, and finally I let my tears of emotion spill over.

... knowing and trusting...   1979 ES

The following day I walked for a mile or so in actual Oregon Trail ruts. The Donner Party did not walk that way however. They took a slightly different route called Robideau Pass. I continued for 15 miles on an empty stomach. That's how unappealing dry sunflower seeds had become by then. Near the end I ran into a horrendous deer

178

fly attack. Although the heat was terrific, my desperation was evidenced by my putting on my heavy turtleneck shirt and the mosquito netting over the hat. The deer flies gathered on my mosquito net like polka dots. What a choice: bugs thick enough to eat one alive or protective clothes and netting thick enough to roast one alive. My heat headache, which lasted far into the night, made me wonder if I'd chosen the lesser of two evils. Paul Henderson's insect warning scared me for possible things ahead.

I ran into the first (and only) dangerously mean dog of the trip, a Doberman that circled to attack. The golf cart threw him off momentarily, but he bit at my pant leg until the owners casually called it back after viewing the clash with mild satisfaction. I was disgusted.

I stayed two days in Morill as the only guest in the elegant, old Park Linn Inn run by Bill and Elsie Parker. Seventy-seven-year old Bill (who works full time as a carpenter) regaled me for hours with enthusiastic reminiscences of his days long ago as a cowboy, his love of western lore, especially Fort Laramie and its military heroes, and his fascination with General Custer. Incredibly the anniversary of Custer's battle was the very day I spent with Bill in June. Bill showed me slides from his fine times in the days that are gone. "Sometimes when I'm down," he sighed wistfully, "I like to look at these and just dream about those times. The only sad part is that I know that those days can't ever be lived again."

Dressed up for memories of long-ago cowboy days. ES

Bill in later years, a carpenter. 1979 ES

So far in my journey things had always seemed to work out well with the strangers whose lives I invaded. My stay with the Parkers, however, became a comedy of errors that I felt helpless to stop. (It still pains me to read this.) First, I was invited for supper and slept through it in exhaustion. When I finally awoke, I found no one home. Actually, the Parkers were in their private section of the inn still keeping the food warm and waiting patiently for me. I felt I could not leave that morning without thanking them so I slept till a reasonable hour to thank them. By that time it was too late to beat the heat with an early departure, so I stayed another day (gratefully). Bill and I were elected to make Sunday dinner while Elsie went to church. Elsie came home 45 minutes later (enhanced by a clock 15 minutes fast) than we expected and by that time I had cooked the pork chops to the ruined toughness of shoe leather. (I'm not much in the kitchen even under the best circumstances.) To add insult to injury, I had used Elsie's $100 frying pan incorrectly, thereby risking its ruin. Later that day Bill was to take me to see his favorite horse out in the pasture. Not wanting to cause any more inconvenience to these people than I already had, I sat by the front door ready and waiting for Bill. After ½ hour I figured something was wrong. Sure enough, Bill had been sitting quietly by the side door waiting patiently for me to get ready. Oh woe!

10

WYOMING

June 26 – July 6
(159 Miles)

"I can see for miles and miles and miles and miles and miles."
The WHO, Peter Townshend

Moonrise over the treeless open range, Wyoming.   1978 MK

The sign said, "Welcome to Big Wonderful Wyoming!" above the silhouette of a cowboy on a bucking bronco. I was now incontrovertibly in the WEST!

Immediately I sensed a change; it was in the air. The land was more vast, less tamed. The occasional dusty towns, in sharp contrast to Nebraska's, had a saloon on every corner, and the "hard drinkin'" saloon ritual was reflected in the aggressive swagger of the cowboys. Cowboy boots, cowboy hats, cowboy belts, and a marked decrease in the ratio of women to men lent the land a distinctly masculine air. The neat streets and flowerbeds gave way to boardwalks, dry grasses and dust. Gone were the grid-pattern section line roads. Distances between towns increased. Lingle was all tan, dusty with blowouts and bluffs. The biggest change, however, was in the sudden lack of people. I was in a time machine, catapulted back to the days of the pioneers. For hundreds of miles in Wyoming, one can follow the ruts and trail of the emigrants and see virtually unchanged the scenery they saw, feel the heat and storms they felt, smell their sage and alkali dust. Wyoming, wild and empty, is the closest thing to the way it was.

Emigrant Trail ruts   1978 ES

But my first few days in Wyoming were colored
sour. As I reread my journal, it becomes obvious that those
days had their usual share of good and bad, but because I
was physically sick, my view of the world was skewed by
self-pity and bitter defensiveness. It is true that in
Torrington I was eyed with suspicion and disgust and turned
away by the managers of the seediest trailer park I ever saw,
but it is also true that a kind and supportive woman named
Betty gave me a discount on the health foods I bought from
her store.

Ruins at Fort Laramie   1979 ES

As I approached Fort Laramie I could feel some vague physical complaints turning into alarming symptoms. I was miserable with diarrhea and backache, but my nausea scared me the most. A park service man, the Fort Laramie night watchman, stopped me along the road. He assured me that Mr. Hennessey, the man in charge of the fort, was a nice man who would let me stay on the grounds there. A second park man stopped his vehicle and suggested that when I arrive I should "go and have ice tea" with the employers there. Two more retired men along the way kindly encouraged me, saying "they'll be nice to you there when you get to the fort."

The last miles before reaching the fort were hard, sun, heat, nausea, (I even had splurged and bought a root beer to try to settle my stomach) and my back ached mightily. As I arrived, Mr. Hennessey, the head man, came out and talked at me...about himself...and then told me I couldn't stay there, not even somewhere on the ground in my sleeping bag. "But please, I'm feeling sick" I groveled.

"No. If I let you stay I'd be flooded with requests. We have no camping facilities."

No iced tea, no chair, no three mile ride back to town. Then he lectured me that "the young woman mauled at Yellowstone last week died yesterday, and it was her own fault." Also, that "the two women who died at Glacier, it was their own fault." Then he left. So I left.

Meanwhile a thunderstorm had boiled up with stabs of lightning. I was sick, miserable, and worst of all, hurt, my feelings bruised and battered. I walked on, weak with self-pity. A park woman drove up in a truck going my way. She stopped and asked, "Are you the woman walking the trail?" "Yes. Could I possibly have a ride to town?" "No." And she drove away. Why had she even stopped?

Fort Laramie, "the crown jewel of the Park Service" and I barely even saw it...no connection with the Donner Party for me there. It had been a major stopping place along the Emigrant Trail, and the Donners had mentioned it in their diaries, but I couldn't get away from that place fast enough. Oh, well, the Donners had found it disappointing, and so did I.

(A year later when I returned by car I tensed up expecting the same critical treatment as a park official ran toward me through pouring rain. To my astonishment, he wasn't coming to chase me away as I expected, but rather he handed me a park information pamphlet and even said a few words of welcome.)

But leaving the fort in 1978, camping was out; I was too sick, so I toiled on hoping for a dry motel bed. But later that too went awry with the first place too filthy even for me, which is saying a lot.

WYOMING

With the storm raging outside I waited in Margaret's Café and had soup trying to settle my stomach. An odd handicapped 30-year old man circulated while I talked with his stepmother/aunt who ran the café. She told me of how the man had been beaten on the head with a log at age 15 months. The next day I returned to the café with the brain-damaged man and had a big dinner (which set my stomach back), but I wanted to even up the score of the bad day before with Fort Laramie by giving this little café some business.

For a measly $2.75 I got coffee, bread and real butter, salad, a large steak burger, mountains of French fries, green beans, and ice cream. How the place makes money I'll never know. It's in a dying town, vacant storefronts, sleepy, forgotten, left behind, dead. Do people really live here? The slamming screen door at the front, the smiling eager brain-damaged man with plastic figures on the wall he made to sell, the woman running the place— cook, server, janitor, with the weariness of working in that place 7 days a week, 12 hours a day for 20 years, the young daughter living there and coming out to show off her 5-week old baby, the old man telling stories. I eat at Margaret's Café all I can to give them money (while my cheese spoils in my pack), but after the Fort Laramie fiasco, I feel better for it anyway.

Later I noticed that both legs were covered with a strange rash. I recalled how early that bad day I had kept getting caught in a smelly white cloud from crop dusters spraying heavily for a local grasshopper plague. My sickness? My rash? Any connection? I wondered...

Looking back I remembered how a few days before: *An old Mexican man stopped in his jalopy and wanted to give me a ride. His pants were holey and held together with pins, but he surely had a good heart. I feel sick. I wish my*

188

backache would go away. When some people are so nice to me it makes me a million times more outraged at the mean ones. I'm frustrated. There must be some way I could reward the nice ones and punish the mean ones. It just doesn't seem right that the contrast is so great, but there are no consequences fitting to each. What's wrong with me? There are nice people all around but I'm letting the jackasses get me down.

I do think I'm overdosed with experiences. Apparently the pioneers also became so jaded with new astounding sights that they barely mentioned the Rocky Mountains. I am in sight of Laramie Peak and other mountains, and it gives a shivering thrill of getting somewhere and leaving the plains behind, but I'm too saturated with experiences to really groove on it for a long high.

I can feel I'm recovering. I always do in the evening as the sun sinks low. It is the sun which gets me tetched every day, anxious, confused, and embattled.

As I approached Guernsey many miles later, a strange man in an expensive car pulled up and said in an Italian accent, "BarBarA! I saw a friend of yours last night. Father Russo!" (The effervescent priest from Yonkers, New York who had sent me off on my journey on his bubble of enthusiasm.) My day suddenly turned bright with the anticipation of seeing a familiar face. Indeed Father Russo had hit the town only the night before, but the place was in an uproar in the wake of his dynamic blitz. As I walked through the little village, people came up and actually smiled warmly, saying, "We've heard about you." "How ya doin'?" "How far'd ya come today?" To my inquiries they responded, "Father Russo? Oh, he moves fast but I think you'll find him down at Crazy Tony's" or "The Bunk House Motel" or "the Catholic Rectory." I ran from spot to spot with mounting excitement and anticipation, thrilled with the prospect of seeing a familiar face until the last lead fell through. Apparently he'd gone on. My bubble burst. I was lost and crestfallen. I walked through town toward the famous Register Cliffs.

Virtually within the shadow of Register Cliffs sits Frederick's Ranch, a shining example of the best of the western ranching tradition. Descendents of the original pioneer homesteaders of the area, the Fredericks today are pillars of their community (and state), and leaders of modern ranching, yet they still preserve the original relics and buildings of their ancestors. Their property and lives are a tradition-rooted blend of the old and new, of the rough and the cultured. Frederico, "the super duper million dollar bull," an Italian exotic, lounges in the dappled shadows of the weathered 100-year old barn. The restrained and elegant new ranch house rests gracefully and modestly beside the original log homestead of their ancestors. Modern pivot irrigators send their lacy spray above the Platte River, which encircles the ranch and its historic fields. Those fields and pastures once twinkled with the glow of pioneer campfires. Looming above all of it is Register Cliffs, the sandstone rock face on which the immigrants carved their names and dates in a wonderful testimony of their endurance. *"The old names look strong as if written by capable competent people. After all, they did find the time and energy to carve them."*

One name out of thousands, Register Cliffs   1979 ES

But as I neared the Frederick's ranch on that blisteringly hot afternoon, I was still carrying the defensive paranoia of the past few days.

As I approached Frederick's ranch I screwed up my courage. A bustling pleasant woman answered my knock, "You must be the lady walking the Oregon Trail." Warmly, "Come right in and have some iced tea." A rush of gratefulness and relief floods through me. Wiped away is the frequent early suspicious sparring and battle to gain acceptance. Smiling, warm, western, bathed in safety and good will. I'll never get used to the contrasts which follow so closely, yesterday treated like dirt, turned away sick, today welcomed without inspection.

While I was gulping iced tea, a car roared up to the house in a flurry of dust and out hopped Father Russo followed by two young tourists he'd found somewhere. They had obviously been swept away by his euphoria; they wore that overwhelmed glazed look that we all get in the presence of this human dynamo as they repeatedly embraced all of us strangers. Father Russo, with his large head yet body short as a peanut, looked so vulnerable in this outlandish cowboy outfit with the vivid, huge kerchief, the fringed leather vest covered with badges and pins, and the leather pony express hat, also smothered in memorabilia and braids. He sort of levitated into the house as we all formed an awed entourage hovering around him. We all beamed and laughed with this more vivid than life character who rattled on with engaging explosive mania. He left in a flurry of haste with plans to drive many hundreds of miles yet that day, but his sense of presence lingered on.

Sheepherder's wagon   1976 BM

Harriet Frederick offered me her heart as she spent the rest of that day giving me a tour of the area. We saw Warm Springs where the pioneers did their laundry. We saw her mother-in-law's private museum of Indian and pioneer relics. We saw the old iron ore mining town of Hartville where EVERYTHING was coated, incorporated, with red greasy dust—tree trunks, roads, building, sidewalks, EVERYTHING! We toured the Greek goat areas from the past, the Italian, Mexican and sheepherder areas. In Crazy Tony's Café we bumped into two old-timers more colorful and authentic than any characters in westerns, with weathered leathery skin, squinting eyes, and cowboy clothes. They greeted Mrs. Frederick with a familiar yet respectful demeanor (as did everyone). Incredibly, one of the men had supplied the horses for a TV documentary about the Donner Party. An independent old cuss, he cared not at all and knew nothing about the Donner Party or the show. Although he was unimpressed, I found my chance meeting with him an amazing coincidence.

Harriet   1979 ES

Harriet Frederick drove past the Guernsey Cemetery. She mused a bit with her memories of when she first came to Guernsey as a bride. "When I saw that cemetery sitting out here with no trees and nothing but dry, brown grass and dust all around, I thought 'my, my, what kind of uncivilized place have I gotten myself into?' The thought of being buried in that awful place seemed like the end of the world to me. I just wanted to turn around and go right back home again."

The little graveyard has changed over the years, probably largely due to the taming influence of strong gentlewomen like Harriet Frederick. As we drove by, the green grass was being watered with sprinklers, and small shade trees were holding their own against the open range. "How do you feel about it now?" I asked. "Oh, why it's just fine now," she said. "I've accepted this as my home. I've raised three sons here. The town has changed, and so have I."

In the evening Mr. Frederick took us across his pastures to turn on the pivot irrigators and show off their exotic Chianina herds (super duper exotic bull, Frederico) and simply exult in the beauty of his farm tucked between the Platte and Register Cliffs in the cool soft evening air. Quiet pride, understated importance, low-key confidence, history. That night I slept in an antique bed in an elegant room after a luxurious bath. Next morning a gift of jerky from the shy, ancient hired hand who'd been on the ranch in the same log building since 1926, and a heartfelt, honest, emotional goodbye from Mrs. Frederick, and I was on my way, alive and able to soak up the western beauty, wide vistas of space over each long hill, miles and miles of ranch land.

———————

The trail ruts in Guernsey are the most dramatic of the trail. Worn into sandstone over rough terrain, they cut a swath up to four feet deep in some places. Each wheel line cuts narrowly into the trail, and the outer sides of the wheels' grooves are lined with the side gouges made by the axles. I was touched and moved by how small and frail the ghostly wagons seemed as I stood in their path. The wheels themselves were skinny and the axle width almost like a child's wagon. There in the vastness of Wyoming I asked myself for the thousandth time, "How did they ever do it?"

Guernsey's deep, deep trail ruts.   1979 ES

As I walked deeper into Wyoming the grandeur of the western scene carried me out of the deadening self-preoccupation that had plagued me a few days earlier.

Ahead was the nine-mile trail shortcut that I'd worried about for days every time I'd looked at the map. Before the day was over, I'd have received 20 different stories from 20 different people as to whether it was a road, whether it was passable, whether it was dangerous, etc. I tried it and then turned back in uncertainty. I feared rattlesnakes alone in the wilderness. If I got bit help was out of reach.

The iconic rattlesnake   1979 ES

I met a bearded, recently matured and transplanted hippy type who assured me with the certain superiority only a youth can show that rattlesnakes were NOTHING to be afraid of. "Why my three-year old carried one into the house just last week," he fairly snorted.

I walked across a high plateau with distant strip wheat farming stretching to distant horizons becoming indistinct in the haze against the dark faraway mountains. A tumultuous storm in the northwest streaked lightening and downward smears of gray and white (hail?), and another dark mass gathered to the southeast. I kept an anxious eye on both, seemingly destined to be caught as the two came together over me. It had been a long day of exposure in the brilliant western sun, and despite wearing my big hat all day, my face and arms were badly burned and swollen.

Walked on next morning still uncommonly gray outside. Later the sun held sway but the rare humidity stayed, enervating. The road dipped into a canyon right out of a cowboy movie, the gulch where the rocky ledges and bluffs provided hiding places as the posse rode by the hidden heroes. Suddenly the contrast between the west and east became clear. Here in the west there are no soft, broad-leafed plants or trees. Everything is stingy with its surface grasses, stiff and sharp yucca, long-needled pinon pines. Even the milky blue-green sagebrush leaves are smoky silver slivers. The sandstone ledges and blowouts and bare ground are a pale beige, baked-adobe shade. The coloring is stingy with its greens, the effect dramatic and lovely, austere and ascetic.

At one point a Vietnam veteran (I learned later) nudged his wife and pointed to me in the distance walking along with my flowing white pants and shirt topped with a wide straw hat. "That looks like a Vietnamese peasant!" he exclaimed. Their curiosity won and they drove to catch me and invited me to stay the night with them. These were good people, kind and generous, sharing and confiding, yet the vet spoke with the passion of frustration about wanting to "kill the niggers," "kill the illegal aliens," "kill the green plates" (Coloradans). Just as I was leaving the vet confided sadly, "I'm so jealous of your trip. I'm trapped here with the irrigation and all..."

At a horse farm far from any town, I learned how extremely spotty and select a western thunderstorm can be. While eating in the old dining room, we sat and looked out the back window as the skies opened and poured a heavy shower in long streaming lines onto the back pasture and sluiced off the house roof. We looked out the front window where the sun shone brightly without a single drop of water to be seen. Some eastern house guests and I leaped up in amazement and ran back and forth from front to back scarcely believing our eyes. The difference was not a matter of degrees or a gentle taper. It really was pouring out the back while clear, dry, and brilliantly sunny out the front.

WYOMING

I had trouble getting into the swing of walking. I kept stopping to eat, to change pants, to pee (in sight of the interstate requires waiting till no cars are in sight), to put on sun lotion and then to adjust pack on cart and retie shoes, recheck maps, drink, eat and then repeat all these again and again. I kept thinking I was at Oren Junction but was at least 8 miles off.

Finally I noticed, with a disgusted, alarmed start, that my hubcap was gone and my wheel about to fall off. What good incredible luck, a gas station one mile ahead! What bad luck, no welding there. What good luck, a friendly young man said he was a metal worker and would fix it! What bad luck, his shop was 50 miles back in Guernsey. In the end the friendly young man drove me ahead to Douglas where we found a welder. We then returned to Oren and together walked the 13 miles back to Douglas in the evening.

The "friendly young man" looked to me like a chubby 15-year old with pale red hair and tender skin. As usual, my first impression was wrong. He was 30, a journeyman, iron worker, Vietnam vet, twice married, and a complex person. His name was Mark (although he seemed more like a Charlie), and the fates couldn't have conspired to send a more welcome companion for the next two days. Mark was an instant soul mate, the only person on the journey with whom I felt free to be me—the puzzled, sometimes angry, sometimes irritable, sometimes prejudiced, sometimes unreasonable me. I started right off by grumbling about the unbroken façade of the macho cowboy image in Wyoming. "I know," he said, "which is why I'm wearing these," pointing to his work boots, not cowboy boots, "and this," pointing to his fishing hat, not a cowboy hat. "And my recreational thing is pot, not liquor. It's just my way of not knuckling under to the cowboy attitude around here." Later when we went into a café Mark left thousands of dollars of camera equipment lying on the seat of his unlocked truck. When I exclaimed about this he said, "There is one thing to realize about the western cowboy and that is their code of honor. They'd never touch another man's property. And that goes for women too," he added with a glance at me. "The men are tough, macho, and heavy drinkers and carry on noisily, but they'd never touch an honorable woman." I assumed his stereotype description was not universal, but it was nice to hear anyway.

Mark   1978 MK

That evening we walked the 13 miles into town. At the end Mark was wincing with blisters, but I was OK and delighted to make it my 32-mile day, longest of the trip. The evening walk was cool and like a fresh start. The sunset was peaceful and the antelope posed in perfect silhouettes against the sky. Herds of Hereford cattle mooed and the little calves stampeded in the dark. Over one final rise and the tiny bright lights of Douglas sparkled in the distance invitingly, altogether a lovely walk. I would walk every evening if I had a partner.

I listened in rapt attention to Mark's stories of his life, stories of his days living in a commune, and how, despite honest labor from all the good people, they steadily lost ground; stories of his nightmare of two years in the evacuation hospital in Japan where he carried amputated legs and arms to the incinerators and where he watched 26 men die of their wounds; stories of his satisfaction and fear working in the select fraternity of iron workers; stories of how he works on the power plant by day and attends citizens' meetings to help try to stop its construction by night; stories of how he joined the motorcycle cult only to give it up suddenly when he found himself early one Sunday morning pointlessly making a racket through the center of town.

Mark told about the dark streak within himself and about his violence toward his second wife. Once when I fulminated about the Bible, he astonished me by gently chiding me about my prejudice. He defended the Bible and Jesus, and I felt properly chastened.

I wrote the most poignant story in my journal.

The Vietnam war left Mark scared, withdrawn, isolated, alienated. He came home and wanted to hide in the woods. He had an antique gun collection. He went hunting. He shot a deer and it dropped. He ran to it in time to still see the shine in its eyes. Then before his own eyes the shine faded and the eyes glazed over, "and I would have done anything to make that shine come back." So he went home and sold all his guns.

I was morbidly fascinated with his stories of the years in Vietnam. In the café at breakfast I pressed him for more and more details of the evacuation hospital. I felt ashamed of my snooping when in the middle of one account of a "young boy from Montana who used to show me pictures of his horses…" there was a pause, and I looked up to see a tear spill over Mark's face. He didn't finish the story; there was no need to.

That night Mark slept on the floor in my sour, moldy sleeping bag and I in the bed. He paid the hotel clerk for the second occupant, and it certainly had a suspicious look. I had rented the room alone earlier, and later Mark came and we hauled a ton of his expensive camera equipment up there (before the startled eyes of the desk clerk) and then he stayed for the night. I learned one lesson: things are simply not always the way they look. And people are not what they may seem. I'm naive and a poor judge of people, yet knowing this I still trust people according to my instincts. And I like me for that.

Mark stayed with me in the hotel all the next day and left in the evening. The friendship (not romance) for those two isolated days was real and valid. I look back with pride and satisfaction.

On the walk to Glenrock I descended into a pretty valley with a red ranch tucked in the treed oasis. Harsh dry mountains loomed to the north. Ahead I spotted a cowboy riding zigzag on a horse and then spotted the round gray-cream milling soft lumps that can only be sheep. I reached a narrow bridge from the east as the sheep did from the west. The cowboy herded them across, baaa, baaa, baaa, a real din. They trotted past me over the bridge, grains of sand slipping through an hourglass, the little black-footed lambs wobbling right in with the crowd, one tiny, tiny lamb struggling in the rear trying to keep up. Then, in a cloud of dust, they were gone, but I could hear the vibrating quivering "baaa" long after they were out of sight.

I walked 24 strenuous miles to Glenrock where I occupied the last vacant room in an old hotel. It was the 4th of July. I had come a long, long way physically and mentally since April 28 when a frightened me started those first painful steps.

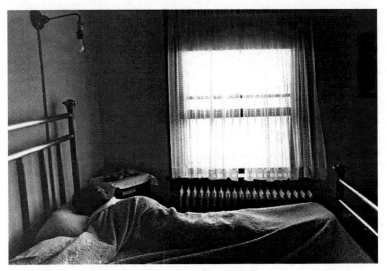

Peace in the old hotel   1979 ES

The past few days it has suddenly dawned on me: this is the happiest, most satisfying time of my life. I'm in an old, old hotel, $8 a night, sharing a bathroom with a man next door and sleeping in an antique brass bed. There are fireworks outside that I see from my big old hotel window. Earlier I walked through town (population 1,000) and ate in the café. The deeply satisfying part of this life is that I'm completely at home and at ease in any town anytime. The hotel becomes an old familiar, comfortable, dear home, even if only for one night. The strange people seem like not-so-strange friends, and most of all, I'm alone but not lonely. I have no fears, love being far away and on my own, confident and comfortable with myself.

The rewards, I realized that evening, were worth every inch of the struggle and went beyond all early expectations. The realization of my deep happiness came almost as a surprise revelation. It emerged uncovered in the Higgens Hotel, but I now see clearly that it had started growing with my first scared steps in Independence, Missouri.

WYOMING

Today in the lounge the women were talking almost proudly and fondly of their phobias, spiders for one, snakes for another. How strange it seemed to cling to these crippling fears.

Wyoming boom towns are something I never anticipated on this trip, the excess of transients and construction hard hat workers and low proportion of women, tight housing situation and high motel rates, all with the evening saloon ritual. It's the kind of situation I should find threatening, but when I really look at the faces of the workers driving past me at 6 or 7 AM, I simply see a long parade of pleasant and often lonely faces, not the insensitive, tough and callous animals the cultural myth paints.

Later, in a swank lounge in Casper, a very proper man, an author, asked loudly and eagerly if a lot of men had been really leaning on me heavily for sexual favors. I was disgusted with his vicarious fantasies and for his assumption of the slurring myth of the wicked construction worker.

I was thinking of the woman who represents many who said, "ALONE?! Oh no, (finger wagging) I wouldn't do that, not in this day and age." My unspoken question to her is, "Why aren't you at the forefront of the women's movement, or do you accept the hobbling and crippling restriction of the free movement of women by culturally sanctioned fear? How can you accept a society where this restriction is so accepted?" Why aren't all the women imprisoned by fear out demanding that this situation be changed?

I keep thinking of a newspaper story and TV report about an assaulted woman. The police or "authorities" say with much head shaking, "These women who get assaulted always think 'it won't happen to me.'" The implication is that these sentiments are self-deluding and stupid and in some way this stupidity led to their demise. Actually, those sentiments are perfectly rational. Percentage-wise the odds are overwhelmingly against being victimized when one considers the thousands of women who do venture out. And yet society's myth approves and rewards the sick, irrational woman's feeling that "if I venture out I'll be assaulted." Thus, once again, society condemns the rational, healthy woman who ventures out and approves the unhealthy, irrational, frightened woman who hides in her prison of fear. Nothing ventured, nothing gained, surely the prison cell of fear.

As if to add to the confusion, there's been a series of seven rapes in Casper within the past two months, women from 16 to 74, a man cutting screens, posing as one wanting to use the telephone, climbing in unlocked windows, etc. I fear that the women who let him in to use the phone will be made to feel guilty, stupid, or naive, and that's infuriating because women are already crippled by the sense of obligatory fear that society hangs on us. Just as there's no way a president can be protected against a determined assassin, a woman should not be expected to imprison herself for life to foil society's lunatics. The exercise is futile anyway, me 880 miles alone on the road, and the poor old lady in the nursing home gets attacked. There's no logic. There's no sane or healthy way to protect against insanity.

Entering Casper:
Glenda, a sexy, blond grandmother, bursting with youth, swirling with effective energy, going many directions, editor of the woman's page, stopped me along the highway in a wonderful assertive flurry and taped my story. She drove away only to return shortly to insist I go to lunch with her. She loaded my impossibly large golf cart into her

204

impossibly small Ford Pinto by sheer force of will, unconcerned about the massive grease spots she got on her smart pantsuit. She escorted a disheveled and tattered me into the plush restaurant where a beautiful, gray-haired (hair in a bun, I think I shall copy that dignity some day) woman waited for her interrupted interview with Glenda. Suddenly I was in the frenzied, exciting tempo of the east, vibrant people pushing their exploding, expanding interests. Later Glenda dropped me off at her tiny cottage. How I loved the careless tumble and jumble of plants and books and warm pictures and bric-a-brac and country fabric and, most endearing, an over-stuffed refrigerator smelling distinctly sour (no matter, just keep the door shut.)

Glenda   1979 ES

205

11

FAMILY

July 7 – 17
(140 miles)

"You're going WHERE through Wyoming?! Lady, I don't even like to drive through there."   Wyoming man in Casper

1978 HM

When I first started the trip there were tentative plans that my family would join me vaguely somewhere "out there" when school was out. I had repeatedly used the image of the "family walking together later on" in relating to strangers because somehow the image of mother and family was reassuring. In reality I had thought very seldom of the time we would be together so that when they actually arrived, it was almost a surprise. It had become obvious by any glance at a map, however, that the family as a support system would be absolutely essential for the next stretch through south-western Wyoming if I were to walk anywhere near the original trail. Not only would it have been foolhardy to attempt the unknown route alone, but it would have been impossible to carry adequate water and food supplies without help.

So I waited at Glenda's cottage in Casper. On Friday morning I recognized the sound of our car's motor followed by the sound of my husband Howard's voice, and then I saw them all. Paula, my daughter, almost 15, was grinning, and my son, Cliff, age 13, shocked me by having grown taller and needing a haircut badly. In seconds it felt like we'd never been apart.

We spent the afternoon buying supplies. In the evening, utterly exhausted, we tried to get organized for a 4:30 departure in the morning. We were all tense and snappy by the time we fell asleep. During the night Cliff called, "Get me a pan; I'm going to throw up." And soon Paula said, "I have a wicked bad pain in my side." And shortly I thought, "Us? Backpacking for 4 days? Alone? In the middle of nowhere?!" And then I realized, "We must take the car." And fell asleep.

A local TV station did some filming and taping on our first morning on the trail. So much for the image of the family gathered together with warm pride for the mother. On the TV interview the kids were decidedly unenthusiastic. "What do you think about walking the trail with your mother?" Cliff, "It's boring." "Paula, what do you think of your mother doing this?" "It's alright." A year later, Paula

207

confessed that at age 15 she felt mortified to be filmed pulling a golf cart across the prairie.

Near the end of our first day of walking, hot, exhausted, miserable, Paula burst into tears of rage and frustration when her golf cart snagged on a boulder. "Mom," she said evenly, her voice tightly controlled, "this trip is your thing. This is not my thing. I hate it."

From then on, I was the only one that pulled a golf cart. The others were stashed in the trunk for good.

At the end of our walking for the first day, we plopped down in the empty yard of Poison Spider School in the middle of vast openness. Paula, leaning limply against the wall, observed, "Usually I'd be bored doing this, but now I'm glad to be sitting." Then with their exasperatingly quick recovery rate, both kids were soon exploring and finding baby birds and "taming" a baby rabbit.

Camping that night behind the closed school, Paula and I slept outside under the stars. Middle of night, started to rain, Paula ran to the tent, squeezing in with Howard and Cliff, and I (the rugged pioneer) retired to the car. We fell asleep and WHAM! Hail!! I in the car was shocked with the sudden fury of the storm (which damaged cars in Casper). I held the car door open a crack for emergencies and shined the flashlight for a beacon. The hail whitened my knuckles and poured in the crack. Outside I got an occasional glimpse, through lightning, of what was the little tent, but it was so grotesquely out of shape, it didn't look like a tent. (Howard, I learned later, was inside holding up the pole desperately). The hail and howling wind and thunder and lightning, what was happening out there?! The fury subsided slightly, and Paula darted to the car soaked and shivering violently. Suddenly the storm moved on, and the lightning flashed to the south as the stars shone overhead despite some lingering rain. Whew. Thank God we had the car.

Cliff, 13 and Paula, 15   1978 HM

From then on for much of their part of the trip, Howard, Paula, and Cliff lumbered along in the distance slowly and often not gently in our faithful car. Or Howard would drive ahead three miles, leave the car, and run back to walk with us when one or both kids were with me. He repeated this again and again for miles and miles. Some days I walked alone from dawn to dusk while the others took side trips. All together we covered roughly 300 miles. The gaps in my original journal became large, but the important times were noted.

Next morning: red buttes, fresh, delightful, saw elk, antelope. The broad trail running across the prairie that we grooved on and followed breathlessly turned out to be the Oregon Trail alright, but the gas company had gone right down it for miles, dug it up, laid lines, etc. Quite disillusioning.

We saw the "grotesque shapes" in a desolate area that had amazed the emigrants and had been described in so many diaries. Toward evening, looking for a place to camp,

Howard became anxious because of "barrenness, no trees and lack of water." At one point he left Cliff ahead in the car and ran back to walk with Paula and me. Later when we approached, there was the car completely surrounded by a herd of cattle and Cliff's little head peeking out over the herd from inside the car.

Later... *Alone, up the big big pull, Rattlesnake Range, an air of tension hovering with the blobs of building storms in various directions and the large herd of cattle milling ahead, behind, and to the south. Suddenly off to the north the ruts (freed from the gas line mutilation) pulled in a wide swale up the hill. Their appearance emanated a sense of strain and exhaustion. Near the top the cattle departed in a noisy clamber of hooves, and then the highest point, physically and emotionally of the journey so far. Was I gasping from the long pull or the sight before me? In the distance the jagged horizon of the honest, genuine Rocky Mountains, at last, range upon range behind range fading forever into the distant mists, black and violet and gray and blue and a vast breathtaking space of emptiness ahead between my hilltop and the mountains and a thin bright skyline above the mountains and then massive rolling thunderheads, black and turbulent, emitting dramatic shafts of light here and there as if to heighten the dynamic throbbing of the soaring miles. The frail dirt road tilted downward for nine miles, nine miles of exhilaration. I went on with a wary eye on the distant lightning and a communing attention on the precious trail ruts accompanying me to the north. Later we all met and camped half way down the nine-mile descent, not a tree in sight, just the tiny dot of our car on the hundreds of small sagebrush clumps and white flashing antelope rumps.*

That night alone outside I slept like a rock, foolishly gripping my sleeping bag tightly around my neck to keep out rattlesnakes. I didn't even hear the coyotes sing, the loudest and closest Howard had ever heard. In the morning the still dawn air had allowed the dew to collect and soak through my sleeping bag. The cloudless bright sunny sky did a remarkable transformation of last night's awesome scene. It flattened it into a brown, desert-like, frightening expanse, no longer the optimistic beckoning of the night before. Did the pioneers see it both ways? Surely yes.

The kids and I started off down the hill, startling herds of antelope. We all bathroomed behind our own selected too-tiny sagebrush clumps and walked on.

We took the actual Oregon Trail ruts for the last 5 or 6 miles, very very realistic on the flat desert-like expanse, the scene virtually unchanged to what the pioneers saw, exciting. Independence Rock lay ahead.

The kids and I continued on the actual ruts toward Independence Rock. Paula wanted to see "exactly" the ruts and artifacts. "Do you think they walked exactly right here?" she'd ask, pointing down over and over. Horse silhouettes, Steamboat Rock, rock mesas, soda lakes, bird nests with eggs right on the ruts on the ground, alkali lakes (tiny glorified puddles smelling chemical, crusty) dramatic swale and us right in the middle, and then the deer flies came attacking and the horror show was on: Cliff frantic, Paula in tears. The swale became a hard-packed sand, claylike pavement, a treat but unappreciated. The bugs blew away with the breeze, but the fear of their return ruined the walk.

This was the dreaded section of the trail where a hundred years ago the stench of rotting carcasses polluted the air. The thirst-crazed animals would break from their traces to gulp the alkali water and die, ironically only a few yards from the life-saving Sweetwater ahead.

211

We came upon a woman who noticed my red raw face which felt like an open sore. She said it was probably burned from uranium dust and alkali dust in the wind. Then she complained bitterly about living too close to Caspar (50 miles away) and too close to Jeffrey City (50 miles away) saying that the "city folk" bothered them, "cut our fences." She had lived 26 miles farther back over the hills before and had liked it. She had had to drive her kids to and from the bus stop, 64 miles per day.

Independence Rock, an elongated dome of granite rock, sits squarely in the middle of the campgrounds the pioneers used upon first reaching "the dearest little stream this side of heaven," the Sweetwater River. Dazed and recovering from their agonizing dry drive from the Platte River in Casper to this, the Sweetwater, the emigrants must have counted their blessings (or their losses) grimly as they recuperated by the clear, sparkling water. It was an interlude conducive to leaving their own personal marks of survival which they did by carefully, proudly, and with the artistic calligraphy of that time, chiseling their names and dates into Independence Rock, called the great registry of the desert.

The graffiti of the pioneers bears little resemblance to today's crude and sloppy vandalism. It took time and patience to chisel the flawless block letters into the hard granite. It was amusing to see the work of a latter-day traveler who scribbled his own name and statistics sloppily with a can of red spray paint. Nearby the exquisite handiwork of a pioneer carver still defied the elements after 100 years. Times have changed our styles if not our basic impulses to leave a mark.

Unfortunately, we were not able to do justice to Independence Rock. The hot wind and the dry alkali dust-laden air sapped our enthusiasm, and Howard went into a near panic to get to water and shade. With detached amusement, the kids and I had observed his preoccupation with water through the dry stretch just covered. "Everything's so DRY!" he'd mutter over and over as his eyes darted ceaselessly over the landscape. Instead of getting used to it, his anxiety became more raging until one day we interrupted the journey to pile into the car and drive off the trail the considerable distance to Alcova Reservoir. Even that did little to calm his terror as the dry red cliffs surrounding it looked to him like the bastions of hell.

Howard is a veteran outdoorsman but an eastern one. For an easterner who grew up among the moist lushness of streams and ponds and lakes and whose vacations were spent at the seashore or in canoes, the dry western landscape can indeed be frightening. One can imagine the nervous stress some pioneers must have endured.

From Independence Rock (back on the trail), one glimpses the famous Devil's Gate in the distance. The rest of the family chose to do that stretch by car, so. . . .

I set out alone cross country on the trail. Devil's Gate looked closer than the actual 8 miles. Then the trail ran out, so I followed some pasture jeep ruts and squeezed under my sixth fence. Over a hill and, Whoa! A black bull the size of a hippo stood guarding a few cows, quite a way off, but the dire warnings about bulls I had heard earlier from a rancher rang in my ear. I tiptoed back near the fence and began a dangerous (so I thought) trek cross pasture in rattlesnake territory off trail toward Devil's Gate and over another hill and Whoa! Eight Hereford bulls, nearer this time and no fence to provide cover. Heart thumping with aimless anger and frustration and fear, fear of bulls, fear of rattlesnakes, I edged near the Sweetwater, planning to jump in if the bulls charged; and the river was suddenly ten feet deep and swift. The bulls stopped grazing and lifted their heads as I crept around. They gathered and walked toward me, but I was gaining distance. Now my fear of bulls surpassed that of the rattlers, and I plunged recklessly on. Finally the bulls lost interest and I breathed easier until I saw one more pasture, full of horses. I got through, and ahead was an utterly gorgeous Oregon Trail swale up and over the hill, Devil's Gate to the northwest. But, no thanks. I was in no mood for more surprises over hills, so I took the long way around.

With Howard, Paula, and Cliff in the car and out of sight on distant roads, for the next few days I continued to walk alone. The long empty stretches cut by highway for that section held little interest in the shimmering heat for anyone but me.

One night we gathered and slept in an ancient bunkhouse with squared logs and an inch of dust built in 1900. It had a fine old wood stove in the center of the open room and smelled good. It was the famous Tom Sun Ranch by Devil's Gate. The cook, a kind woman, served us iced tea (sun tea in the west) and then rang the old bell for dinner. As it often is with range cattle, the well-cooked meat was tough as shoe leather. The ranch hands there ate fast and silent. We couldn't tell if they were unfriendly or just shy.

We saw the pitiful rock cove where the Mormon handcart company led by Martin, an early Saint, was caught by a blizzard and sought shelter. Without draft animals, they had harnessed themselves to their heavy carts and pulled them, human beasts of burden, as far as I had walked.

In his book, *The Gathering of Zion,* Wallace Stegner describes the scene, page 245:

> Hopelessness ate like a slow acid at their spirits. There was a gray October morning when the people plodding in a ragged column along the Sweetwater felt something brush their faces and looked up. Snow. They did not pause; they dared not.
>
> Fatigue, malnutrition, cold, failure of faith, wore them down…the men who had labored all the way to protect their families…stumbled into camp with their faces drawn and set and sometimes if they rested a few minutes before putting up the tents, they lay down and died without knowing how completely exhausted they were….Chislett, a rescuer, wrote, 'Life went out as smoothly as a lamp ceases to burn when the oil is gone.
>
> Another rescuer, Dan Jones, wrote, "A condition of distress here met my eyes that I never saw before or since. There were old men pulling and tugging their carts, sometimes loaded with a sick wife or children—women pulling along sick husbands—little children six to eight years old struggling through the mud and snow.
>
> *From The Gathering of Zion, page 252*

We saw the famous Split Rock and Split Rock Ranch from the east and for *many* days from the west as I, usually alone, walked beyond it. And Muddy Gap Junction, oh, the great names…

Two miles before Jeffrey City, the uranium trailer-town, one glimpses the Wind River Range of mountains, snow-capped. What exclamations of excitement must have run through the wagon trains! Snow in the middle of summer!

Leaving Jeffrey City, I was up early and left alone. The rest of my family chose to sleep late. Breakfast in a café. Cold air, crisp and wonderful. Alone again on the road. Is this my escape? I feel so at peace and in the swing, on top of the world. From Jeffrey City to Sweetwater Junction was the friendliest stretch yet, lots of smiles and waves. People stop and smile and give food and wish well. How can I describe this land to my friends in the east? Today the scene, 20 miles of walking, lonely wide open spaces, the most desolate empty landscape so far. Not a tree in sight. Mountains can be seen 125 miles away, walk through wide slightly rumpled plain of blue-green milky fragrant sage and sharp, sparse, brittle, brown grass.

Ant hills 10 inches high and 20 inches wide. The ants scurry with such industrious purpose! As I look down on them I realize they are so alive but know nothing of the great world around them: human beings, symphony music, football games, air flight, books. I can destroy their world with a catastrophic heavy footstep. Are we humans too unaware of greater things around us? Are we like the little ants? Are we too limited by our small-brained ignorance of much, much greater things? On I trudge, feeling like a tiny ant wobbling across a vast ballroom floor.

Later, this is how I recorded one of the defining incidents of the trip:

Just beyond the ice slough, saw a rattletrap pickup with a poor looking man stopped ahead. Waiting? Saw a knife blade on the ground. Picked up the knife. Would I attack immediately if grabbed, or wait and use it after tied in back of the truck? Knife in pocket. Approach. Man ducks behind camper. I pass and turn and say hello. All OK but somehow, for certain, something different had happened in me with the knife in my pocket. My assertive humanity had reined in a bit. A faint echo of defensiveness had crept into my repertoire of options. Animals are said to sense when one carries a gun. I was different after feeling it and thinking about it. It would be so easy to carry the knife under my golf cart, just in case. . . . I held the knife and then, strangely, but with certainty, threw the knife into the empty plains as far as I could and smiled confidently and assertively at the uranium miners driving by and waving. It will be a sad and dangerous day when I carry a weapon. I am committed to assertive non-violence and feel safe.

This paragraph is from a loose journal fragment of unknown location: *Today for the first time after so many miles of empty trail, a paved road was punctuated occasionally with cyclists. I am a person who doesn't get things in perspective until I lose it; I don't realize how I suffered from sore feet until my feet are healed. Today I didn't realize how lonely on the long empty areas I'd been until the bikes started rolling by, not stopping, just a friendly road-weary wave and hello. It was just enough human contact to realize how I miss its lack.*

I turned off the frail pavement into a maze of jeep trails. It was a long day because I wearily and slowly toiled up hill after hill after hill as the continental divide hump neared. I had a satisfied sense of accomplishment as the terrain changed to mountains, and Split Rock finally faded into oblivion behind me, although I occasionally strained to see it from the hill crests. The snow capped mountains of the Wind River Range came closer, and at one point I was on the rim of a magnificent deep canyon valley, a speck of a ranch nearly lost on the wide bottom far below and the snow peaks high above and far beyond. (Unknown to me then, we would later all attend a cattle branding right there on that distant ranch.) *The ground became a moonscape, irregular rock out-cropping crumbling here and there, grass between the sage almost non-existent, yet herds of cattle, distant dark specks on far away rises. Up forever, up the long hills, and when I could not go up one more step, we all gathered and camped in a slight depression between hills where the extra moisture from runoff made a small grassy meadow. A bull lay at the grassy edge, and we eyed it warily until finally it became evident that our fear arousal was ludicrous. Howard dubbed him "Affie the affable bull," and we regarded him fondly thereafter, while he ignored us with studied indifference.*

Miles later, deep in the endless stretches of emptiness, many miles from a paved road, where we were perilously close to becoming lost, we crossed paths with the Woolerys (Violet, Harvey, Nancy, Clyde and Terry) who were on their remote summer ranch to do some final calf branding. They invited us to the branding.

To reach the tiny summer camp we followed the truck ruts over the rim of a precipitously steep walled canyon to the broad bottom far below. The tiny speck we saw from the lip of the canyon rim was their summer ranch, virtually unchanged for half a century. Its location was determined then and now by the spring nearby. In a parched land such as this, a sweet spring is more valuable than gold itself. Water for the little ranch house was procured, as it always had been, by walking out the unsteady plank to the center of the spring and dipping in a bucket. Inside the bunkhouse the clear, cool water sat in a tub. Dippers and tin cups around the tub served as do-it-yourself faucets.

Harvey   The branding corral   1978 HM

    The small wooden corral held some cows and their late calves to be branded. A roaring fire was built, and the long-handled branding irons were set into the hot coals. The horses from another corral were saddled up and mounted. Mr. Woolery, his son, and grandson rounded up the small herd of cattle and drove them to the branding corral. Out came the rope and lasso, and the grandson twirled the thing over his head and practiced roping, looping either the horns or legs and dragged the calf toward the fire. The calf was wrestled to the ground and held by two people, the Woolery's daughter and one of the cowboys.

Nancy   The acrid smell of the branding
1978   HM

Paula   Some mothers hovered nearby... 1978 HM

Mrs. Woolery kept statistics on the cows and calves as the branding team went to work. The calf was given a vaccination injection. If a male, it was castrated. To do this the skin was cut exposing two shiny round balls, which were pulled outward on their gleaming cords. The cords were swiftly severed and the balls thrown unceremoniously into the fields. The branding irons were then taken from the fire and pressed into the side of the calf one at a time, a lazy sideways V and a 3. As the brand was burning through hair and into flesh, the calf could let forth with a most heart-rending bawl with tongue extending and eyeballs rolling upward. The air was acrid with the hot smell of burning hair and flesh. Before releasing the calf the ears were notched quickly with a sharp jackknife. After all this, the calf would quickly scramble to its feet and trot quietly back into the herd to join its mother. Some mothers would hover nearby throughout the branding while others meandered about with bland unconcern. The cutting, branding, slicing procedure is certainly barbaric, but the saving grace was that the calves showed no evidence of distress within seconds after being released. This then is the routine of the west, performed thousands and millions of times every year as it has been done throughout the west for decades. To my easterner's eyes it was incomparably romantic out there on the range in that deep remote canyon. Paula even renewed her passion for riding horses.

In the evening Mr. Woolery and his daughter bantered jokingly. Mr. Woolery found it incomprehensible and hilarious that an easterner would actually pay money to come to a dude ranch and ride horses around aimlessly. To him horse riding was a chore to be tolerated in the work of handling cattle. His daughter turned to me with twinkling eyes. "Do you know what HE thinks is the greatest pastime in the world? He likes to go east and ride the escalators all day!" We all had a marvelous chuckle. East meets west.

Alone again, the trail struck out on a high flat plateau toward the pass (South Pass), Pacific Buttes in the distance, desert scene to the south, snowy Rockies to the far north and hundreds of square miles of sagebrush range land visible in between, the trail ruts striking out across the

221

center with a patient determined sense of destination. The harshness of the dry, hot, windy climate had sculpted the sage into zillions of perfect bonsai, none over six inches tall, their tight little leaves bunching in shapely formations over the thick, woody, splintering, twisted trunks. Some plants massed against the crunchy dry ground like flat leafy granular pancakes, a rock gardener's dream. Such a sense of happiness and deep satisfaction welled in me! The wind was a cooling antidote to the clear brilliant sun.

12

SOUTH PASS AND TO THE UTAH BORDER

July 18 - 28
(120 miles)

"At the end of the storm is a golden sky and the sweet silver song of a
lark."   Oscar Hammerstein, II

Crossing the continental divide was a big moment
for the pioneers. This is the full journal entry for my day
reaching South Pass. My whole family was with me. We
had left the car behind in a complicated logistical plan.

*This morning up early and off to our big day. Very
cold. Drove and parked at start and set out, only to run into
impassable Willow Creek at once. What an obstacle so soon
on our big day! We walked 1/2 mile upstream looking for a
spot to ford. Howard heard a riffle and found a beaver dam
overgrown with thick growth of willows. We plunged,
jumped, and dragged through the dew dripping mass and
reached a center peninsula, one more stream branch yet to
cross. After more exploring (an hour gone already just
trying to cross this creek) we found some planks and logs
and built a wobbly bridge and finally with some decidedly
damp feet, made it across. We retraced our route on the
opposite bank and re-found the Oregon Trail, conveniently
(and essentially) marked with cement posts (a brass Oregon
Trail medallion embedded in each if not already
vandalized).*

*The South Pass saddle is 30 miles wide and flat
with a gentle steady slope, almost imperceptible in pitch.
Our map showed a final crossing to the Sweetwater in 5
miles, a hurdle that gave an edge to anticipation. Again that*

sense of being more deeply satisfied than ever in my life, the sense of power that miles were churning steadily beneath the effortless rhythm of my own walking. The feeling of being into life, not above it, not beyond it, not escaping from it, but deeply into it. The stillness of the air under the bright cloudless sky had been a nagging concern. When the early morning chill was gone, would we wither in the merciless heat?

Then, as is so often the case, my anxiety swiftly increased and changed as the unmistakable deep, dark blue on the horizon signaled stormy weather ahead and heading toward the snowcapped Wind River Mountains to our north. But would we also be caught? Constantly gauging the wind direction, sky, trail, assessing our preparedness (none), and mentally sorting options and contingencies. The clouds edged toward us and the sky darkened to the northwest. Darkened? BLACKENED! So, amidst the edge of concern, the edge of appreciation and sensitivity increased as antelope with their twin babies flew majestically and soared in every direction. The sun still painted the sage, and this against the black sky was simply stunning. Ahead the Sweetwater crossing question was to be faced shortly. The clouds' edge slipped under the sun, and a sudden windy cold enveloped us. Paula wanted to catch a horny toad at a time like this!!? I almost had a fit. The storm was nearly upon us, and as we approached the alley of the Sweetwater to get low so as to avoid lightning, we all shivered, unprepared for cold rain. Then, as a miracle for sure, the empty buildings of Burnt Ranch! The ranch house was padlocked so we dashed for the barn. It and the house were built a thousand years before (so it seemed) of large squared logs. The only problem was that there was no chinking and 3 and 4 inch spaces gaped between the logs, walls and ceiling. It was like being in a Tinker Toy house. But no matter, it seemed like a haven compared to the lashing elements on the open range. We huddled in the ancient horse manure under an old horse blanket as we watched between the logs while the wind bent the willows double along the river bank. The sound of the wind humming and screaming between the logs probably made it sound worse than it was. We sat and pressed our backs against the dirty cobwebbed horse blanket against the wall, and the wind pressed it against us. Howard and I were more alarmed than Paula and Cliff. The horizontal rain came in gusts but never made much headway. Far from the blazing heat I'd feared, we suddenly found ourselves with teeth chattering and shivering and so ate the sugary dried pineapple and chewed beef jerky, "just like the Donners eating hides in the storm," Cliff said. Then, with astonishing suddenness, it stopped. "The eye of the hurricane," I feared, but then some birds started to sing outside and blue sky peeped through the logs. The storm had vanished in an instant.

We stepped out of the barn, blinking unbelieving, into a glorious, bright, cool day. The storm was past us, the brisk breeze pushing it farther away. First the problem of crossing Willow Creek had been solved and now the storm problem had disappeared. Such ups and downs! The next immediate problem was crossing the swift and turbulent Sweetwater. Perhaps the hundreds of square miles of empty dry sagebrush range had primed me, but the brief green grass of Burnt Ranch next to the Sweetwater seemed like the most perfect heaven. The tiny, tumbled, weathered log buildings, picturesque and homey, just proving again that everything is relative, I guess.

The problem was to re-find the Oregon Trail and to figure a way to cross the river. Despite the fact that I knew it was the wrong direction for the trail, I said with confident authority, "Howard, my instincts tell me to go this way,"

225

and I clumped unerringly and blindly toward—a cattle bridge! Another miracle: intuition, instinct or greater self or guide? Whatever, it was a wonderful and irrefutable sense of self-discovery. We crossed and climbed up onto the parched plateau and searched and spotted the essential cement marker and were off, happy and exuberant after some more snacks. On and on, mile upon mile, antelope buttes, distant cattle, and then my eyes could no longer deny the signs, another storm brewing on the horizon, heading toward the snow caps, but clearly we were to be brushed.

Looking back eastward on the trail just walked.　　　1978　HM

The fear of lightning on the flat plains is the nerve-wracker. The black clouds assembled while our sun shone down on us oblivious to the threat. An hour later and the first clouds dimmed the sun, and then the chill wind engulfed us and then tore into us. The black band of clouds moved above us, and one by one icy drops of water pelted us like peas from a pea shooter. But the sky was light beyond the wide storm front, and before long it passed, and we had weathered another problem in triumph.

The trail ahead looking westward, South Pass with the Wind River Range in the distance.   1978   HM

The hot blaze returned. Despite its uniform appearance, the composition of the ground changed occasionally. Crunchy

desert rock turned to chalk-white powder and then to sharp, cruel, slate-like stones as if recently blasted by dynamite. I caught a note of anxiety for the sore feet of the pioneers' oxen. For a stretch the baked adobe-like clay held glorious, translucent, gem-type stones. I impulsively gathered a few (the first time in 1,000 miles I succumbed) and unbeknownst to me, Paula did the same when she passed. I've noticed that as we weary, we spread out and straggle, great distances opening between us as we plod on grimly. At a snack and toilet stop, Paula dragged up and showed me her stones. I nearly jumped out of my skin, "Holy Dear God, Paula, that's an Indian scraper!" She had unknowingly picked up a perfectly worked Indian scraper. Amazing. I am sure I'll never find an artifact on the trail simply because I BELIEVE I won't. With this frame of mind, I'll probably not even pick one up if I stumble on it, yet I can't seem to shake this mental set.

The miles wore away, and Howard jogged off to pick up the car, yet the kids kept on. South Pass was only a couple miles ahead. And then, there it was, South Pass, designated by two monuments. A more forlorn anti-climax I cannot imagine. Two lonely and touching monuments in the sage, marred suddenly by a railroad track, high tension power lines, cattle fences, yet here we were, incontrovertibly at the continental divide. I felt nothing on the outside, but something inside stirred with quiet satisfaction. No one could ever take this from me.

After a treat we started down the Pacific watershed. Immediately the land changed, closer hills and chest-high sagebrush. The trail turned in a curving meander, and we silently pushed ourselves the last five miles, exhausted at the end of a brimming full and important day.

SOUTH PASS AND TO THE UTAH BORDER

That night the sixth storm of the day passed overhead.

Today, alone again, I walked on a plain with the snow mountains to the rear, finally, and desert with mesas ahead and to the south. The traffic was not friendly, and I knew there was not a house or ranch or tree for 30 miles. The family had driven away to get supplies. There were more dead and rotting and stinking antelope, badger, and jack rabbits on the road than ever before. One gas-bloated dead jack rabbit lay on the pavement. As I approached it a high speed car ran over it. There was a loud POP and intestines, entrails, and all manner of guts exploded and shot in every direction. The stench was horrifying, and I was hard pressed not to vomit.

Yesterday while I walked an old man stopped to check his car and then I passed him. He was, I think, in a bit of an alcoholic haze, seemed a bit confused. Anyway, after trying to orient himself as to whether or not I was a ghost (in the middle of nowhere) he said, "Hey, isn't that a bit dangerous? I mean some man could stop and take you in his car by force and ravage your body." His slightly pornographic description has rattled my nerves because he was obviously off on his own sick fantasy. This morning the waitress said, "But aren't you scared?" Honestly, my nerves are suffering. A great weariness has set in. I'm tired of being afraid and especially of handling other people's gloomy assessments. I study the maps, and the long stretches ahead look menacing, and I wonder where I'll get the will to walk assertively and not defensively.

SOUTH PASS AND TO THE UTAH BORDER

The passing of the 1,000-mile mark and South Pass I had thought would be a cause for celebration, not the ho hum attitude it seems to bring. It seems that completing 250 miles brought a greater atmosphere of excitement than 1,000 miles from self, family, and others. Gloom. Gloom. This too will pass, I'm sure.

Howard had backed over a sign reflector at a rest stop and cut the brakes, requiring an urgent 100-mile repair trip to Rock Springs.

On July 20, 1978, I walked into Farson and met the family again. For two days there Cliff was sick with a fever that spiked to 104 degrees. *Since we have no tub here I sponged him. His body radiated heat. One stroke with cool water and the wash cloth became warm. During the night he was speaking in fast, choppy cadence and mumbling nonsense. He recovered quickly, but we know that many children died during the emigrant crossing days. A mother's fear and sorrow can still reach across the years*

———

On July 20, 1846, exactly 132 years before, a large wagon train of California bound emigrants halted at the Little Sandy River near today's Farson, Wyoming. A fateful decision was in the making. The season was late, although not unreasonably so, and *the* chance for a 350 to 400 mile shortcut loomed ahead. Although the shortcut route was an even more unknown quantity to the virgin emigrants than the regular California route, it had the enticing lure of a promise. That promise was that its discoverer, a daring young man named Lansford Hastings, would return personally to lead any wagon train attempting it. The legendary mountain man, Jim Bridger, arrived at the Little Sandy with his partner and conferred favorably with the wagon train. The discussion among the emigrants adjourned with the wagon train splitting, the larger section taking the longer more northerly tried and true route to California. The smaller group, soon to elect a captain named George Donner, took a thoughtful risk and chose the shortcut. They did only what any rational humans can do; they soberly gathered together all the facts they could find and on that basis made a decision. No one could ask more than that. Their decision, reached so rationally, would seal the deaths of half of them and leave the rest a testimony of unspeakable endurance. The facts they had weighed and relied upon turned out to be false, but at the time there was no way of knowing that. And so the Donner Party took the left fork in the trail, headed for Fort Bridger and then for the shortcut beyond. By the time they realized their mistake, it was too late in the season, way too late to turn back, so they did what was really their only option: they pushed on as best they could.

A year later after her rescue Virginia Reed, a mere child at the time, summed up their fatal decision in a famous letter to her cousin: "Never take no cutoffs and hurry along as fast as you can."

In the motel room were two cheap paint-by-number pictures on the wall of New England church scenes, but I stared and stared at them. The west is grand and vast, majestic and stirring, awesome and harsh, but my God!, for beauty tender enough to make your heart ache with longing, there is nowhere on earth that can touch New England. The memory of its scenes in the fall, in the midst of summer, in the deepest winter and in the fragile spring have haunted me for hours.

At the Farson motel a sudden (why is that word so appropriate for so many many phenomena in the west?) wind arose without warning of another ominous storm edge, and howled menacingly. Instantly the world was a beige blur of blazing dust, not unlike the sensation of a snow blizzard. Boxes and miscellany whizzed past the window in streaks. The car outside rocked violently, and then all was quiet. Later a local woman said these tornado type winds are becoming inexplicably more common and more frightening. WOW. I've had enough of this dynamic weather. I recall early in the trip how it thrilled me. Now it's wearing.

On the morning I left Farson alone, I took a wrong turn, became lost, and returned to town to recheck my maps. On setting out again, incredibly I again took the wrong turn and had to double back to start over. My third try at getting off was foiled when I found I'd left behind some equipment, and by then my trudge back to town was frightening as well as frustrating. In my journal I wrote that I was "at war with myself" and "self-destructive." A year later I realized an uncanny coincidence. That was precisely the spot and date at which the Donner Party agonized so vividly over their route and took their own ultimately self-destructive wrong turn. Tamsen Donner is recorded as having been especially "dispirited" as the fatal path was chosen.

After a brief rain the sky overwhelmed my self-destructive mood with its enchanting clouds, and the air was cold, fresh, and invigorating. The clouds determine how majestic and large mountains look, and the Rockies (now at my back) looked astoundingly imposing with the clouds even below the peaks in places. I kept gulping the cold fresh air and craning my neck around to see again and again the mountains. Around me the sage range flattened much like Nebraska, and the desert mesas were mere silhouettes in the distance. The Emigrant Trail cut a deep swale next to me. Once again it became obvious that nothing pleases me like the flat plains. I can't fathom why.

I ate lunch right in the swale with a retired Wyoming couple "driving" a 100-year old wagon pulled by two mules. They fed me royally and invited me to camp with them on the Big Sandy. (Regretfully had to refuse.) It was so peaceful there on the bright cool range that I fell into their relaxed manner and stayed lazily 1½ hours while the man showed me how the pioneers greased their axles one by one from a big bucket of goo hanging from the wagon. When a brief rain squall sneaked up on us, their mood was so peaceful that they unconcernedly let everything get wet as they slowly repacked the pillows and quilts we had been lounging on. My own underlying uptightness became obvious to me as I tried to dash about in a panic. The man had bought the ancient wagon for $2.50 (plus a ride to town to buy whiskey) from an Indian. The man had trained the mules, sold their home, and been on their way - mountains etc. - since April - 100 miles. They were to sell the whole rig in 50 miles. They were so peaceful that they treated me as if I were an everyday occurrence and perfectly ordinary - a pleasant feeling of acceptance for me. We never even exchanged names.

One day as Cliff and I walked, the trail dropped into a desperately dry, baked badlands, eroded into carved beige moonscape. The baked adobe mud made me squint even through my dark glasses. Although it was hot the extreme dryness made it fairly comfortable. After five miles

233

of this, Cliff and I emerged onto the little Colorado Desert, a flat five mile plain leading to the Green River, marked as a distant black fringe of trees, presumably along the river. For a while the white powdered or baked clay was spotted with shiny black stones, but this changed to crunchy dry desert gravel in a sage plain, the trail stretching straight and out of sight toward the black tree fringe and distant bluffs. Cliff had had enough, gestured for the car, and rode the rest of the way to the campground miles ahead.

Despite the fact that I'd read of it in diaries and had a map for contrary proof, I misjudged the distance to the black fringe of trees, estimating a quick and easy two miles. The desert air, occasionally softened by a mysterious sweet aroma, and gravel crunch and dry, clear atmosphere and bright, hot sun made the first miles thrilling and fun, but the dark fringe of trees appeared no closer after an hour of walking. My crunch crunch crunch walking took on a treadmill aspect as I could discern no landmarks but the seemingly receding black trees. For the first time on the trip I experienced a rage of impatience, frustration, and near despair at my seeming lack of progress. After another half hour the ground suddenly dropped, and the river wound bright blue and green grass fringed. The trees never did change much in appearance until the last 100 yards.

Another day we ascended onto a dry sage area which looked like Nebraska's sandhills. Paula noticed the prints of unshod horse hoofs and a colt's among them. Cliff and I continued on and over a small hill and came upon a wild horse band. The breeze was not carrying our scent, so they were as startled as we. Their coloring, their wildness, the setting, the lighting, something or everything made them exalting in their sheer beauty. The mares started

234

toward us. Curious? And the stallion, alarmed, also galloped to check us out, and Cliff and I waved frantically for the car. At that point the stallion wheeled and herded his mares away from us. There were 6 lovely, sleek, varicolored mares, one small colt, and the stately brown stallion. Their gallop, flowing manes, and graceful tails were breathtaking.

The rest of the day was an introduction to parched desert. My arms and face burned. My feet blistered for the first time in months. My eyes hurt despite glasses. We're camped in a dry flat, huddled in the thin shade of the car. My eyes and feet are shot, rendering me quite helpless. We're all quite devastated and awed by the pitiless power of the dry air and the blinding sun. As the evening (8:30) shadows lengthen, the land takes on a softness, but the damage has been done, and we can only wait impatiently for the cool and soothing darkness. I'm unnerved by the thought of the deserts ahead.

Today is about the last day of back country trails. It has been priceless, the heart of the trail and the raw land. We're the better for its indescribable experience.

The Wind River Range is now gone out of sight at our backs. We first sighted them many days ago by Split Rock. To approach, come even and eventually leave behind such earth-marks gives one a sense of power. Inch by inch even one small person can pass by a great mountain range. Now the snow-peaked Uintas lie ahead. And then the Wahsatch and then Salt Lake City and then the Great Salt Lake Desert and then...and then...and someday the end.

We camped on the desert, a tiny speck on a planet of baked sand and scratchy plants. I slept under the stars as usual. Shortly after we had climbed comfortably into our bags (incredible to easterners, it cools down the instant the sun sets), I lay peacefully and then stared with interest and amazement as an enormous black insect zoomed overhead sounding exactly like a small airplane. I was more fascinated than alarmed until the damn thing started to hone in on my face. I shrieked and covered my head. Cliff said its passes were 6 inches above my face. The whole family watched and listened to it circle the tents and land on Paula's side of the tent to walk around and explore until darkness engulfed it. We all marveled and agreed it was at least 3 inches long with a 3 inch wing span and sounded like a small airplane.

I slept tensely at first, the bag pulled tightly around my neck.

Today will be a rest day in the terrible heat. Yesterday when we arrived here in Lyman, we all gasped and choked and ached as we peeked into the valley. There were the first green, irrigated, lush grass meadows and trees, leafy trees! for an eternity. Actually, everything is relative. A regular easterner would sniff at it unless desert numbed as we were.

Yesterday, passed though a prairie dog town. There's nothing as charming as the erect posture of a prairie dog standing tall outside her entry hole.

Along its western edge, the Wyoming terrain gave way to unmistakable mountains and valleys. The tiny towns of Lyman and Fort Bridger were oases on the edge of the dry range that had been our toil for weeks. In Lyman, we rested at a campground. While taking a side trip to a store, our car broke down. Howard went ahead to see about repairs while I waited, bored, in the car. We were approximately half a mile from the campground. "Oh phooey," I sighed, "it's too far to walk back. I'll just have to wait here." I idly let this musing thought rattle around in my head, and then I sat up with a start. I, who had just walked a thousand miles over plains, mountains and deserts was thinking that a paltry half a mile back to the campground was too far? Quick as a wink I hopped out of the stalled car and scurried back to the campground, all the while absolutely amazed at how I could have been so dense.

Desert aromas, today a spice rather like poultry seasoning. Some vicious seeds rather like harpoons on tiny coiled rope stick into socks. I stepped barefoot on harsh burrs and spent time pulling them out of my tough soles like porcupine quills.

After Fort Bridger I stepped onto Interstate 80. The interstate was OK today. I got blown off the road periodically, but it's rather like being buffeted by waves at the ocean, no harm done.

Too many putrid dead animal smells, I'm getting a phobia about it. The odor actually gave me a kind of instant earache. I touched under my ear, and the glands hurt, but 50 feet later all was well. It's like the sour pickle test for mumps. I do believe the odor of rotting flesh could eventually drive me crazy if I couldn't get away.

Today was a long, windy walk, hot, through and over the mountains called the Bear River Divide, up 4 miles, down 4 miles, up 4 miles, down 4 miles, up 4 miles and down 8.

We reached Evanston and I said, "we're going to EAT for a change!" So we ATE. I had one pint yogurt (potato chips and dip), 2 giant hamburgers, 1 quart milk, 1 quart water, strawberries, all in all a heavenly pig-out and, honestly, I can't remember when I've been so satisfied.

Lots of woman truckers today. One gave me an especially big smile, a small brief incident, but I'll remember it.

13

SALT LAKE CITY, UTAH

July 29 - August 16
(80 miles)

"It's not where you get at the end of the day, but what
you've seen along the way."   man on the trail

1979 ES

*The sign said "Welcome to UTAH." I allowed
myself a deep, daring breath and unabashed smile and then
the thought ever so fleeting, "I think, I'm pretty sure, I
mean, I think I might actually make it." It was beginning,
just beginning, to seem, possible.*

Feeling a little bit like "The Little Engine That
Could" in the child's story, I walked on westward.

Soon after entering Utah, I-80 and I began the
gradual descent into Echo Canyon. The landscape grew
more dramatic as the canyon walls steepened and reddened.
For the Donner Party the descent was a funnel leading

unknowingly into a trap. Ahead was the blind wall of the Wahsatch Mountains. Crossing those mountains would exact a three-week toll in time and backbreaking effort before they would be left behind. But for me Echo Canyon was an exciting land form change, an accelerated experience in beauty.

Today fragrance of anise or licorice is in the air.

That night we gathered, all four of us, and:
Camped high on the side of Echo Canyon. Listened to the hum of traffic all night. Tried to imagine sounds when pioneers streamed through, then realized that today's traffic hum will also some day be extinct, so I tried to absorb today's historic period movement too. Watched also today's historic trains far below. One had 110 cars, all kinds. Very peaceful to be so high above the activity and to have such a panoramic view. At night we watched the stars, shooting stars, and satellites, later a half-ish moon.

Next morning we walked up Echo Canyon, step by step becoming more dramatic. Everyone and everything throughout history streamed through here: old roads and trails next to the railroad and the dominant Interstate 80. At one time in the morning there glided a plane, train, trucks, cars, motorcycles (no bikes), and us walking. The north canyon wall steepened into dazzling orange cliffs and caves and holes and fissures and grottoes. As the sun heated, the colors became more vivid until I realized I was seeing my first really verdant greens in 3 months. The startling side canyons, winding back and up to secret Indian places, captured enough water to flourish cool groves of trees and wild, green, grassy meadows, while high above the orange walls faded again into the familiar harsh sage and desert sand. Frosty clouds swarmed in the deepest blue sky which pulsated behind the orange cliffs. I could nearly drink in the verdant, almost forgotten green. How many months the blue sage range and tan grass plains had been my reality.

Cliff said, "Mom, in the book 'Sing Down the

Moon,' in the end when they got married, this is exactly, EXACTLY the kind of place I imagined!" We peered up the perfect heaven of another side canyon and I gave silent tribute to the beauty which equaled a New England idyll. Howard jogged up the canyon. "It's the greatest road you'll ever walk," he marveled.

Then a few miles up the old road I looked up for the millionth time and spotted some old graffiti, the careful and fancy calligraphy of the olden days, dated 1885, with two names plus the word "artist" after each and an old, carefully lettered advertisement: Salt Lake House, Salt Lake City. The perfect elegant touch to tie in the human history of the canyon.

Through all this my feet were protesting the feat more and more insistently until they felt like mush spiked now and then with shooting pains. Am also finding tiny watery blisters on arms and legs more and more.

Next morning the sun and clouds had changed, and yesterday's fiery cliffs had become a wintry brown, the atmosphere now cold and unfriendly.

———

Like the stem and cross bar of a T, the west end of Echo Canyon leads smack into the Wahsatch Mountains, a virtual blank wall. The Donner Party turned north and followed the Weber River as it paralleled the mountains to the west. Ahead, the Weber cut through a narrow impassible canyon with precipitous walls, and the emigrants were blocked. Lansford Hastings, the dashing young guide who had promised to personally lead the emigrants, had failed to meet them as planned. He had pressed forward blindly with another group of emigrants. The shortcut over which they'd agonized back at the Little Sandy was virtually impassible. The Donner Party was on its own. Impossible as it looked, there was no other choice but to turn toward the ominous mountains and start up a side canyon. The struggle was unlike anything yet encountered on the journey. For the first time the wagons had to contend with a forest of willows so thick they had to be cut and chopped one by one. For the first time they assaulted mountains straight on with no trail to follow. The slopes were so steep that at times for long stretches no ground could be found flat enough to allow a wagon to pass without toppling over. Somehow they struggled to the top.

Wall upon wall yet to cross   1978 HM

The long, arduous pull up a mountain range was rewarded by the most incredible and discouraging sight of the trip, impenetrable wall upon wall of mountains yet to cross. The sight of deserts and plains was discouraging, but crossing them "merely" required dogged plodding determination to just somehow keep going day after day after day. This mountainous spectacle, however, was horrifying. It actually looked impossible. The Donner Party, lagging with the lumbering wagons and no trail to follow, must have vomited with horror. It took them 17 days to hack through the mountainous tangle foot by foot, a miracle of accomplishment in itself. I would cross through it by road in a comparatively easy two days. With a blazed trail they would have been able to do it in three, as did the Mormons a year later.

We camped at East Canyon Reservoir, the same

spot that we had come to in 1976.

About 1 1/2 miles beyond East Canyon Reservoir, Cliff and I were enjoying the brief cool of morning and walking steadily. A car sped by ahead and Cliff said, "Hey Mom, what's that thing?" I looked up the road and about 50 yards ahead a large animal was casually, relaxedly, crossing the road in the wake of the vanishing car. Its languid graceful movements, its facial profile and tiny ears, its soft paws all said CAT, but its size was impossibly large. Cliff said, "Is it a bobcat?" I said firmly, "No, too big." And Cliff said, "It's a mountain lion." It then, cat-like and with consummate grace, leaped over a barbed wire fence and disappeared into the brush and trees. I swore softly, "Holy dear God almighty, what WAS that?" Clearly it was a mountain lion. Our view had been too long and too close to doubt our vision, but I quickly ran through the reasons why it couldn't have been: 1) too close to civilization. It had stepped behind the car and in front of us. In fact, I immediately voiced a fear of rabies since its casual behavior had seemed so strange; 2) too unlikely in such a heavily hunted area. I couldn't imagine any living thing surviving the army of hunters we'd seen there 2 years ago; 3) too relaxed. It didn't live up to my image of the frightened hunted animal, tensely crouching and waiting and hiding and dashing in fear from place to place. But there it had been, clear, unmistakable and unbelievable, but really there. Then I searched for explanations: escaped from zoo? Someone's pet? Nope. Try as I might I couldn't refute my senses. We had seen a real mountain lion, a rare privilege. I kept looking over my shoulder — Attack? My senses said "No, of course not." My cowboy-movie training said, "Watch out."

The Wahsatch Mountains reminded me of the Adirondacks in their jumbled contours. They're not laid out neatly as are the Rockies but are a jumble of mountains and ridges and canyons running all at crazy and undecipherable angles. The Donners struggled through this maze half blindly, taking three weeks to hack and push through this tortured mess. We rapidly lost our comprehension of how anyone could do this in three years let alone three weeks, and after hours and hours of aching legs we reached the divide. And our route had been up a graded modern 1978 highway.

(For the Donner Party, they were to be by far the hardest mountains of the trip, barring the short impossible stretch in the Sierras at Donner Pass.)

A year later I returned to the Wahsatch. I stood and gazed again at those steep steep mountains. My eyes teared briefly. "How did they ever do it?" I whispered to the mountains looming before me.

———

After weeks of heartbreaking toil in the cursed Wahsatch maze, with blind alleys, wrong turns, and false illusions of shortcuts, the Donner Party halted for the night, and a few climbed the hill bordering the creek they were following.

The steep 300-foot hill emerged onto a barren plateau which dipped finally into the broad treeless valley below. That valley stretched, unhindered, 25 miles to the Great Salt Lake shimmering in the distance. Below them in the tangled thicket of willows sat their 20-odd wagons by the little stream. The brook also emerged a short way ahead onto the treeless plain, but that "short way" looked like an eternity of hellish tree-cutting misery to the bone-weary emigrants. It is an eloquent measure of their advanced state of exhaustion that a desperate decision was made: they would try to scale the hill with the wagons and roll down to the plateau without having to cut another tree.

The next morning it required every team of oxen hitched to every single wagon to accomplish the feat. Somehow they did it, but they had taken an awful risk. Any misstep would have meant injured animals and broken wagons. On the other hand it has been conjectured that perhaps they lost the gamble after all. Perhaps it was this near perpendicular 300-foot wall that pulled the hearts out of the oxen beyond recovery and set them staggering more dead than alive out onto the 500 miles of desert yet to cross.

In 1978, the hill is distorted by utility buildings and a nearby modern apartment building. Those living in the building can gaze out on the unobstructed view that so lured the Donner Party, but now the treeless plain is the thriving bustling Salt Lake City. As I tried to picture oxen straining to keep their footing on the hill before me, a fashionable man walking his Dobermans strolled along the little stream bed.

A monument and plaque entitled "Donner Hill" sits vandalized at the base. The monument notes that in 1847, one year later, the Mormons under the leadership of Brigham Young cut through the willow thicket along the stream in only four hours. That Mormon vanguard had over 100 of the strongest select men of that entire religion at its disposal. There were less than a handful of women and children in that Mormon group. Brigham Young's contingent had rolled in on the trail that the Donner Party had blazed with their pitiful weakened crew of less than 27 men, many old and feeble or sick. The Donner decision to scale the wall could only have been taken out of desperation, certainly not from laziness or stupidity.

It was almost time for my family to leave me. Howard had done more than his share at campsites. Paula had read dozens of books, Cliff too. As well as the good times we had all experienced boredom, lethargy, irritability, and downright ugliness on occasion. The kids had taken turns walking with me. Each had walked at least 100 miles. I had spent hours and hours alone with each. These were virtually the only times in our lives when we had each other's undivided attention for such long periods. There were no legions of dishes to do, appointments to keep, house cleaning nagging, or books waiting to be read, newspapers to catch up on, and no phone ringing. It was just us walking forever across vast sage range. Often they talked of things far removed from our endless walking, old friends, future horse stable dreams, coins, and pets at home. Paula chattered ceaselessly with her thoughtful, creative energy. Cliff was more circumspect, his sentences carrying the weight of one who uses words sparingly. The kids, and Howard too, shared each other. We shared the heat and the antelope, storms and tired legs. We shared short tempers and shooting stars. We shared the first sight of wild horses and the fresh gaze over the old swale. We shared the Trail. And when it was over the kids were still not particularly impressed with my venture. It was not quite the warm family scene that people pictured when I'd say, "My family walked part of the way with me." But it was good. I'm glad they were part of it, and I couldn't have done those desolate stretches without them.

Next morning Howard dropped me off on the Wahsatch divide before sunrise in incredible windy cold after a day in the 100's. I cried. Howard cried. Later he returned with kids. Paula gave me a beautiful hawk feather she'd found on the trail for good luck, and I cried again. Quickly the little red car was gone. I raced 24 miles into the city to get my room at the YWCA before 1:00 PM. Today my feet and legs are very, very lame. I must put a search on for vitamins; something drastically wrong with my recovery rate.

I love the "Y." Haven't penetrated it yet. Strange mixture of women: unwed pregnant, battered, recovering from surgery, old, young, foreign, hookers, blind, brain damaged. I almost feel guilty of being so well off, so I bought a membership.

I wanted to stay on the Donner schedule as well as on their trail. Their three-week struggle through the Wahsatch compared with my two days set me way ahead. So I decided to stay at the YWCA for a couple of weeks. Immediately I was faced with a problem that had been pursuing me relentlessly for weeks: my money was running low. After avoiding the inevitable for a few days, I finally faced myself, ignored my embarrassment and self

246

consciousness, and went looking for a job.

For two weeks my trail mentality would be shelved as I readjusted from the empty wagon ruts of Wyoming to the press and stress of big city living. The contrasts couldn't have been more vivid.

I went to a temporary job service and sat briefly among some scruffy looking fellow job seekers. I wore my trail-ravaged clothes but somehow still feel that I fit in with the group. Within 30 minutes I was offered 3 jobs: secretary, maid, or production work. I chose production work and after catching the bus outside, was working within a half hour, minimum wage $2.65 per hour, in a clanging, banging, chop chop, whir, squeal, screech, grinding factory, making and packing surgical masks. I felt I was out of my element but was determined to fit into the job, so I applied myself diligently. All my old sociology courses and academic snob analyses hung in the back of my mind, the demeaning, dehumanizing, deadening qualities of repetitive factory jobs sapping one's vitality, etc., etc. "Hey!" I thought, "That was all baloney. This is terrific!" as I assembled, glued, stuffed and packed box after box. "Why, this is even fun! Not hard, even satisfying!" I worked fast and tried to be a model of efficiency, ever the good little girl seeking gold stars. Then I remembered the academic studies that showed the system of the unspoken code of the workers: don't rock the boat by working too fast and productively. So I slowed down to what I guessed was a moderate fellow-worker acceptable pace. But good little girls don't disappear that fast, so I worked through my coffee breaks and my lunch break. Somewhere between 3 and 5 hours the early conclusions about work speed became theoretical as I had burned myself out in the first three hours, and my 1,200-mile feet began to ache, and my back wanted to lie down, and my mind screamed for a rest, ahhh sleep. The hours which had slipped by so easily earlier suddenly froze, and every five minutes took forever. I felt trapped and defeated. One and a half more hours to go and I summoned up some grit and hung in there to the end, when I limped (sore and fatigued) to the bus. Oh yes, my *grand pay? $17.23.*

The busses kept turning before they reached me, and I repeatedly inquired if this was really the bus stop. It was. So I sat and broiled and seethed and stressed in the oven-like supper time evening rush sun. After an hour a bus came, and I got on. This was harder than walking 30 miles of trail any day.

Back at the "Y" I was handed a sheaf of messages from media people. There it goes again, the roller coaster effect, from beaten, haggard, minimum wage assembly line factory worker to media star all in one day,

Friday at work was a robot torture day; no desire to set new records enlivened it.

After a week's factory work I was beaten and drained. I could feel fatigue distorting my face, a fatigue that has a different quality from the fatigue of a long day on the trail. My eyes were expressionless and a heavy drooping sensation pulled down on my facial muscles. I had a weak impulse to say a nice thing to the sad person next to me on the bus, but the impulse drowned in exhaustion. It was a deadening life.

Just as much as I love the majestic feeling of being alone in the wilderness, I also love the excitement and people mixture of a big city. But coming in fresh from the clean health-promoting trail, I saw city life with sad new eyes. City stress was everywhere, in complicated bus schedules, in bungled phone messages, in long lines at the checkout counter, in thousands of tense and sallow faces, in shrill and sobbing children, in obese bodies straining to hoist themselves up stairs.

But these people had a lot to teach me. One evening after work I helped a young woman find her way across town to a hospital clinic. Mary had behaved strangely on the way in the bus. She laughed hysterically at inappropriate things (the sound of the money dropping into the coin collector), and she became agitated over peculiar things (whether or not the traffic light would change before our bus reached it). In retrospect, I must admit with shame that her odd behavior was an acute annoyance to me. At the hospital she was led by a nurse into the examining room to see the doctor. I waited for her to emerge with medicine for her sore throat. Past midnight, five hours later, I was still waiting. The nurse approached to question me. Marys strange behavior had so alarmed the doctor that she was being evaluated by a psychiatrist. In the early hours of the morning Mary was released to return to her temporary home, the YWCA. Alone in the big strange city, looking for her lost baby (her husband had taken it away), Mary was having a nervous breakdown.

Every day a woman waited eagerly for the 5:37 bus on the corner of 78th Street. As the bus approached she would strain to see through the windshield if the driver that day would be Ronald. On Thursday her face lighted when she recognized him. He ignored her as usual as she dropped her fare into the money machine. She sat in the front seat across from him. She ran a comb through her wispy brown hair, her eyes still on Ronald. She hoisted a large tape recorder onto the seat and flipped the switch. The bus carried the quivering sugared tones of an electric ukulele. With a shy yet determined look, the woman rummaged in her large bag and pulled out the final prop, a huge Hawaiian lei made of shiny pink plastic flowers. She arranged this carefully, draping it over her shoulders, and pulled the strands of her thin brown hair forward. She waited, her pleading wistful eyes never leaving Ronald. She turned the music up a bit and waited some more. "Lovely hula hands, graceful......" The bus route ended. The woman packed up her tape recorder. She took off the enormous plastic pink lei and put it back in the bag and climbed off the bus with the rest of us. Ronald never looked up. I wanted to tell her that I enjoyed her music, but I didn't.

Walking to the food store yesterday I passed drunks

asleep on the curb, a puddle of blood where an old lady had fallen, and the overpowering stench of urine by the phone booth; the pee was in the newspaper vendor next to the phone.

Back at work a young woman, Sandy, got her middle finger chopped off in one of the machines. In a flash I found myself in a car with a driver, Sandy in the middle, and me in the passenger's seat. With my left hand I held the chopped off finger stub tightly to stop the squirting blood. Someone had handed me the chopped off finger which I held gently in my right hand, cradled carefully and tenderly by my curled fingers around it. At some point in the ride to the emergency room I surreptitiously uncurled my fingers a bit to see the detached finger. It was a cool gray-blue color which shocked me...that color... Later I was told that they sewed it back on in surgery.

One day in the crowded bus station I was watching an exhausted woman with six young children coping patiently with one baby in her arms, another sleeping in a pack on her back and four others crying or lying on the dirty bus station floor eating candy. An old lady offered kindly to hold one of the babies. The scene was abruptly interrupted when from the far side of the waiting room a well-dressed, very handsome athletic-looking man began shouting and stomping in an unearthly authoritative voice: "GAMES! NO MORE GAMES!! ALL YOU PEOPLE STOP PLAYING GAMES!" He strode through the terrified, hushed crowd with an air of barely controlled violence. The two frightened ticket salesmen marched up from behind, each firmly grabbing an arm, and ushered him outside. The scene had suddenly rocketed every one of us in the crowd out of our normal and varied preoccupations—every one of us, that is, except the one sleeping baby. We all remained motionless and stunned for a few eternal seconds. The berserk man returned a few minutes later, a changed and now sane but pale expression on his face. A muscle throbbed rhythmically on his temple.

He purposefully walked here and there about the

station as people averted their eyes. He walked out of sight into a side room. In about 20 minutes, he emerged looking upset and tense, but with charisma and infinite self-control, he apologized individually to everyone in the bus station, going from person to person with extended hand saying quietly, "Thank you for understanding.'" "I appreciate your understanding." "Thank you, sir.'" "Thank you, madam." "Thank you for understanding." Then he left. I had wanted to communicate something to him, but my fleeting chance had passed.

What had happened? Could it have been a Vietnam flashback? A bad drug trip? An LSD flashback? A nervous breakdown? A weird experiment in social psychology? The man had emanated something special in carriage and manner: mysterious and fascinating, insane one minute and showing exceptional poise the next.

There were three beds in my room at the "Y." I had a steady stream of roommates. One day I dragged my weary self home from the factory, and the operator in the lobby stopped me. "Barbara, this is Dorothy. She'll be staying in your room tonight." Dorothy hovered like an emaciated wraith in the corner of the lobby. She had the thinnest head and the sallowest face I ever saw. On her hunched and motionless frame hung an exquisite white dress, almost a bridal type of gown. Two suitcases seemed to stretch her long thin arms nearly to the floor. I led her to our room. She stood mute and expressionless. "You can sit down, Dorothy. Make yourself at home." Dorothy stood motionless. "Dorothy, sit down, " I said rather firmly.

Bit by bit I extracted Dorothy's monotone story. Dorothy lived in the Bronx in New York City. She was from an old world ethnic family. She had been extremely sheltered all her 22-year life. Her family fairly adored, even worshipped, the Osmonds singing group, especially Donny and Marie. (At that point I had scarcely heard of them, leading one to wonder who was more out of the mainstream, Dorothy or me.) Her family, although poor, had scrimped and saved to buy a plane ticket, a new white dress, and presents for Dorothy to deliver to the Osmond family. "The cops" had picked up Dorothy wandering aimlessly and lost in the Salt Lake City airport and had delivered her to the "Y" to the "women in jeopardy" program. Indeed, this surely was one woman in need of help. Dorothy opened her suitcase, and sure enough, there they were, presents, a suitcase full of them for the Osmond family. The next morning I took Dorothy to the Travelers Aid office where a kind and amazed social worker took the problem in hand. When I left, a bewildered Dorothy was sitting like a haunted statue in a chair while effort was being made to at least get her to a recording session of the rich and powerful Osmonds.

Helen stayed in "my" room one night. She had a black eye and a swollen face. Her husband had beaten her again. She was slowly losing sight in one eye from the beatings. "I begged him, 'Honey, if you think I'm bad and need to be hit, then please hit me on my rear where it won 't show.' But he always goes for my face, and then I have to miss work." It was Helen's fourth marriage. This was the only husband who had ever hit her. The second husband had divorced his abnormal wife to marry Helen when she had weighed 340 lbs. "He must have been a real winner too," I thought with grim sarcasm. Helen was waging a terrible internal struggle, fighting the temptation to go back to her violent husband. When I returned from work the next day I found a note on my bed. "Goodbye, my friend Barbara. I am on my way to Arizona. I think I'm going to make it this time. Love, Helen." I hope she made it. Somehow I think she did.

In the past it had been so easy to overlook the casualties of the city life. Here for a while that was all I could see. I was appalled at the obvious poor health of those around me. Having just walked through the rosy-cheeked ranch and farm population, the human condition in the city seemed all the more tragic. The distinctly different body odors, the rotting, crooked teeth, the style and colors of the clothing, the pasty skin, the stringy hair, oily and dark near the scalp, brittle dry and light nearing the split ends, the expression in eyes. Looking for simple (simplistic) solutions I pounced on the poor American diet as the culprit. My journal fairly steams with indignation:

I'm appalled at the realization of how utterly sickening, weakening is the American diet, and the poor people seem drawn to its very worst elements. Is there a conspiracy somewhere to dominate the market with these sickening products? One must struggle to eat or even find decent food. The whole factory where I work is hooked on Coke and soda and horrible vending machine candy. Garbage and worse, all of it! Sugar and chemicals. Sugar addicts, unhealthy people, weak, sick, fat, pouring this horrible stuff into already debilitated bodies. Who is it that floods the media this week with warnings about hazards of drinking too much milk or eating too many eggs while the Coca-Cola pipeline is pumping chemical sugars into protein-starved gullets unchecked? The government and media chortle about how health foods are rip-offs. Is there any bigger rip-off in this country than $.25 for a Milky Way which has no redeeming food value at any price? In the middle of a busy day at the factory, it is impossible to find decent food, yet the vending machines surround one's growling stomach with sugar and salt in every chemical form and flavor. No wonder the rural farm families seemed younger and healthier than their years— fresh eggs, meat, milk and the backyard vegetable garden. Now I am on the rampage.

This morning at the "Y" ate breakfast with a young woman, vivacious and attractive with a neck brace, nose patch, and covered with bruises. She'd been raped a week ago after hitchhiking. Another woman, an attractive 40-year old nurse, had been raped at age 19. The young woman said, "Of course I'll continue to hitchhike; in fact, I have since. I felt I had to. It's like getting back on a horse after being thrown. It's a way of life for me, and I meet so many people."

I said, "People expect women to cloister themselves for life and that's unfair." The older woman said, "Look at me. It's been all these years, 20, since I was 19, and nothing has happened to me since."

In that brief conversation I learned 2 things: 1) Every woman must draw her own rules and lines about how she is to live. I will never hitchhike, but more power to those who do, who, as these women, do so with real (too real) knowledge of the risks. 2) My 2,000 mile walk is a baby step as far as subjecting myself to risk. Women do more "brave" living commonly year after year than my trek. I just haven't until now run into them.

But there was also other inspiration in Salt Lake City. The Mormon history, if nothing else, demonstrates the Herculean problems that a determined populace can surmount.

I have an unquenchable thirst for being bowled over again and again by the feats of the Mormon pioneers. The bare facts of their early accomplishments seem to put them out of the class of ordinary mortals. Persecuted and driven, they died by the hundreds, yet they managed to escape to this godforsaken desert, make it "bloom like a rose," erect a tabernacle, begin work on a temple that still awes, lay out plans for a city that had 100 years foresight, all within 2 or 3 years. They combined the back-breaking toughness of the crudest muscled pioneer, the genius of the NASA lab scientist, and the refinement of the most cultured Bostonian. Inside the old civic building, matching in elegance the finest furniture in the Louvre, one can see even today the old richly carved piano that was brought with the first group across the plains in a wagon.

I heard a free organ recital in the tabernacle. Built by the pioneers, the tabernacle remains one of the great buildings of the world, all of wood, held together with pegs and leather thongs, acoustically considered supreme, housing one of the world's great organs, seating 6,000 intimately and cozily. One can feel the vibrations of greatness and history there. The great organ throbbed a favorite Mormon hymn, "Come Come Ye Saints, no toil nor labor fear, All is well, All is well." I'm told it was penned by the irritable William Clayton while on the first vanguard to find the promised land. Having just walked hundreds of miles where William Clayton travelled, often, no doubt, in his very footprints, I found myself choking back tears. I returned later just to hear again the majesty of that hymn, its yearnings and final triumph.

Unfortunately, next to the dignified and inspired tabernacle stand two modern visitors' propaganda centers. Although herded and guided by attractive and poised Mormons, the centers degenerate rapidly into simplistic, sentimental Disney-style gimmickry. They reminded me of the red spray paint next to the elegant granite chiseling on Independence Rock.

While waiting for the cafeteria to open, the "Y" women often gather in the lounge to watch the evening news. On August 15th the news switched to a boat off the coast of Florida where the young woman, Diana Nyad, was making her well publicized bid to swim from Cuba to Florida.

I detected then and since a great antipathy toward her, generated, I assume, by her vigorous self-promotion. It rubs against the grain of our image of the modest self-effacing woman. But tonight Diana was failing in her attempt at greatness. I'm afraid that many people were smugly satisfied at her failure. "It served her right for being so commercial." But there in the "Y" lounge we all saw just a woman like us trying desperately hard to achieve something important to her. We saw her vomit in the water while trying to keep swimming. As she put forth the ultimate in effort and failed, we did not separate from her, we joined her. There went up an agonized sigh from our lounge when she was pulled from the water. I was proud of us all at the "Y". My eyes were wet. That night I dreamed of her struggle.

I was in my own struggle that was important to me. I did not feel competitive with her. Somehow I felt we were on the same team, and, in a way, her loss was all of ours.

Today talked to a newspaper reporter. She asked thorough questions. I went into my "Good American

255

People" theme. On leaving she said she hopes the publicity will bring me no kooks or harm. I said, "It brings out the good people."

She said, "We can hope that maybe only 1 out of 10 will be bad."

I said, "No, only one out of a hundred thousand is bad." And that points out the pervasive attitude (even in the wake of my strenuous speech) that the world is very dangerous, strangers likely evil, etc. But again, "Strangers are simply friends we don't know yet."

It was time to leave Salt Lake City. A TV reporter, Adelle Tyree, and a cameraman walked with me for about nine miles westward out of the city. While walking together, Adelle and I talked opening and intimately about everything from women's lib to Mormons. There was an unusual rapport, instantaneous and complete. Unlike most conversations this was balanced, neither of us dominant, but both of us taut with the excitement of sharing, expressing and receiving each other's opinions and emotions. Near the end of our walk together, Adelle interviewed me for TV by the edge of the highway. She gazed intently into my eyes and asked deep and thoughtful questions. I put all of myself into answering her as truthfully and deeply as I could. The cameraman filmed a "farewell" scene, and Adelle and I awkwardly but with mutual impulse embraced each other. Adelle said "Barbara, I like you." The cameraman had "technical difficulties" so we filmed the "farewell" again (more polished this time.).

Adelle is a professional reporter. She pulled from me the best interview I have ever given. She worked for it; prepared thoughtful questions, established a rapport with me, and yet nothing on earth can shake my faith that our brief sparking relationship was genuine all the way.

style Section A   Monday Morning, August 7, 1978   Page 16

trail

up in the East. She first got cold chills in she spotted hills. Then in the Dakotas began traveling, she was awed and seeing her first mountain.

y part is that I don't feel I've walked that 't seem that far. I guess the paradox is g the walking, the distance doesn't seem I think it's less boring to walk 'cross n to drive."

walks, she worries. About her feet, the er golf cart, the work and family she left of the weather. But there's anticipation ahead.

great fear of highways and people has out. What I can't figure out is that everyone's smiling, laughing, calling ent to me. Two days later, I get scowls, 't know what goes on from day to day to hanges."

tops, she stays wherever she can. She's urches, motels, in farmer's yards,

Keep Weight Down

e weight down, she carries no tent or are out. So she eats sunflower seeds, nuts, wheat germ, peanut butter and red milk — all high in protein, calories it.

els, she thinks of cheeseburgers, junk food.

andwiches one day. That's 12 pieces of such cravings. The other day it was think about Oreos and milk. I stopped ought half a gallon of milk and the ge of cookies I could find. I ate the

a of the end of the trail. She'll climb on meone else drive her home back over she once walked. The golf cart will go It's become her modern handcart. tional attachment for anything she's he trip. Losing anything is a trauma.

Keep a Journal

a journal, but has no real plans for g. Part of the problem is too many much to tell.

i with it."

s white cotton long-sleeved shirt, socks and running shoes. She tried orts, T-shirt and hiking boots.

tton, cover up protects me from the bugs."

if she can't make it?

n't, I really haven't considered not k I can do it. If I don't, I won't try

Barbara Maat left family, home in Boston behind to spend six months following route Donner party took into the Sierras.

Salt Lake Tribune   August 7, 1978

Somehow it felt like Salt Lake City should be the end of my journey. I had absorbed all the experiences I thought I could hold, and 1,200 miles seemed like enough journeying for any pioneers. But a quick look at any map showed I had come, incredibly, only a bit over half way. Ahead loomed the deserts. The scariest of all would come first, the Great Salt Desert. A newspaper article about me had brought a flurry of telephone messages piling up at the front desk warning me of the terrible dangers of the desert.

A dazzling, creative woman named Karen Graham (who had forthrightly summoned the press on my arrival in Salt Lake) presented me with a creation that she had whipped up. It was a concoction of white sheets and silver mylar for my "dangerous" desert crossing. The silver layers were to reflect heat and make shade (which they did very well) and to use later in the snowy mountains to reflect heat inward (which they also did very well). The layers of sheets had brilliant orange sparkle words printed on them in huge letters. One word was my name, MAAT, to signal the possible helicopter search parties that I was OK, and the other message was SOS to signal for rescue. She had notified and inquired of all sorts of officials (like jeep posses!) and rattled off assorted facts to me about sand temperatures, salt requirements, and desert water collectors. With a "can do" person like Karen behind me, how could I fail! Her friend Bill made a packet of boullion, sugar, tea and assorted goodies that he estimated would keep me alive for 10 days in a pinch. I accepted Karen's and Bill's thoughtful, serious gifts and found room somehow to add them to the pack on my groaning golf cart.

That was not the end of my safety equipment, however. A very official and intimidating military car pulled in front of me soon after I was under way. My paranoia flared, and I braced for a lecture and prohibition about walking the desert. (I had already heard about the miles and miles of military test site with the thousands of rounds of live ammunition peppering the innocent-looking sands.) Out stepped two men in military regalia who stood before me and all but saluted. To my utter astonishment, they rather formally (and somewhat bashfully) presented me with a heavy ammunition bag stuffed full with more safety equipment: smoke flares for the day, fire flares for the night, matches that would burn in 50-mph wind, mirror signal devices for search planes, tarps for water stills, charts of distress codes for signal flags, and lots of other little weighty goodies. I was overwhelmed with the unexpected thoughtfulness. Whoever heard of the U.S. military, whose image to me was one of bureaucratic inefficiency and snarls of red tape, managing this little quirk of kindness! Surely it is not covered in any of the procedures manuals. Somewhat nonplussed I stammered my thanks rather foolishly and then said earnestly, "Please rest assured that I am not going to do anything dangerous that would require any possible inconvenience of search and rescue by anyone. I'll be within sight of I-80 all the way. I'm doing this trip for experience but never never for narrow escapes." Then I added, "Gee whiz with all this safety equipment you'll make me feel that somehow maybe I OUGHT to try something a bit more dangerous." "My God," I thought, "was I letting someone down? Were people expecting me to risk myself in hairbreadth escapes with my life?" My trip carried no such image to me.

The kind officer and sergeant shook my hand (positive and supportive) and drove away. I stood by the roadside searching my already overloaded cart for another spot to tie on some more safety equipment. ''My safety equipment," I mused with irony, "will do me in yet." The extra weight was wearing my axles thin and was wearing me out. I might be better carrying extra water. But my policy, perhaps superstition, was firm: anything given to me out of kindness would never kill me, and I would carry it all the way no matter what. The power of kindness was the greatest fuel I'd found yet. "But where, oh where was the ammunition bag going to go?'' With an anxious chuckle I turned and walked on, carrying it in my free hand. Laden down with my safety equipment, I headed west.

It was the middle of August. I looked back at the city that had been my home for two weeks. The backdrop of the Wahsatch Mountains was topped generously with freshly fallen snow, and yet I was already well out onto the scorching hot desert. Only in the west could the paradoxes come so frequently. I was mentally shifting gears, getting into my "alert for any contingency" frame of mind that went with my "woman alone on the highway" situation. It was a stress that I carried along with me all the way. Sometimes I scarcely knew I carried it; sometimes, especially early in the trip, it dominated me. Probably none of it was necessary.

I also had to shift gears with my sense of time and distance. There was no sense in trying to rush toward the landmark ahead. It was still four miles ahead to the edge of the Great Salt Lake campground, and four miles took over an hour regardless how fast my mind raced or how impatiently I strained. Finally after an eternity of city-tense anticipation, I lowered myself into the skimpy shade cast by the public restroom. I had forgotten how weary my bones could feel. I would have to get used to this again too.

The families of George and Jacob Donner represented well-to-do respectability and responsibility. Tamsen Donner, an educated woman, had plans to start a women's academy in California for the benefit of her five daughters and others. George, the captain of the train, and Tamsen were solid people, the kind who brought civilization to the west. It was only natural that they took in Luke Halloran, a consumptive, traveling alone with the train. Tamsen nursed the sick young man, but within two days after escaping the clutches of the deadly Wahsatch, Luke Halloran died. Out of respect for his death the emigrants, who had shunned a day's rest after their escape from the mountains, paused one day. "When you throw bread on the waters, it comes back to you" insists a successful businessman I know. Maybe so; after he died, Luke Halloran was found to have carried $1,500 in coins that he willed to the Donners on his sick bed.

Despite the horrors of the trip so far, the emigrants by this simple gesture gave testimony that they were still a viable, functioning unit practicing the accepted civilized decorum of the day. Later, in Nevada, their common standards of decency would begin to crumble under the stress of their increasingly desperate situation.

At night by the Great Salt Lake it actually became cold (jacket) and very windy. The wind blew hard, and a splattering noise and feeling covered the windy side of me. I thought it was sand and salt and then rain drops, but when I looked down, I was amazed. I was thoroughly speckled with black dots, crawling bugs. They would be blown against me and stick; face, jacket, pants, etc., thousands of them, and then I realized that in the twilight I had been eating them in the beans.

A storm seemed to be brewing, so I dragged the picnic table to some sand (away from the sea of boulders) and weighted some plastic on the top with rocks. I pulled 2 garbage cans to the windy side and squeezed under the table into my bag, looking like a bum in a garbage dump. The wind had blown sand into my bag, and the bugs were speckling everything. I raised my head, brushed the bugs from my "pillow" and quickly put down my head to avoid squashing bugs, then pulled the bag around my neck to keep out more sand and bugs and went to sleep—sand collecting on me like snow.

The other tents around me blew down, but I slept well enough through the tumult, once again proving mind over matter. In the morning the wind was gone, and the mosquitoes were out and the stench from the garbage cans awful. When I rolled up my sleeping bag, I found that the garbage cans weren't the only objects emanating stench; there was a dead rat in my sleeping bag. Its rotting entrails had smeared between the bag and the groundcover, and I had slumbered oblivious and peaceful during the night. A string of bad luck quickly followed. I could not find my food bag and assumed (mistakenly as it later turned out) that someone had stolen it. The bathroom and water supply were locked. Sometime during the walk the day before, I had lost one of my wineskin water containers. I checked my golf cart and noticed with horror that my axle was virtually worn through. So I headed toward the little village of Grantsville with a smelly sleeping bag, thirsty, hungry (thinking of the food I had overbought the day before and had given away to lighten my load) and with a wary eye on my thread-thin cart axle.

Then on the way to Grantsville a man in a dump truck motioned slyly for me to go to him. I did and he talked silkily about wanting "a chance to get to know me," and I said there was no chance. He was the very first obvious skunk to try to pick me up. Later a car of young men

261

careened past and tried to scare me (I was startled and annoyed) by leaning out and screaming at me while banging on the car door. Three people with wormy dispositions and cesspool brains in quick succession unfairly but inevitably colored my impressions of all of the Salt Lake City area. It's amazing how a few incidents, good or bad, can leave an impression of a whole area.

Then magically my luck changed. Two men in a cafe were very nice; they'd seen me on TV, and then I became aware that the kitchen help and people all over the cafe were recognizing me. When I left, people waved or stopped or called "good luck." One man got a camera and returned. Then the senior citizen van returned from distant Grantsville and delivered to me a hot lunch.

Approaching Grantsville, people emerged: the reporter from the paper, friendly townspeople, the city councilman, people with cameras, and pictures for me to autograph. At the city hall, people crowded in to see me. I was tired and dazed but found myself escorted to the local Donner museum, which was unlocked for me. A wonderful Mormon family opened their home to me; another gave me $5 for courage. It had been a full and long 20 miles from the dead rat in my sleeping bag so long ago that morning to the safety and goodwill that the people of Grantsville extended.

14

GREAT SALT LAKE DESERT

August 18 - 26
(140 miles)

No high mountains,
No lowly hills:
At the earth's limits
before my eyes
the heavens fall.
Sachio

On endless white salt   1978 WS

The remainder of Utah is an account of my trip across the Great Salt Desert. Because I always feared this section as the most dangerous of the journey, I asked a healthy male friend to accompany me as a safety back-up. Although he had trained for this by running six miles every day, ironically he immediately succumbed to the desert rigors, and the helper role switched to me. He soon rented a car and followed me as I completed the crossing easily.

———

Emerging disheartened and shaken from their ordeal in the Wahsatch, the Donner Party immediately ran into another cruel deception. The Great Salt Desert had been depicted loosely as a dry drive of forty miles. In reality the bad stretch was over eighty miles, much of it over a soggy salt mush impossible to drink and nearly impossible for the weakened animals to pull through. To carry enough water for animals and people would have weighted the wagons to immovability anyway. The dilemma was insolvable and untellable suffering inevitable. The agony was all the more bitter as the thirst-driven immigrants would strive half crazed again and again to the dot of the next ridge, expecting water and finding none. Five wagons were abandoned on the salt flats when the thirst-crazed oxen broke from the wagons and stampeded out of control in a futile search for water. It was from one of those abandoned wagon mounds that the bone and bit of wood had been taken in 1976 and eventually given to me.

While researching my trip I stumbled upon a picture of the Donner Trace on the salt flats taken from a helicopter. Because of the peculiar nature of the water and mineral ecology of the salt desert, wheel marks, oxen prints, and even human footprints had been preserved vividly for over 100 years. The wheel marks are still visible, and it is just within the past two decades that the footprints of the men, women, and children have faded. The photograph that I found brought tears to my eyes. There on an eternity of featureless salt, there on the terrifying landscape of nothingness, there wavered the frail and feeble tracks of one lonely wagon. The sad little marks entered from the lower corner of the picture and wandered with a heart-breaking quaver off in the distance at the top of the photograph, coming from nowhere and going nowhere, endless.

I met Warren, an old family friend, at the airport. He was the one recruited to add a measure of safety for the salt desert crossing.

Wind, sun, a peek at the Donner relics through the museum window, and then we were out into the desert, readjusting and redistributing weight on carts, dry jagged western mountains, brown, and brown valley with 20 Wells greenery. Warren, basking in relaxation, business stresses far behind, walking. Sun quickly became very warm, long rest in shade of a factory (Dolomite) relay station. Walking hours and lunch on I-80 in shade of "fallen rock zone" sign, cars whizzing close. Warren spotted a Conoco gas station sign, "even read the word 'Conoco'," he said, but it turned out to be merely a triangular tiny YIELD sign. It was the first indication of desert distortions in size and distance, of desert heat and mirage. We discovered a leak in our gallon water container. As the heat intensified I called a halt on a flat, and we used Karen's mylar to rig a sun shade over the golf carts. I was vaguely puzzled at Warren's haphazard rigging of it. Shortly he said, "Is that an outhouse over there on the railroad track?" I again faintly stirred with alarm; the "outhouse" was a railroad signal control, many miles from any possible customers for an outhouse (except us!). Any worries I had were dispelled by my own physical well-being. I was not tired or particularly hot although raising a hand into the sun brought a sobering oven-like blast. We mused and dozed in our meager shade and walked a few more miles at dusk to find a drier spot. The Great Salt Desert is brutally dry and hot, yet everywhere under a ¼-inch crust of salt, it is extremely wet, like a slick gray clay, amazing paradox.

We marveled at the other-worldly atmosphere as the sun set, touching the pale bare landscape with deep blues and rosy pinks. The I-80 traffic hummed and an occasional train roared, but the feeling was one of being on another planet and peaceful. At 11:00 I was awakened by moon-rise, indeed one of the great spectacles of the trip, glowing dusky orange on the horizon and seemingly nearly as large as the earth itself. It was distorted, lopsided with a knobby top. Hours later it awakened me again like a blinking white street light overhead, brilliant white and casting deep blue moon shadows by the salt sage.

Earlier the sun sank low, giving a warm golden

265

touch to the sands and flats with long blue shadows extending eastward from every clump of salt sage.

In the morning we pushed on to Delle eager to refill our water bottles, especially since the loss of one gallon. We were stupefied to find the place totally closed down, even the gas stations, because of no water. The hauling truck was broken. It was a serious development but not disastrous since we had 2 gallons left and "only" 20 more miles to Knolls and water. Two miles beyond Delle, Warren discovered that he'd lost his sunglasses, a very serious loss with prospects of sun blindness on the white salt flats ahead. Warren decided to return to Delle to see if they'd fallen from his pocket when we climbed the fence. As he left I was horrified to see him jogging, insane in the heat, and hoped he'd taken money to buy more. He hitched, thumb out, as he ran, and did not get a ride, a very, very disconcerting phenomenon since I had confidently relied on the humanity of travelers on I-80 as a final safety backup. This failure to pick him up, running in the heat of the desert, haunted me for days. Warren returned, no glasses, and he had not thought to see if Delle even had any. By now I began to wonder about his thinking processes.

We resumed walking, having lost a precious "coolish" morning hour yet pressed to continue by our water situation. We spread Desitin on half of his eye glasses to cut the glare, and he pulled his hat low. We were prepared to break a flat whisky bottle as soon as we found one along the road and clothespin-clip the colored glass to Warren's glasses for makeshift sun glasses.

I felt fine, energetic, and not too hot, but Warren's face was terribly sunburned. He asked for a break, and I was suddenly very alarmed, a sense that all was not well with him despite his protestations to the contrary. He admitted he was very hot, strange since I was reasonably comfortable. He agreed to stop in the shade of the next road sign, but we headed for a railroad underpass instead. We crawled and squeezed through the barbed wire and found ourselves in a dirt dusty gravel platform sharing the shady haven with a dead porcupine. The situation became clear. Warren was burning hot, as if in high fever, his face flushed from near heat stroke, not sunburn. Thank God for the underpass. We rigged Karen's mylar for a wind-break. The wind was funneling dirty dust at us, and we began the long process of cooling Warren, using water for drinking, not enough to spare for sponging. The breezy dryness of the desert kept sweat evaporated even though we had drunk huge quantities of water and eaten salty beef jerky. I was amazed how seldom and little I urinated despite the water consumption. We noted Warren's cooling skin with relief as the hours passed. I dozed but awoke feeling horrible. Something goes wrong with the body's cooling mechanism when one sleeps on a hot afternoon.

At one point we were rewarded by the rare sight of a badger wandering casually in a zigzag path along the railroad embankment. As with the mountain lion, I was struck by its relaxed movements, and then I realized that the various Wild Kingdom type TV shows generally are filming nervous, tense or alarmed animals, giving a wrong impression of how animals generally behave in the wild state. The badger continued his contented amble as we glanced at him now and then to check his progress. A few trains roared by, a powerful experience at such close range.

Warren had cooled completely by evening, and we climbed out of the dirty little haven and continued. The mountain pass we emerged from opened into yet another broad valley, the very one the Donner Party had traversed. Again the setting sun painted its magic light, and we walked lightly down the 15-mile flat valley between mountain ridges. I recalled a half-forgotten phenomenon that the great west had taught me years ago. The human eye can perceive relative distances only a few miles. Beyond this, distances and positions appear to collapse so that 15 miles appears no farther than 4 miles, etc. The desert scene is particularly vulnerable to mistaken space perceptions; mountain ranges and ridges and broad plains and valleys constantly shift and collapse and expand as one's position changes. A mountain range behind another mountain range appears to be separated by 2 or 3 miles when in reality it may be 50. Sometimes the 2 may even appear as one, as the human eye cannot perceive any distance between the two.

To be lost in this situation would be indeed terrifying since landmarks appear to shift position as one approaches. It is speculated that this phenomenon might have occurred to the Donner Party, and they might have confused Silver Mountain with Pilot Peak. It would not even take their exhaustion and thirst to confuse any easterner.

The sun set, and the stars appeared, and we walked in darkness. The moon had 2 hours before it would show itself. I experienced the pleasant sensation as if gliding effortlessly on roller skates, as faint images of salt sage loomed out of the darkness briefly and disappeared. We churned away the miles. I felt good enough to consider going all the way to Knolls — we would arrive about 5:00 A.M., and we'd been told a motel was there. Warren looked terribly pale even by moonlight, but I ignored this. Finally he said he wanted to stop and I agreed. We unrolled our bags on the flats, the salt bushes eerie clumps here and there, the warm wind faintly howling as if protesting the presence of humans on this alien land. The moon appeared and I fell asleep, only to be awakened shortly by the sound of Warren vomiting from exhaustion. He said he felt as if he'd "run too far" and then lay down, confessing that even during the dark hours he'd been hot. Now it was borderline heat exhaustion.

Suddenly across the years I was touched by the similar utter horror that the Donner Party must have felt. I felt I could have reached out and touched them as they had struggled through the night, exhausted yet urgent in their need for water. The balmy warm breeze was a grotesque mask covering the endless miles, the pitiless empty stretches, the loneliness of their ordeal. The eerie soft moonlight masked the harshness of the situation. The land was a nightmare screaming "You are not welcome. Leave!" My horror was awesome but not panicky, amazed more than frightened. It was clear that Warren (without sunglasses) would have to make Knolls in the morning, and walking the actual salt flats ahead would be doubtful for him.

In the morning Warren said he felt fine and would like to do the salt flats. I was amazed he could even say such a ridiculous thing and marveled at his erratic thinking patterns. In a few miles he was pooped again.

As we finally approached Knolls, a terrific wind arose. We struggled mightily just to keep moving and passed through some dramatic desert dunes and sculptures as we bent forward. Knolls was an unspeakable disappointment. It was a decrepit outpost of hell. No motel, a junk yard, a sagging paint-peeled cabin as a gas station, and a sour man who simply turned his back on my wave as we painfully dragged in through the wind and sand storm. Warren nearly spilled a tear as he said wistfully, "It's amazing how you get expectations built up in your mind..." There was a diner of sorts (apparently unchanged since the 1930's depression) but the hamburger was surprisingly delicious.

We had emerged on foot, hot and tired from the desert heat and winds, yet the sour man was totally indifferent to my pleas for renting a shack or a corner of a garage or anything to let Warren recover. Obviously we'd have to return to Salt Lake City to rent a car for Warren for the salt flats ahead. I geared up and began begging a ride from every car that drove in for gas. Warren said, "My God, you have one hell of a nerve." I was beginning to get mad enough to feel everyone ELSE had one hell of a nerve for turning us down.

A middle-aged couple drove up, and I put them on the spot. The woman squirmed uncomfortably and looked afraid. When they emerged from the cafe they wavered and softened. We climbed into the car and all was well. The woman confessed that she had been afraid of us, but the husband had felt we were not to be feared. Our ride to Salt Lake City was pleasant. They were religious, their daughter on a church mission with the Indians in Salt Lake City. They did not know what tribe.

Spent the night in a cheap motel in Salt Lake City. The radiator leaked and the carpet was wet, garbage under the bed, shower stall a mass of mold and gaping holes in the blanket and spread, but Warren, chivalrously on the floor, and I in bed fell into an exhausted sleep. I could hardly remember even lying down.

Next day rented a car and drove back to Knolls in the evening, and a brother of the Knolls family snarled at me with unbridled hostility. "There's a word for what you're doing, but I'm not going to say it."

I walked onto the really flat salt flats into the evening, with Warren following in the car. We used the old abandoned road all the rest of the way across. Eating the unrefined salt is a definite no-no (arsenic and other poisons), but in spots the salt crystals were delicate and feathery and they tasted delicious, soft crystals that gave a softly satisfying crunchy crumble between the teeth. In the next days I ate more than a few.

Walked far into the night   1978 WS

The sunset was dramatic against the snow-white flats. Warren took pictures gleefully. Walked far into the night, an occasional train shaking the ground as it passed. I saw an unusual shooting star, a reddish purplish bluish head with a purple-pink tail streak. It looked similar to 4th of July fireworks.

Next morning walked again, squinting painfully even behind sunglasses. I marveled again at the distance deceptions. I remember how the Donner Party had seen mirages, and I smugly remarked to Warren during a snack stop that I could easily see in the distance what must have looked like a lake with trees to exhausted pioneers. The heat waves made it look like shimmering waves breaking on a beach with breeze-blowing trees. Mountain peaks curled and lifted to the horizon in points at each end and edges and appeared to make perfect reflections of themselves in the "water." A bunched row of dark shapes indeed looked like a line of people and vehicles. At one point a low section in a mountain range disappeared and became a pass, so much so that Warren took a picture showing what he assumed was a real pass. Imagine this kind of confusion to water-craved pioneers... I jeered at Warren's mistake and went on. I was mildly interested in a large truck and some jeeps to the southwest (Dugway Proving Ground?) and saw someone get out. A few miles later I realized the truck and jeeps and people had all been mirages! Tiny objects out on the flats cannot be judged for distance, and my trucks were shadows of tiny lumps. I was considerably humbled.

Then ahead I saw a huge, white, cascading fountain in the distance against the mountains. "Wow! There's Wendover... Well I'll be damned. Another mirage got me. That can't be a fountain because Wendover is still 20 miles away, so that fountain would have to be a thousand feet high." Another mile and a dark fringe of trees and tiny houses appeared around the fountain. "Holy smokes! That IS Wendover! What a joke... I thought the real fountain was a mirage..." Nope. In the end the white fountain was a small building omni many miles from Wendover, and the dark green trees and houses were actually blades of grass no more than 6 inches high.

Pilot Peak really appeared at hand when still actually 50 miles away. The Bonneville flats seemed squeezed into an impossibly narrow strip at the foot of the mountains. One tries diligently to compensate for the known distortions, but the attempt is futile as distances and positions shift and objects assume vivid new forms. The sensation is one of being in another dimension, a dream world whose perceptual rules follow capricious whims. Only a fool could not respect the desert.

We spent the hours of intense sun in the shade of the car. I resumed walking in the evening. Wendover appeared "again" far ahead, and I became tired. Warren spotted the rest area on I-80 and calculated mathematically by telephone pole count that it was 1/2 mile more. I agreed to meet him there. Fooled again. Even with the poles to count, the distortion put it 2 1/2 miles ahead. We decided *to drive into town where I got an ice cream cone, a craving I'd had all day. An ice cream cone never before (or ever will) taste so wonderfully cool, creamy and sensuous on my desert-heated throat. It is surely one of those rare moments; the memory of its satisfaction will linger with me. (The Reed children had such a memory of their Christmas dinner while trapped and starving in the snowy Sierras—for me like the smell of my mother's spaghetti cooking as I rush off the school bus as a child.)*

We drove back onto the flats, where I had stopped walking earlier, and then backtracked a few more miles looking for dry salt. We ended up sleeping literally on the shoulder of the old road, the only dry spot. Next morning went into Wendover where I was given a complimentary suite at the luxurious hotel casino. I reveled in the contrast, one night sleeping on the shoulder of an old road, the next in a silken-sheeted king sized bed.

From the hotel window I looked out at Nevada ahead and recoiled in horror. Somehow I marked crossing the Great Salt Desert as the final hurdle, not even thinking beyond it. Now, before me stretched a brown landscape devoid of any human influence, with mean mountains and hot, baked, broad, treeless valleys 15 miles wide. I scrambled for the maps and began counting miles between towns, searching in vain for little black squares that would mean buildings. Warren looked at me with pity, and I burst into tears. Obviously the worst was yet to come. Nevada, lying quietly and overlooked, would get its revenge. It would be the biggest challenge yet...sixty miles between towns and not a ranch or a shack anywhere between. I crumbled, demoralized. Then Warren said something true. He said "If I weren't here, you'd not be upset. You'd be sitting here figuring it out and getting ready, not be crying defeated." And immediately I knew it to be true. There are times when sympathy and pity are deadly debilitators. One had enough challenge just to cope without handling and defending against another's sorrowful sympathy.

Another notion was begging to be recognized. Although my leg muscles were nearly as small and soft as before my 1,300 miles of walking, I was forced to entertain the notion that I was in superlative condition. In Wyoming, where I was horrified to learn I couldn't jog, I assumed that my body was unchanged much from pre-trip days. Now I had to reconsider. I had easily outlasted and out-walked 4 men (with the possible exception of my husband), all of whom were supposedly conditioned. Despite this obvious evidence and despite my women's orientation, I instinctively felt I needed a man to "help" me over the tough spots. Incredible.

To know I can walk probably 40 or 50 miles in a pinch gives one a confident, even safe, feeling, a less vulnerable feeling than the flabby soul, even in a Cadillac, must feel with 50 miles of emptiness ahead. In the latter case, one is dependent on the car machine, but in the former, one relies safely on one's self, a surer bet.

After Warren left Sunday evening, I had my wheels cotter-pinned at the Mobil station. A group of people had seen me walk in and poured around to say hello, one woman nudging her husband saying, "See, I told you I'd have the nerve to talk to her!" Three minutes before this I was standing mutely in a corner being rudely ignored by the attendant. The mechanic fixed my wheels. "If you're dumb enough to do this trip, I'll be dumb enough not to charge you." And we all giggled with him.

15

NEVADA

August 27 - September 18

(210 miles)

"The country couldn't run without the illegal Mexicans."
prosperous Clover Valley rancher

"The illegal aliens are ruining the country."
struggling Ruby Valley rancher

Just Keep Going   1978   MB

Nevada, Four Hundred miles to go. I had learned the physical part, how to Just Keep Going. The Donner Party too, somehow beyond my understanding, somehow had just kept going, actually making a fast crossing with animals dying, tempers raging, Indians harassing, hunger increasing, fear growing, but somehow they just kept going…somehow…

It was time to tackle Nevada.

NEVADA

In the morning I awoke by 5 AM as I instructed my faithful psyche to do. There is a brief period on awakening in the dark with the unknown road ahead that is hell to contend with. Thank heaven it seems to leave no scars. I tore away from my plush safe hotel womb in Wendover and headed out into the brown Nevada road scar. A flag signaler on the road said, "Lady, aren't you taking an awful chance?" Later, others talked of murders on the Nevada stretch. It was a grueling re-entry into the road life alone. My water was too heavy. The golf cart sagged, and I worried. The bag of flares from the army fit nowhere, but I have that superstition that I must carry all gifts. My safety equipment may do me in yet.

A scary Indian in a battered car drove off the road and onto the service road to ask me to ride with him. He probably meant well, but it required self-discipline to think so. I was tired, weary, and dispirited.

And then I heard a friendly European (German) accent, "Hello." I looked and saw an engaging smile, a boyish young man on a bike, a disarming miracle from heaven here a million miles from nowhere. And unlike all the other bikers who grunt "hi" and churn by, he was actually stopped! Heaven couldn't have sent a more welcome gift, and I actually felt nervous that I'd overdo my enthusiasm in my momentary desperate need for companionship. (Donners upon seeing their rescuers: "Are you the men from California or from heaven?")

He was tired, having crossed the desert from Salt Lake City during the night, so we pulled sweating and panting up the pass and camped over a side hill in a sandy stream bed while Pilot Peak loomed over us to the north. He talked of families and Germany and bike adventures. He talked of liking old-fashioned domestic women and disapproving of modern independent women. I talked of my being a modern independent woman and hating the role he

275

*so admired. Yet his manner was so engaging that I felt
myself nearly blurting, "Would you marry my daughter
please!" and frankly I now wish I had. I kidded him about
his German cleanliness, and he won me completely as he
tactfully ate my evaporated milk and wheat germ with only
a somewhat restrained gusto. His English was excellent,
proper and melodic (having learned it from grammar
textbooks). He struggled to describe German character
saying, "Germans try to keep not a dirty mind" and then
found the phrase he'd been searching for: "try to keep a
clear conscience."*

*The German student said he'd heard of a man who
biked across the U.S. and got to the Brooklyn Bridge and
threw his bike over the rail. I recounted the story of the old
lady in the Mormon handcart company who pulled her cart
all the way to Salt Lake City only to promptly throw it over
a cliff. We both laughed heartily at the stories. Would I
heave my golf cart off the Golden Gate Bridge?*

*In the evening the bats seemed amazed to find people
in their stream-bed flyway and repeatedly dive bombed our
heads. (We were in a long line in the narrow sandy arroyo.)
At one point a bat brushed my face and I clearly heard the
wing beats. In the morning we said goodbye and the
pleasant interlude was over.*

We had some important things in common that felt
like a bond that no one else seemed to understand. We
both were traveling alone, a long, long way. We both had
tried to find someone to share our trips but had found no
one interested. We both were doing something that lots of
the homefolks and relatives thought a bit daffy. And above
all, we both loved it.

As soon as I re-emerged onto the highway, a car
pulled over and said that someone had been calling on the
CB all morning searching for me. Unbeknownst to me, the

big rig truckers had been calling each other to keep track of my progress and protect me. A few hours later a camper circled and stopped. I looked up and saw the faces of some old, old friends, the Thompsons, who had moved to California years ago. They had seen the AP picture of me while on their Colorado vacation and had kept a lookout for me on their way home to California. Again the "barren wastes" of Nevada had yielded a happy surprise.

Seeing the Thompsons was fun and important. Old high school friends change over the years. I'm afraid I was even more sweet and meek in high school than I like to remember. George's brother, Billy, my classmate since second grade, couldn't even remember me. DeEtt said with emphasis, "You would be the last person from high school that I'd imagine doing this."

George, best man at our wedding, said, "Poor Howard. He thought he was marrying someone sweet and shy and now look."

DeEtt on the other hand, in high school was sharply aggressive and seemed to scorn feminine trappings. She's now become a Mormon with all the Mormon subservience to George. "George, will you let me walk 2 weeks with Barbara?"

George: "I think, Honey, you'd better come home with us together."

"OK, George."

Biblical: The lion will become as a lamb and the lamb as a lion...

In Oasis, a crossroad only, I ate a double cheeseburger with the Thompsons and another as soon as they left and then asked for vanilla ice cream. The lady was "out" but gave me the cardboard bucket with a long spoon for a final cleanout. There was a lot of ice cream there, heavenly delicious, and I fairly waddled away when it was gone. Painfully aware of my own insatiable appetite, I had long ago lost comprehension of how infinitely beyond mine the Donner Party emigrants' hunger must have felt. They had so little food and later... nothing.

Nevada, like going against the grain of a washboard, one mountain range after another, 4 miles up, 3 miles down, 10 miles of plain, repeat, repeat, repeat. The mountains are dotted with scrub cedar, the plains with brown low shrubs and sage. Yesterday I saw one single broadleaf tree, small, but the way it swayed softly in the breeze was a beauty to me. The cedars whir nicely but never rustle.

The notion of camping over a tiny hill near I-80 appeals, but I can't lift my cart load over the ubiquitous freeway fence. (Where are you, nice German student?) I tried an exit but found every spot deep in human toilet paper, a lesson learned: don't use the exits. I also found a drugged hippy in a horrendously junky VW Beetle who talked with a glazed intensity. "I might walk from Salt Lake to the east coast because I'm out of money. I'm looking for the social center of the U.S., but it's hard to explain it. I found San Francisco too gay." His desperation and bizarre thought processes made me wary, and I wished him luck in "whatever," and he me. I left in a hasty departure. No thank you to camping with him (am I too uptight?) but I am VERY regretful I didn't offer him food. Kindness was sorely needed there.

I have no mirror. My nose peeled easily yesterday to bare raw flesh and bled profusely. What does it look like today? It feels pitted and scabby and begging to be peeled again.

278

Karen Graham had given me the name of a woman, Marvel, who would "certainly love what you're doing and would surely want to talk to you and put you up in high style for a night."

"Oh, but who is she?" I had asked.

"Well, she practically owns the whole town" I was told.

There was a pause and then, "She's loaded with money, a shrewd woman. She ran a string of girl houses when prostitution was in its heyday. But now she lives outside of town in retirement in a swank Mexican ranch. Everyone likes her. She holds her head as high as anyone even if she is a madam."

I approached the little desert town and could find no campground, so I asked a passerby where I could find Marvel.

The woman said, "Well, you'll probably see her riding around town with a young gigolo in her fancy car, a Lincoln Continental." The woman gave me a curious look and then continued in a friendly way, "I suppose you know that she used to run the uhhh, well, you know... girl houses here. You'll see her sooner or later; you can't miss her. She has platinum blond hair. She's put on a little weight the past few years but is still a good looking woman. Why don't you try the Spigot Casino first? She owns it and stops in there every day to check on things."

I headed toward the Golden Spigot more curious than ever about Marvel. But I just missed Marvel. "Oh, she just left. I think she was going down to the hotel."

And again I just missed her. "I think she said she was going to the beauty parlor. You'll see it down there next to the Sunoco station."

I was beginning to feel a bit silly dashing to and fro about town, my loose white pants flapping in the breeze as I pulled my little golf cart behind me.

Hot on the trail of the elusive Marvel, I arrived fairly panting at the beauty parlor. "Marvel?" said the hairdresser, "Yeah, she's here. Whadda ya want her for?" With an implicit deference and defensive protectiveness, the hairdresser had placed herself between me and another woman nearby. But then the other woman stepped forward and spoke for herself. I knew at once it was Marvel: the platinum blond hair, a steady eye and straight back, the wrinkled skin, and authority that she emanated. She was heavy but not quite fat. "Yes?" she said with a tone intimating the controlled patience of a busy person.

Suddenly nonplussed I stammered who I was and what I was doing, feeling more foolish with every word. Marvel, meanwhile, was carefully scrutinizing me up and down with her professional eye, and I can only assume her assessment found me lacking. I just wasn't the type for her type of business.

"But what do you want from me?" she asked sensibly.

"Well, I ahhh, I just wanted to say hello from Karen" (who, as it turned out, Marvel couldn't remember) "and ask if I could stay in your hotel," I finished rather lamely.

"Sure, tell Rubin (one of her former husbands) at the front desk I said to rent you a room. Is that all?"

"Yes."

As I stumbled out the door I tried to remember just what it was I had been looking for. The legendary Marvel at that point was probably trying to figure it out too.

I felt that the hotel with Rubin was too expensive for me ($16.50). I found a cheaper one, a flophouse for $6.50, run and owned by two old men. One, Larry, ("But aren't you afraid of wild animals?") is nice enough with no teeth, a bearded stubble, and bowed back, who does the cleaning. He "cleaned" (well, sort of) my room and made my bed while I conversed with two alcoholics in the lobby.

"Hell yes, you can take my picture." Pete   1979 ES

I came to love the old place, which smelled like a wet dog. Pete, the other owner, wore an undershirt and cooked and kept up a banter with the steady stream of old-timers who came in to read the papers. They all loved looking at my maps. Pete hadn't been to Boston in 30 years but knew every street, and when I left he pressed on me a free sandwich and a huge cup of strong coffee. Generous. And the caffeine, EXHILARATING.

Walked on and found a thick (tiny) scrub cedar forest on the freeway side of the fence and camped out of sight yet 60 feet from the traffic. Although I am not ever afraid, I have a tense sense of being on guard. It lessens after dark when darkness tucks me away safely. I'm worried about the weight on the golf cart. The water and food I need even for 2 dry days is too much for the wheel and axle system.

Everyone is obsessed with my keeping warm, but that's NEVER a problem. I sweated all last night trying to elude the damn ants. What should have been a perfect spot was alive with ants, all solid black, solid pale orange, or one segment black and two dark red, the black either front or rear. Thank heaven they didn't bite unless caught between clothes and skin tightly, but otherwise they tormented me incessantly. I had thought at nightfall they'd lay off but no. What were they looking for? Their explorations seemed to come in waves. I awoke to feel them in my hair, over my face, in my ears, down my neck, on my legs (deep in the sleeping bag), on my back and even in my underpants. Ahhh well... if it won't kill me, I'll not get genuinely alarmed, only aggravated. Coyotes musical last night.

The money situation has been a nagging worry, a relentless pressure. I'm caught by having to slow my journey to keep the Donner schedule, but this is more expensive in food and lodging. I can camp free in the wilderness, but I run out of food and water, or I can stay in towns near grocery food, but the campgrounds cost a fortune (and are carpeted with dog shit).

I can see clearly in the mirror that my top lip has become longer (nose to lip) and is thinner (lip part). Why?

I can scan my face in the mirror again and like what I see. Tan, peeling nose, lots of happy wrinkles and creases, joyful, deeply alive eyes and an infinite kaleidoscope of changing expressions as my thoughts change. I like my thin body. It's all me and I'm comfortable in it. I like my hands, long, strong, graceful with dirty nails and angular beauty. I have my very own style it seems. Hey. Why this exhilaration? Pete's strong coffee still?

I have a dream that all the people I've loved on this trip will not fade in isolation but will come together in mutual celebration. For sure it will happen in the afterlife. Could they all be part of a book in this life? Would they like each other? Appreciate each other despite extreme disparities? Could they bridge their differences?

———

Beyond Pilot Peak the Donner Party followed a western course with the repeating monotonous pattern of up, over, down, and across the desert plains as each mountain range was scaled and crossed. This pattern was interrupted abruptly when they came face to face with a mountain range much higher than the rest, with craggy snow-covered peaks and no passes in sight. At that point they were following the feeble wagon trace of a lost party that had gone before them. It was a clear case of the blind leading the blind. The lost party, faced with a blank mountainous wall, could have turned north or south in search of a pass. Had they turned north, they would have shortly found a pass and continued their westward course with only a minor jog interrupting their journey. Subsequent routes to the west would take a northern route. But, unfortunately, the lost party turned south, and the ill-fated Donners were doomed to repeat the fatal mistake. For three days the little wagons inched straight south before finding a pass, and for three more days the wagons repeated the wasteful exercise, this time heading straight north on the opposite side of the narrow mountain range. The sad detour stands out sharply as an erratic waver on every map of the Donner route.

But for me the Ruby Mountains detour was a most pleasant surprise. The kind people who ranched in Clover

Valley and Ruby Valley would pass me from ranch to ranch, calling ahead and paving the way as solicitously as any mother would for the welfare of her child. But I didn't know that when I first turned south to follow the long way round those endless mountains.

I tore away on a 2 lane highway tense and angry and defensive and walked or raced with hostility south on the hostile road. A drugged psycho had assaulted a woman and kidnapped her and her 2 kids the day before on I-80. My pack was too heavy for the golf cart again, and the heavy flare bag cut my hands. A fat man in a camper sat in a desolation of sage plain and simply smoked and watched as I walked by. After a couple of hours I turned onto the side loop closer to the mountains that were dotted with ranches on the map. My body melted in grateful relief as the tension of the highway disappeared. Sometimes I'm not even aware of the stress of battling highway potential danger. My pace slowed, and I drank deeply, letting the wonderful water spill all over my clothes as usual, and noticed for the first time the gentle warmth of the morning sun.

The Ruby Mountains majestically formed a rugged snow-patched backdrop for the tiny dots of ranches below. Then the alfalfa fields, emerald green and dotted with fresh bales wafting their sweet and tender fragrance. A tractor moved in gentle harmony far away, and the peace of the scene flooded my senses. My God, it's paradise. Here in Nevada, parched and brown Nevada, tucked secretly in this state of bad press, here was the greenest, loveliest, loftiest paradise of the entire trip. My surprise made its reality all the sweeter. I walked in awe, blinking and overwhelmed. The 12,000-foot mountains, high enough to hold melting snow all year, were the key that made this valley bloom while the others lie silent and brown. Tiny sparkling streams gurgled through willow brush ditches. Cheerful birds darted in the undergrowth, oblivious to the rare miracle of this Clover Valley.

Again, I'm thinking, My God, I'm in ultimate happiness, exalting, inspired, bursting with triumph and meaning and optimism. How could I lose this so quickly and forget, "Oh ye, of little faith"...

A battered pickup stopped and a 33-year old man, huge black beard, sweat-stained brim on felt hat, friendly face and friendly eyes above that beard, offered a ride. I declined, and then he started talking, helpfully drawing maps, invitations to his ranch (too far off my route), and generally took time to be encouraging. He had a severe case of stuttering, and I tensed, but he in no way let his speech impediment prevent him from extending friendly gestures. He said, "This is the best time in history to be alive. One can do anything if one has the guts, even walk across the country. There is freedom now to do whatever you want with your life. My wife and I worked on shrimp boats in Alaska to get money to buy our ranch. I'm the living proof it can be done. This is the best of times to be alive." We parted, and I felt great optimism. He was someone not only devoid of complaints but actually endorsing life itself. It was a bold statement, and coming through a crippling stutter, it seemed all the more affirmative.

The wonderful ranch people who invited me for lunch or asked me to spend the night somehow cast me instantly into the role of an eastern representative who was in dire need of western enlightenment. Mingled with their gracious and genuine hospitality, I was urged, even commanded, to listen carefully so that I could get it all straight. Western anger was a force to be reckoned with. My opinions were never solicited; it was assumed that I was their own version of an eastern stereotype. "Massachusetts? I suppose you're one of the Teddy Kennedy lovers."

"Next time you're in Washington, D.C...,"

"I've only been there once in my life."

"Well, all those places are right close together back there anyway."

"Those people in the east don't appreciate us. All they think of is the price of beef in the supermarket. Do you know that every farmer feeds 40 families?"

"Those ecologists from back there who've never even seen a coyote think they can come out here and tell us not to kill them."

"Now the environmentalists are trying to say that we have to do something about the dust on the roads to the mines. Did you ever hear anything more ridiculous? First they come up with so many stupid rules that the copper mine has to shut down and now this. That copper plant meant the livelihood of 40 families. Kid, you ever hear anything more senseless? Way out there in the middle of the desert and they're worrying about how clean the air is. The wind blows up more dust in 10 minutes than all the copper plants and gravel roads."

"Now we have to go running to the archeologist every time we want to dig a hole in case it might be some Indian ground. I don't care what anyone says. No one will tell me where I can dig or what Indian artifacts I can pick up."

"I heard that they stopped the construction of an electric power plant because of some little fish or snail. It's just crazy depriving thousands of people of electricity because of some little fish or frog that no one could ever care about or ever even heard of."

"Oh yeah, they want to keep this land government owned so people from back there like the Sierra Club can stomp around up there. They can't find their way up a hill without a guide, but they think they need to set aside good grazing land just to tramp around on."

Again and again I heard about the wildlife preservationists' biggest blunder, the "save the wild horses campaign." That one mistake is cited like the black mark it is every time the word ecology is breathed. I fear they'll never live it down.

"The thing that we don't like is all you people from the east coming out here sticking your noses into our business, telling us what to do with the land here, where we can and can't build dams, when you don't know what you're talking about. Why don't you just stay back where you came from?"

"Who are you talking about?"

"All those people from Washington who come out here and try to tell us how to run our lives."

"Massachusetts? I suppose you're for the ERA."

"Yes. "

"That figures.'"

The perplexed and angry west.   1979 ES

The last wonder of it all was that, feeling as these people did, they still exuded warmth and hospitality as if to a dear friend. I had not seen such political passion and bitterness since the Vietnam debate at its height. We in the east simply have no conception of the animosity they have toward us. And they have no idea how surprised we'd be to learn this. They would be surprised to learn how splintered and divided are eastern points of view. Perhaps sadly and closer to the truth is the fact that most of us never think of Nevadans at all, not in animosity, not in sympathy, not at all. Our visions of them are vague and hazy. Theirs of us are sharp and definite and probably inaccurate.

Kathy   1979 ES

It was just my good luck that I stumbled into the home of the Neffs, where I found myself face to face with the chairman of some district against the ERA and getting the whole passionate lecture parts I and II. Kathy, an animated and intelligent woman, was speaking breathlessly, passionately while I sat dazed and tongue-tied by the onslaught. The more she talked, the more I realized that we disagreed on everything. We were at odds over welfare, farm issues, gay rights, women's issues, religion, families, on and on. The strangest thing was that the more areas of disagreement we explored, the more I realized how very much I liked her. Having finally found my tongue, we both kept up a rapid fire of exchanges, not even pausing as we climbed the stairs to get me settled, not even pausing to get supper underway, not even pausing more than an instant to answer questions fired hopefully by her children. Off we were on the subject of books, and there we were again, deadlocked in disagreement.

"As far as I'm concerned," said Kathy, "I consider reading anything besides the classics as a waste of my time."

"The classics!" I shrieked. "I wouldn't touch them with a ten-foot pole, too boring."

Kathy's eyes snapped and sparkled and her face glowed with the exhilaration of a vigorous exchange of ideas. It's hard to explain even now, but there was a fondness between Kathy and me that was unmarred by our passionate arguments about everything.

Months later, back home, I was trying to give a sympathetic description of the conservative western viewpoint to a very liberal friend of mine, Karyl.

"How could you stand to be around people with those attitudes?" she said.

"What?" I asked, dumbfounded.

"I mean, these are the people who vote against aid to the inner cities. How could you stand them?"

"'Stand them? I love them!" I shouted. "I don't know anything about their voting, but those conservatives were the warmest, most humane group of people I've ever met. They were wonderful to me when I needed it, and beyond that who's to judge?" All the Mormon families said grace at every meal, and although they knew we disagreed on every topic, without exception, they always asked for blessings on me and my trip.

Farther south in Ruby Valley I stayed with the Smiths, a family with impressive Mormon ancestry.

JoAnn with her genealogy album   1979 ES

JoAnn and her husband, Paul, spoke with the most gentle yet riveting voices I've ever heard. In the evening they knelt around a chair with their two daughters and all clasped hands in prayer. The hairs stood up on the back of my neck and little shivers danced on my spine. Their voices floated and caressed each reverent word. Afterward, not wanting to break the spell, I asked JoAnn to tell me about the Mormon practice of tracing back their genealogies. She took an enormous album from the bookcase and sat with me, intoning the names of grandmothers and great uncles. She turned the weighty pages slowly and moved her pointing finger while reading short stories of people long dead and nearly forgotten. The atmosphere was hypnotic, and I felt carried away.

Dinner with the Smith family was a lesson in nutrition, all food grown or made on their shambly farm. We ate homemade cottage cheese and butter, home-grown beef and vegetables, eggs from the farm chickens, honey from the meadow hive, homemade bread, fresh milk, berries and cream.

The next day my walk was through the most dynamic and magnificent geography and weather of the trip. The high, high mountains caught and swirled the black and white storm clouds while the valley and I were burned briefly as the sun cut through the cold air. The rain had set the mountain streams sparkling and gurgling down to the valley pastures where the cattle grazed, thousands of tiny brown dots, tweed. The wind increased, and I did battle. The clouds above swept violently and noisily down the peaks through the draws, and the sun was blackened frequently. I arrived exhausted and exhilarated at a ranch where the foreman showed me the ancient bunkhouse. There I learned about ranch people's pride in hand-stacked bales of hay (not machine-stacked!) waiting for winter.

Days later I had long ago left the ranches and walked many miles alone. A ranch ahead meant a decision to make: stop or go. I walked on trusting an inner guide to make the decision. Answer? No. I walked on...

Another day, hot and weary I looked for a camping and hiding spot, juniper trees. Dragged my bag under branches and ate and waited. Stormy clouds gathered and sent brief spits of rain. I ate evaporated milk, wheat germ, baby food and tuna. I battened down hatches and crawled into my sleeping bag. It was 2:30 in the afternoon and I stayed there till 7:30 next day. Somewhere during those hours I realized that I was as alone as I'd ever been, 50ish miles from a town and 10 from the nearest ranch on a back road with no cars. A hundred miles of wilderness stretched ahead of me. I felt a grin spread. Somewhere on this journey my fear of wide open spaces had completely disappeared. I watched a salmon-colored bug, scorpion or spider, climb about the sage and sand. The coyotes howled during the dark hours. Rain squalls sent me deep under my cover. A loud determined gnawing told me something was in my seed pack. I turned on the flashlight and was greeted by 2 bright beady eyes and large ears, the alert and wistful face of a sweet little mouse. It had run gently over my bag earlier.

Before the trip I was willing to pay any price for proper equipment. Accordingly, I paid $65 for a breathable rain jacket made of the outdoor equipment wonder fabric, the new Gore-tex. The only wonder I found about it was the price. Every time it rained, I walked in a perfect white fury as the damn thing leaked like a flannel shirt. So I cut a hole in a garbage bag which I pulled over my head to keep the rain off my fancy-dancy Gore-tex rain gear. There I walked in all my glory with a plastic garbage bag over my head.

When not in an indignant rage over my lousy rain jacket, I experience a great high while walking in the rain.

It was the first rain the area had had in many months. When the clouds lifted (after a soaking night camping on the mountain) I gazed startled at the higher elevations, which were covered deeply with new-fallen snow.

On the western side of the Ruby Mountains there is a town called Jiggs. It is clearly inscribed on every map of Nevada I've ever seen. The funny thing about this town is not only its name but its population. The population is three.

Three! One approaches it over a pleasant road and comes upon a cluster of buildings. The large, imposing brick building has been empty for years, I was told. A tiny, empty-looking, decrepit building sits unworthy of a passing glance until the neatly newly labeled sign "U.S. Post Office" is noticed. There appear to be holes in the roof and the long grass surrounding it looks untrodden. Across the street a tiny building leaning at a nervous tilt wears the sign "Jiggs Volunteer Fire Dept." It looks barely wide enough for a VW bug. I didn't look to see what kind of fire truck sits there.

Jiggs Bar   1979 ES

NEVADA

Across the street from the firehouse is the Jiggs Bar, a place of community, congregation, Indian artifacts, local cultural history, recreation, gossip center, restaurant and old-fashioned goodwill. Ruby and Oliver Breschini, both in their 60's, run or preside over the venerable institution of the Jiggs Bar. Ruby, a tiny woman, is the bouncer, having ejected 200 drunken Indians the night before I arrived. They kept and fed me royally for five nights in a heavenly state of passivity. I merely sat back and let the stories unfold.

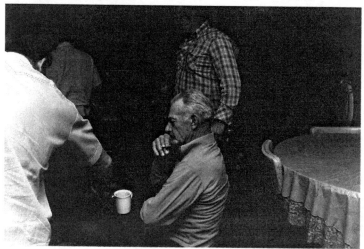

Oliver   1979 ES

Twenty-two years ago Oliver went on a fishing binge. Every single day for six months he arose at 4:00 A.M. and fished till 7:00 A.M. when it was time for work. After work at 4:30 P.M., he picked up his high school son, and they would fish until dark. One day Ruby, his wife, said, "Stop fishing. Take me arrowhead hunting." Oliver went arrowhead hunting with her. AND HAS NOT PICKED UP A FISHING POLE SINCE. For 27 years arrowhead hunting has been their passion.

The next day we went arrowhead hunting to the valley which spilled onto the plain from the mountains. The scenery was spectacular. The quiet hush seemed like Indian air, and I was seeing through Indian eyes the game paths running from mountain to valley. The ground was littered with chips left behind when Indians sat in watch and waiting while tooling their weapons. Pinon pine fragrance, cold air, hot sun, steep hill up from smooth pine floor, rocky ledges, beautiful.

I heard a buzzing noise clearly from a dark rock pile. I call Oliver who, hard of hearing, hears nothing. Whenever he throws a rock, the buzzing increases to a furious pitch. We call Ruby who identifies it as a rattlesnake. I learned later it was her first snake but "when you hear one, you'll know it" goes the popular local wisdom. By this time I move close enough to see the rattling tail curved upright and vibrating. Oliver goes to the truck to get the shovel for the kill. (Not killing a found rattler is inconceivable here in the west.) Oliver moves the rock and the snake emerges, a Western Diamondback rattler. I am breathless but felt great sadness for the snake who is about to be killed. It only wanted to hide and be left alone. CHOP goes Oliver's shovel, and he gives me the rattle.

We continue hunting arrows, but it's prime rattlesnake country. My nylon jogging shoes feel feeble. I imagine fangs piercing the thin fabric. Ruby admonishes, "Now Barbara, don't be afraid of snakes. You must not let anything interfere with arrow hunting." Ruby scrambles over rocks, a spry 67-year old dynamo, while I tiptoe along behind, skittish, every step a potential snake den. The hair on the back of my neck rises yet I giggle with hysterical daring. Ruby urges me on, but I'm afraid to walk easily, so I step daintily with cold chills, sneaking silently. There's no rationale behind this; I'd be better off making noise to get rattle warnings before the strike. I look down in this state of taut snake anticipation and see a sweet little pearl-white arrowhead. It lies there a gleaming perfect tooth, my first whole arrowhead. I call Ruby, who admires it lavishly.

Ruby climbs up the ledges, "You can go here, Barbara, I have already checked it." Then the buzz starts again. Ruby shouts, "Oliver, come here and kill another snake. Oliver. Oliver!!"

I call, "Oliver, another snake. Come up here."

We wait and wait. Oliver comes slowly picking his way carefully since his deafness precludes hearing warning rattling. Ruby is furious at his slowness. Then "Hey! There's TWO!!" Oliver kills them. One falls between the rocks out of reach.

Oliver says, "Let's get the hell out of here." All agree.

Wow. I found my first perfect arrowhead and saw my first rattler all at once. This is the life.

Ruby with a few frames of their thousands of points   1979 ES

Days later, Oren Probert, the manager of the Commercial Hotel in Elko, gave me a complimentary room. When I sought him out to thank him, I found myself ushered before a patriarchal figure of a man, almost Biblical in his virile proportions. It was not surprising to learn that he is a leader of the Mormon Church as well as a successful businessman. What was surprising to learn was that Oren Probert had been battling cancer for many years. For three years he had endured chemotherapy so severe that he was able to leave his bed only one day per week. He had lost a lung, kidney, and part of his intestines to the ravaging disease. He was making a weekly 500-mile round trip for constant monitoring by his doctors in Salt Lake City.

And after years of illness, his 27-year old son had died one month before, from suicide. His short, painful life had included 16 surgeries. A week after our first meeting, Oren had to cancel a trip because the doctors had found something new on his cancer scan. Try as I might, I could find no melancholy or self-pity in Oren Probert. An optimistic smile hovered ticklishly around the corners of his mouth, and his eyes rested in perpetual amusement.

Oren and his statuesque wife, Beverly, invited me to attend their church. I quickly accepted and then had second thoughts. My only clothes were my ragged trail outfits, and I felt that my radical departure from the exalted Mormon ideal of the woman's role would put a strain on everyone. My doubts were dispelled immediately as the men and women of the church surrounded me with enthusiastic support and encouragement. I was frankly astonished and asked one woman quite directly, "How can it be that you are all being so approving of me when your church so fervently pushes the 'woman in the home' theme?"

"'Really,' she said, "I think my church would approve your venture as setting a wonderful example for your children, of following your deepest beliefs and goals."

It came out as a beautiful answer although I still can't quite square it with *official* church policy.

I'm bewildered by all the generosity of the people here, Ruby, Oliver, Scott, Oren, church people, store people, casino people, etc. I've almost lost a sense of what I'm doing or who I am. Why am I being so showered with gifts, long underwear, gloves, beef jerky, pants, money? It confuses me. I've done nothing to deserve this. Others are mired in need, in fact, I'VE been more in need earlier in this trip. How should I handle all this, inside my head especially?

The power has been off all day in Elko. It makes it seem special, and the weather has suddenly turned almost bitter cold with snow whitening even the low mountains and flurries in the air all day. I have a need to hit the road again. After one day's rest I'm always surprised at my urge to move on. Moving on satisfies some part of me even when the moving is difficult. I'm especially eager to test myself in the cold and snow and clear my head again. It's so easy to get off track by the reactions of others. This ultra service is even more bewildering than the hostility or indifference. All my thank yous seem inadequate. I almost feel like some kind of imposter. Have people built me into something I'm not? Have I misled people somehow into thinking I'm something I'm not? I am in reality a very, very privileged and lucky person to have the opportunity to do this trip. I'm not to be pitied but more to be envied. Every day every experience is a joy. Every new experience something to be savored...even ants in my sleeping bag.

I almost dare now to let go of some of my ever-present tension about this trip. After the Ruby Mountains, I-80 looks almost possible from there on. I look far ahead and wonder what comes after the trip. Will I ever be this happy again? What will I do? Cliff is at home sick again. This gives me feelings of alarm and guilt.

16

ALONG THE HUMBOLDT

September 18 - October 11
(292 miles)

"Sunshine on my shoulders makes me happy…"
John Denver

A pioneer re-enactment…   1978 MB

It's a blessing to be alone again and clear my head.
The walk was wonderful today, I-80 a real fall situation
with unsettled weather, shifting patterns of snow flurries,
rain and sunshine, clouds dark and sky brilliant blue all

churning and windy. I looked back and saw the distant mountains, snow mantled. Could there be anything whiter and more pristine than the early autumn snows in the mountains? Of course, to the Donner Party, those early snows would have been a scary warning. They were already late in the emigrant travel season.

My alarm was aroused by lateness and no camping spots. Finally I turned into an old road and was forced to scale the fence. I broke my water jug and lifted the cart over in a raging fury. The old abandoned highway skirted the Humboldt River. The only hidden camping spot required a mighty struggle with a cattle gate, opening and closing. I camped in a wash crouched behind a large sagebrush.

The night cooled dramatically, and I went all out for warmth, both sets of underwear, cotton pants, Oliver's 30-year old wool gabardine square-dancing pants, 2 turtlenecks, wool shirts, and my down jacket. I used the mylar groundcover from Karen and the bivy bag under the down bag. I kept an anxious eye on the snowstorm clouds racing by overhead. The lovely Humboldt twisted its way through the haze. Sunset was charcoal gray and pink, reminding me of that color fad when I was in high school. Night closed in with a few friendly stars peeking through.

When it finally got dark, I felt safe. The usual ground mice thumped gently over my bag. Stars multiplied and cold deepened. I noticed some high-tension power lines and realized Nevada is a big UFO state, and UFOs are often seen near power lines. The prospect of a close UFO encounter and abduction swept over me as an unbearable sadness at the thought of not seeing my children any more. Indeed, the sadness longing for them was so overwhelming that I nearly panicked. Then I regained my anchor and rationality reigned. The UFO possibility was utterly remote. This trip has enforced upon me the need to deal with all situations and fears with total realism. Then fear and hysteria and irrationality are banished. What are the actual chances that this horror or that horror will actually occur? (Slim to none.) And then if these horrors occur, how would I handle them, step by step? What are the options? If someone comes, what are the chances he'll (it'll) find me? Small. If he finds me, what are the chances he'll be mean? Smaller. If mean, what are the chances he'll hurt me? Smaller yet. If he wants to hurt me, what will I do? 1. or 2. and 3. then 4. etc. This kind of calculating, rational thinking overcomes helpless feelings of vulnerability with a sense of taking charge and competence and control.

Slept warmly. Moon was so bright (sky had cleared) that it hurt my eyes. One could easily read by it. I noticed that ice crystals of frost glittered everywhere in the moonlight, especially on my sleeping bag and even on my "pillow" of sage. Morning, over 1/2 inch of frost everywhere. Wait for sun as it turned to golden the deeply scoured and rounded brown canyon rocks. Finally it crept down to my gully, and I began the long process of drying my frost-wetted camp.

Birds flapped by, the whistle of the air clearly audible in their feathers. The cloudless sky, first in weeks, the air clean and cold as spring water on a hot day, the sun warming and warming, gently melting, the Humboldt sliding steadily on as it did in 1846, such peace and beauty, seeing, smiling, hearing, feeling. I felt part of the setting, as much as the fragrant sage next to me, its frost turned now to shimmering water droplets in each seed bud. Is this kin to how mystics felt? Blending and melting into nature? Could I merge with these ancient brown rocks and levitate? I sort of tried but gasped and broke the spell as my senses began to change. A breeze had gently started the rabbit brush swaying, and I felt my head reeling.

ALONG THE HUMBOLDT

Time to pack up and move on, 10:30, no hurry anymore, no afternoon heat to beat, no 20-mile quota to meet, just solitary wallowing drunken in this heady beauty. Now I must make noise and disturb it all, the crackle of folding my ground cloth and the scrape of my golf cart. The horrible struggle of the damn cattle fence and then a psyching up to handle I-80 and whatever lies ahead for this day.

While camping in Carlin Canyon the sky ahead was ominous and deep gray, yet the sun had broken through behind my back. It fell on an arching silver rope 300 feet high, streaming gently in the breeze, an incredible mysterious sight, ethereal, gleaming and perfect. I found out a few days later that the "rope" was a fine spider's rope often seen at this time of year. Where do they get the fuel and material to make such a long one? It's many times the volume of the spider who spins it.

Every day I experience periods of what can only be described as euphoria.
It's a sensation of almost bursting with a sense of happiness, well-being, and optimism. It's as if the ultimate secret of life is only an inch away. The excitement comes from being so close to it. Today it came when I heard music from Saturday Night Fever. Usually it comes when I'm alone and on the road camping. It's a sense of power and peace and conquering fear and merging with nature, a timelessness, a different dimension or perspective.

During the night, I awoke to a blending of moonlight and a rhythmic sound. I thought it was the crackle of my mylar, but something told me to check it out. It was distinctly hoof beats. Then I saw huge dark shapes move—cows? No, a faster beat, horses! In a flash I realized

304

the piles of horse manure and barren dry ground between sage bushes as the gathering spot for horses, and there they were, thundering around me. I turned the flashlight on the towering dark shape nearest me. One huge yellow eye shone, still now, and I reared up instinctively, combatively, and all the horses retreated. I was aroused but not scared. Another milestone, I thought, remembering my nervousness in Wyoming when being with unfenced horses even 1/2 mile away was scary. Next morning the great thundering herd of horses was nearby, but it turned out to be just three, kindly and likable looking besides.

Walked on, real Indian summer, the kind of weather that starts deliciously warm and turns to a still-aired sweat producer. I suffered for leaving on my long underwear bottoms.

I had heard twice of an old woman living alone in a cluster of deserted buildings on the interstate. Tired and hot, I headed there. The scene was like a 1930's ghost town, deserted cabins, gas station, old trailers and a motley assortment of small, confusing, abandoned shacks. I roamed through the incredible scene, a John Steinbeck **Wayward Bus** *movie setting, a disaster movie setting, eerie and not quite old enough to be charming or quaint. After knocking on a half dozen unlikely doors, a pleasant-faced old woman called me into a large, low building crammed full with thousands of dollars worth of antiques, glassware, Tiffany lamps, photos shelved neatly on an old ice cream counter, glass apothecary display cabinets, etc.*

Beulah Wallace, 74, in her white, crisp uniform, sat me down amid the dazzling collection and talked compulsively non-stop from 1:00 P.M. to 8:00 P.M. until I tried to call a halt after total darkness had descended, about which she showed no awareness. I was so tired I knew I'd either throw up or faint. She talked frantically with great agitation of her life, deaths, births, murders, suicides, stabbings, robberies, etc., etc. Pistols and tear gas, no fear, chasing away terrified vandals, closing the eyes of dead babies, sex and births of 3 children. Then all over again......Born in Kentucky, she saw her mother's death, saw her father lose the farm, moved to Ohio, helped her father be an undertaker, had 5 suicides in her own house, helped a midwife, had 3 babies of her own, moved to Dunphy, saw two stabbings, has been robbed three times (only three?), drove out some local Morman woman, husband is in mental hospital, has bad feet and, last but not least, the roof leaks. (That damn roof. Was it the last straw?)

Finally! *She padlocked me in a shack for the night to avoid possible crossfire from nightly vandals who try to rob her. That night cars prowled but I barely heard them.* (Who were they? I had heard no cars during the day.) *In the morning Beulah unlocked me and said she'd finally realized my true identity; I was President Carter's daughter-in-law checking up on her. President Carter, she assured me, had been checking up on her last week in disguise. She grabbed my arm, frantic to distract me to stay. The pistol lay on the table between us. I thanked her firmly for a truly remarkable stay and left. She still sits there, I assume, alone in her jumble of shacks, guarding her fortune in antiques with the loaded pistol, alone, fearless, without phone or transportation, many miles from the nearest house.*

Far, far in the distance, around a big bend in the Humboldt, against a backdrop of brown, parched mountains, Battle Mountain lay bleaching in the desert sun. I headed for it hour after hour but seemed to get no closer. By the time I finally dragged myself into town, numbing weariness rode like a weight I couldn't dislodge. The name Senator Rene Lemaire was given to me as someone to say hello to. I found my way to a tall, white house, just the place, I thought, for a retired senator to reside. My tentative knock was answered by a tall, regal woman who bowed slightly and smiled generously. She held the door wide open and exclaimed, "Why, it's just as if heaven sent you here to us. I've heard about you and wanted so much to meet you. Come right in and let me get you some lemonade." Leaving my cart on the stately porch, I followed Thelma Lemaire into the elegant old home. High paneled ceiling, chandeliers, and quiet dignity enveloped me with a sense of peace and history and permanence. The memory of the weary hours on the highway receded like a bad dream. Senator Lemaire was sitting at the kitchen table, and after introductions, asked me what nationality my name was. I said "Maat is Dutch, but of course that's my husband's nationality, not mine."

Ever the consummate host, Senator Lemaire leaned forward and asked, "What *is* YOUR nationality and what was YOUR maiden name?"

"I'm Hungarian," I answered "and my name was Kardos."

"I would like to have you write that down for me," he said, handing me paper and pencil.

I complied with a feeling that I had been honored by his interest and sensitivity. I also was walloped with the realization that I would have voted for this man any day. He cared and had communicated that concern within two minutes of our meeting. Skillful politician, genuine human being, both meeting in the same man.

I spent three memorable days with the Lemaires, basking in their graciousness. Thelma too had developed her hostess skills to a fine art. While talking I had mentioned casually that one thing I dearly missed on the trail was reading magazines now and then. As soon as the conversation shifted to Rene and me, Thelma unobtrusively arose and went upstairs for a few moments. Later, up in the guest room while resting in perfect splendor under a satin comforter, I discovered what Thelma had done earlier in her brief absence. On the bedside table she had quietly, thoughtfully arranged a variety of magazines and assorted reading matter for me.

In the evenings we dined in the elegant dining room, me in my ragged trail clothes, and Rene would speak as if he were still before the senate. Apparently he was given to dramatic lectures and speeches with poses and finger pointing. (Thelma later confided that she had endured them nightly at the dinner table.) His deep integrity was of the John Wayne school with right and wrong views of the world. He would lean forward with steely eyes to the soul, and just at the point of intimidation, he'd pull back with an "aw shucks" modesty, covering his self-pride with a little boy smile, the corners of his mouth pushed down and half-hidden laughter in his eyes. He would fix a stern eye on me and hold forth on subjects ranging from declining national morality to Nevada silver mining in the old days. I was a rapt pupil as much from his charismatic delivery as the anecdotes. When reminiscing about his own successful career, he would assume a bashful, "aw gosh and golly" demeanor, the modesty of a man with a lot to be proud of.

A bit over a month after my stay with the Lemaires, Rene was killed in a car accident and Thelma critically injured. But memories of those evenings around the dining table are as fresh and alive as yesterday.

Days later. Left Valmy and trudged on, buffeted horribly by the big trucks. A wonderful treat was seeing a coyote—it watched me a long time—head high, chest white—then turned and disappeared, walked into the sage. The desert became white—alkali beds, bitter brush, glorious blooming rabbit brush—small furry yellow blooms in huge bouquets, each brush bush separate and on a pale beige floor as clean and smooth as a swept dance floor. Then Emigrant Pass—another huge mountain range. The Indian summer heat slammed me—and I had thought summer gone for good... I crossed the summit and viewed Golconda, far off in another flat, flat valley.

I'm alarmed by my sudden deterioration, partly too much and too many doses of people. I'm strained to be ever gracious and thoughtful and it's cracking. And partly the great stress of the interstate, trucks blow you over, spray gravel, blow off hat, etc. Have decided not to be so uptight about schedule.

Rounding the big bend of the Humboldt was dramatic, vast marsh plain 30 miles across and surrounded by mountain ranges. Nevada mountain ranges run in straight long lines, utterly brown. The color of the landscape here very mute, brown and faint milky green similar to looking through a dirty window or subtle pre-dawn tinge. Dark brown rock, dirt brown, brush on grass, tan brown. The Humboldt is almost always out of sight. No dramatic tree line marks its course as with the Platte.

In the evening the sunset worked its artistry in shades of mauve and deep rose on the mountains. The sky turned auburn and burnished straw and the valley grayed in haze. The stars came out, old friends I wait anxiously for every night. The first twinkle brings a sigh of safety and relaxation, and then after a snooze I awaken and watch the satellites and shooting stars and planes. At one point I was fascinated (and not scared) to see what I thought was a UFO. It was flying low, even disappeared behind a nearby mountain peak and was extremely fast and utterly silent even at close range. It turned out to be a jet, however. The sound was audible later.

ALONG THE HUMBOLDT

———

Much has been made of Donner Party mistakes by Monday morning quarterbacks. They rested too long here; they took the wrong route there, and on and on. The romantics among us would like to picture the emigrant pioneers as daring, courageous, and above all smart. We fairly demand images of competent and trail-wise leaders, outguessing the Indians and plucking edible plants along the way. Is it our insecurities that urge us to expect the impossible? The families that moved west across unfamiliar territory made all the mistakes that you or I would make in an alien land. Why do we, today as yesterday, speak contemptuously of "greenhorns?" The rancher today snickers about the city dude who doesn't know from which side to mount a horse while the city folk snort about the hillbillies who get lost on subways.

Yesterday's adventurers who leave the familiar, faced crises and unknown terrors that boggle the mind, yet all in all they coped with a flexibility that should make us proud of our heritage. When the trees ran out, they burned buffalo droppings (chips) for fuel. They did their laundry in hot springs and used some kinds of alkali for baking powder biscuits. They traveled by night across hot deserts and made snowshoes from oxen yokes. On the other hand, they (so humanly) overloaded their wagons, carried the wrong kind of guns for the large, distant game in the west, and were exploited by Indians because they erred on the side of hospitality. The wonder is that any of them made it at all. From diaries it is apparent that some emigrant trains actually had a wonderful time. Amazing.

As I was getting my room, a sheriff arrived and ominously asked to speak with me alone. There began a most bizarre adventure. I was a suspect in a robbery: 2 diamond rings were missing from the home I'd been a guest in a week before. I offered my stuff to search, incredulous and alternately stunned and giggling. I was horrified that my hosts could think I might have stolen their rings after we'd had a such a fine and trusting time together. The deputy, who was very engaging and even embarrassed, completely dismantled my pack. The sheer amount of stuff was astounding, piled high on the bed and dresser. I'm sure he felt like a fool going through my underwear and sanitary supplies, and he certainly could have missed diamond rings any number of times. My only thought was to prove my innocence to my former hosts, and I readily agreed to a skin search at the police station. Off we went in the police car, the motel personnel already eyeing me as if I were a criminal. At the police station a very uncomfortable woman took me to the ladies room where I stood before her and took off all my clothes, which she examined, even my hair elastic. I found the whole episode ludicrous, some big silly mistake, a good and amusing story for another day.

This is quite an education. It's one thing to be wined and dined in Elko, introduced at the floor show in the casino and at the Mormon Church, newspaper articles running for 4 days, and being given the luxury suite with food and then to be unknown in the next town but actually be a police suspect and searched? The contrast is quite a jar to the psyche. I have a new attitude toward famous or infamous people. They're all more medium than the publicity paints. President Kennedy not as good nor President Nixon as bad.

I'm going through another uneasy stage in this trip. It's almost as if my lucky stars have moved out of position. For about 3 weeks my feeling has been one of unexplainable deterioration. Physically, I've been verging on sickness. My *mental stability seems a bit more shaky, and my luck has been slowly but surely turning sour. In the back of my mind I even fathom attack or death as I near the end of the trip. The most eerie phenomenon of all is that suddenly many people are asking, "How's your health?" No one asked that before and now suddenly EVERYONE is popping that question. Why?*

I vaguely recall a saying to the effect that "there's a tide in the affairs of men (women). To fight it is futile." The tide until now has been with me. Now it seems to be turning. Feeling this way, today downtown after hours of total frustration in every avenue I turned, I suddenly just felt so defeated and victimized that I cried momentarily on the sidewalk. Then I rallied and started making some firm decisions:

1) No, I will not go to dinner with the repulsive reporter.

2) No, I will not pay another cent to the horrid motel people who treat me like dirt. I will move on to town or beyond and pay whatever it costs.

3) I will not be intimidated by my fear of spending money to the point where I exclude other considerations.

4) I will head for Reno and maybe work or see what develops.

While only half awake this morning, I was slowly brought to the realization (by my inner guide) that there is a great generalization that can be made about many of the women I've met. They are apparently more eager to get out and explore life than their husbands. They are stifled and frustrated and bored and held back. They are the closet adventurers. In those situations where the woman holds back the husband, one is immediately sympathetic to the husband, but somehow one overlooks the reverse. The great parade of closet adventurers, Thelma, Ruby, LaVonne, JoAnn, Kathy, Beverly, Erma, Becky, Rose and on and on. I'll have to get out my list and examine it all the way.

I'm sick of and peeved by the universal western sign (is it also in the east?) found everywhere, cafes, drugstores, libraries, news-stands, hotels, barbershops, everywhere, NO SHIRT, NO SHOES, NO SERVICE. Its smart-alec flippancy was catchy, no doubt, the first time it was written, but now its repetition infinitum signals a mindless herd instinct. Ahhh yes, let's all unite against the common foe, that monster that threatens us all, the filthy drug-crazed hippy. Dear God! Did ever so few strike such lasting terror in the hearts of so many? For so long? How many years ago did the hippy movement crest? Still to this day I'm warned occasionally that my greatest danger on the road is the "drug addict who'll do ANYTHING to get money to support his habit." (Here in the middle of the Great Basin Desert?) A great, rabid, insane, crazed, violence is hinted at. It's a bogeyman image.

A far cry from the sickly heroin addict nodding out or skulking nervously after the color TV in the next apartment. But yep, the whole West is on alert against the dread hippy menace, and NO SHIRT, NO SHOES, NO SERVICE serves notice. OK, so what's my gripe? Look in your own backyard, westerners. What about your drunken he-men? Your smelly lecherous drunks, all living in the hallowed tradition of the old hard drinkin', hard fightin' West, utterly macho and utterly obnoxious? Is THAT who you want in your cafes and stores?

Related to this, on the TV news, Howard Jarvis, the Proposition 13 man, was speaking at a gathering and somebody threw a pie in his face. Horrors. (A hippy, no doubt.) Anyway, the startled and horrified attendants wiping the pie away muttered instinctively, "It wasn't one of

313

us. IT WAS SOME OUTSIDER." And there it is, the unhealthy fear and assumption that strangers and outsiders are the problem.

All across the country I had been warned about the bad people in the next state. But, of course, the people in the next state would always be as kind and generous as the people in the previous state.

However, many days ahead I wrote a different story in my journal: *Now that I'm approaching California, I see more weirdos. If these horrors are what people mean by hippies, then I take back all my defense of hippies, and I also beg forgiveness of those I criticized for hating hippies. These creeps are men with filthy clothes, ragged clothes, long, stringy, oily, dirty, smelly hair. Their eyes wander. They seem old—maybe they're the original hippies who never outgrew it. Their filth frightens me.*

When I came to this town, I'd toiled for hours and miles and days across hot (and impressive) sage range. No trees for hundreds of miles in sight. At the motel near the edge of town there were trees, pretty scraggly to be sure by eastern standards, but I stood and gazed gratefully at the lovely dappled shadows they cast on the driveway. Today walking through town I kicked and the breeze rustled some of the few brown leaves the trees had dropped. I turned around and walked through them again, and the sound was a small and pitiful reminder of the swish and rustle of fallen leaves in New England. I hope that this trip sharpens my appreciation for the small, precious signals that every region has. The contrasts draw attention to the little things often overlooked.

I'm learning, or just beginning to learn and understand, the extent to which we are able to create our own sense of happiness or fear. A given set of circumstances can be interpreted many ways. A friend of mine, Barbara Chapin, first pointed this out when I once sympathized with her leadership of a festival which flopped for lack of help. She corrected me. She said, "But I don't think of all the people who didn't help; I remember all those who DID and who worked so hard." Similarly, if 2 out of 10 truckers wave to me, I can grumble about the 8 who glare stonily, or I can bask in the warmth and friendliness of the 2 who do wave and smile. Winnemucca, which seemed so hostile yesterday, today feels safe and friendly. I cannot be strictly objective, try as I might. I am struck again, however, with the force of kindness. It's catching. When I get a break, I come out of my defensive shell and, in turn, feel more kindly toward others.

Earlier I watched some people play "twenty-one." A man and his wife were betting $50 a hand. They were enjoying it, but my nerves were a wreck. I wanted them to win (which they were doing) but when they'd lose $50, I'd nearly die. Finally I left in a state of tension, no gambler me.

I have attacks of unease fearing that I've forgotten to write someone in my address book that I've promised a "victory" postcard to. Even awaken in the middle of the night with memory of someone who stopped way back in Nebraska or wherever.

I watched Pope John Paul's investiture in Clover Valley, and now I'm in Winnemucca, and he's dead. His whole reign lasted only as long as my walk from Clover Valley to Winnemucca, and yet he touched millions. There are so many ways to measure time.

315

This morning a workman here eyed me balefully and said with vague scorn, "Just what is the purpose of your trip!"
And the woman beyond the desk immediately defended me vigorously: "Just because she wants to, and I think it takes a lot of guts." It's taking an overly long time to sink into my prejudiced brain, but women are defending me often, especially in Nevada and especially Mormon women.

Why is it that if not "perfectly" OK, it's at least rather OK for men to pee in semi-public along the highways, to itch their crotches even on full-color TV (ever see a ballgame?), but it's absolutely taboo for a woman to pee along the highway or itch her crotch. All 5 men I've walked with have peed unceremoniously a few feet from me. I have often walked a whole day on a busy highway on a treeless, brushless plain waiting for darkness to pee. I remember with shame my own unfair horror in Brookline when I rounded a corner to see an old woman peeing behind a garbage can.

Yesterday left Winnemucca and walked long and hard. The valleys are broader and the mountains less high and more spaced. Everything is a pale brown, the mountains like smooth cloth draped over bumps. Walking almost due south now. At one point saw 6 wild horses at the foot of the mountain range to the east at least 2 miles away. They were grazing and walking parallel to me for at least 1/2 hour before dropping below my sight line.

Stopped at an elaborate rest area and was soon joined by a young California man. He astonished me by reporting that in 1974 he had run across the U.S. ocean to ocean in less than 4 months. We were compatible souls comparing and sharing similar experiences, food cravings, lack of distance comprehension, shoe problems, etc.

After a particularly sophisticated exchange of ideas about nutrition I asked, "But what did your diet consist of on your trip?"

"Any and every damn thing I could get my hands on," he laughed. I knew what he meant. At the end of a 25-mile day, a hamburger was manna from heaven even to that vegetarian.

I spent the night on the floor of his van, both of us dumping all kinds of pent-up stuff that only a bull shitter from the urban east and a bull shitter from California could stand. I was absolutely hungry to talk to this type (and mine), psychic talk, vegetarian talk, philosophy, exercise, etc., etc. He fixed my shoes (Sho-goo), fed me well and generously, and next morning I paid him $1.25. Afterward on the road I was mortified at my cheapness, absolutely appalled. Despite all the generosity shown to me, my underlying stinginess still dies hard and slow, I guess.

Long hot day. Every camping spot seems a bit worse. Now I'm near the road and in sight if I sit and if I lie, but I think it would take very sharp eyes to spot me.

The California runner said that he did his run partly to encourage people to get out of capsules, houses, and cars, to promote a sense of community. It's true that cars and houses and offices foster isolation, insulation and dehumanize. The jerks who honk and swear at old ladies wouldn't be so inhuman in person. It is unhealthy to travel hundreds of miles by car and pass close to thousands of people (also in cars) and have no interaction. It fosters indifference in people and a sense of personal isolation and alienation.

I told the runner about my distress over the diamond ring suspicions, and he mentioned something true, a continuation of his community theory: if the rings were discovered missing while I was there, there'd be no suspicion, but trust breaks down with increase in time and distance between people. The one main thing he learned is that people are nice, so many.

Runner friend at conclusion of coast-to-coast run sat with his feet in the Atlantic ocean in Georgia. He pulled out his United States map and said with disbelief, "Did I really do that?" I feel the same lack of comprehension. Have I really walked almost 2,000 miles? One almost feels cheated in not being able to comprehend (let alone savor) it. I'm sure the Donners also couldn't comprehend their achievement. Yet the lesson may be that we humans CAN accomplish even more than we can imagine. The human mind is very sorely limited. There are whole worlds beyond our ability to imagine, comprehend. As I look back across the desert I have crossed, I see the road fade to nothing in the distance. I can't even comprehend or appreciate walking the comparatively short distance that I have today. Similarly, at the start of the trip the distance looks impossible, unfathomable. I would never have dreamed of even attempting it if the pioneers hadn't first led the way by the hundreds of thousands. I'm sure they didn't fully realize what they were getting into, and after they'd crossed, didn't fully realize what they'd done. What a pity for all of us! (In this world anyway. Maybe comprehension will come in another dimension, in afterlife perhaps.)

Today I wore my old shoes while the Nikes dried and got very sore feet and blisters. Passed a long white alkali flat. At about 3:00 P.M. exhausted and overheated, I looked for a spot to hide and camp. I finally found a ditch back from the road. I must either lie down or crawl to be invisible from the highway, but it's a pretty setting, light straw native grass, delicate but sharp and scratchy, stretches to the shadow-sculpted, wrinkly, brown mountains about 2 miles away. The high peak rises to 9,000 feet some rough brown rock visible at the top. I can see 5 wild horses grazing at the base.

Had a hard time with the water jug. It kept leaking. Finally, discovered it was through the cap, sloshing out. I have 40 miles to go yet on 1/2 gallon, hope there'll be a refill stop somewhere. Interesting thing, today white truck that said on the front HERE COME THE LOAFERS tooted gently as it passed and out flew 2 packaged sweet rolls that landed at my feet. It was very hot today. Now the sun is setting and it's very cold.

Yesterday saw a little snake, no rattles but a very triangular shaped head. It coiled zigzag and seemed a bit aggressive. Kind?

A strange thing has happened to my hair on this trip. It's never been nicer. It's shiny and manageable and healthy. Most of my life it's been dull and dry and bushy and split-endsy. Something is wrong here. It's been subject to all those things that make the beauty magazines quiver with fright—blazing sun, wind, damaging dryness, but all this seems to have had a good effect.

Last week I realized I was eating an orange while gratefully squatting in the tiny shadow of a "Yield" sign. I don't think people who live in the east very long can imagine the situation of no trees or shade for hundreds of miles. I had actually become quite emotional about that tiny precious patch of shade.

Last night I became so impatient to end this trip I could hardly stand it. As one nears a goal, whether walking the Donner Trail or blacks achieving equality, one becomes frantic for attainment, nervous, energized, impatient.

"Just what is the point of your trip?" said the man in the cafe. Dear God, I still can't even come up with a flip answer or any answer. Do I have a mental block? I know damn well it'll be asked again and again, yet I fumble and strain, and the questioner confirms his original suspicion that I'm nuts.

Last night went on a vegetable baby food binge, 4 jars strained green beans, strained squash, strained garden vegetables, and strained peaches; enjoyed every bit.

Today 12 miles to Lovelock, the blister grew to an enormous size.

My lips scare me. After being burned and peeling for the hundredth time, they are not healing anymore. Skin cancer? I was scared enough to buy some PABAnol but to save money bought it in alcohol base which dries everything, hurts, and makes the problem worse.

In Winnemucca the newspaper headlines screamed, NUDE WOMAN FOUND WANDERING WITH ARMS CUT OFF. In Lovelock a woman brought it to my attention and so did another. One was hostile toward me saying, "I'd NEVER go out alone or permit my daughter to either."
As my runner friend would say, "So that's one in 200,000,000 people." True.

Although I had been urged to stop in and see Marcia (not her real name nor location) I had not been warned about what I'd walk into. Marcia took a long time to respond to my knock and graciously invited me in, pronouncing each word with careful effort. She walked unsteadily to her chair and began her story of horror. The smell of alcohol surrounded her impeccable grooming.

Her father had worked for years as a railroad engineer with the same side of his face continually in the sun. Then for 30 years (30 years!) cancer and acid treatments ate his nose and then his face away. First one hole and then a second hole appeared and ate away his cheek, then his nose, leaving two holes, then the whole side of his face. Cruelly even his eye began to sag. Bone became visible. Food would fall from the huge holes. Eating became an unending struggle, an ordeal. For 15 years he crawled on hands and knees, a madman, drooling and shrieking with pain. The cancer never hit a vital organ as the nightmare intensified. Finally he got hold of a gun and blew out his brains.

The sun set, and darkness enveloped us as Marcia, oblivious, relived her story. It consumed her, enveloped us both, thickened the heavy air in the room. Through her recital I had not spoken a word. She would not have heard me.

The door opened and her husband entered and turned on the lights, his face a mixture of disgust and hopeless rage. He'd heard it all before. Marcia seemed apologetic and frightened toward him. I learned later that he too had cancer in his eye.

Somehow we all got through the night. I left the next morning heavy and haunted. It haunts me still, Marcia (and her husband) trapped in her cycles of remembrance, unable to climb out, even the haze of alcohol bringing scant relief.

I'm getting weary, too many people, too many experiences. I need more days of mental rest and require them more often. Now I'm near the end and should be in a frame of mind to celebrate, but what I'd like is a week alone in a motel room.

Tomorrow I start the long haul, and on Sunday and Monday my great fear is no hiding place. Then Reno and many options, no certainties.

Long hot haul. Alkali flats, Humboldt Sink, Carson Sink. Saw a tarantula. Over crest of hill and 40 mile desert ahead. Still distant brown mountains. Desert gritty here, like cinders, plants sparse and spotty. Exciting and feels like getting there. Wheels, rubber, about to come off, worn through.

————

The 40-mile desert is a barren stretch of waterless alkali wasteland. It was the most dreaded section of the trail with starvation and thirst stalking men and animals every mile. In 1850 a traveler counted and recorded 1,061 dead mules, 5,000 dead horses, 3,750 dead cattle, 853 graves and an estimated $1,000,000 worth of personal property discarded to lighten loads.

Usually overlooked are the animals. Every single one of those 1,061 dead mules, 5,000 dead horses, 3,750 dead cattle—every single one, its suffering would break our hearts if only we knew, if only we could walk on their four feet for a month, or even a day or minute. Thank God we'll never understand because we couldn't possibly bear it.

Day at Lovelock saw train with record 141 cars. Yesterday saw 4 trains stopped dead in the middle of the desert, looked like 4 straight dead segmented worms lying there.

Today saw an exquisitely beautiful large bird lying in a dead fluff by the road. I turned it over and saw it was a huge owl, so clean and delicately marked. I tried to get some feathers for Paula. First I tried to pull, then pull with my foot holding the owl down, then I tried to break one off. Through all this I was breaking bones and twisting wings. I gave up and looked at the bird now grotesquely mutilated, and I felt so sickened and ashamed.

Last evening at the rest area some poor tough, tough-looking guy came coasting in on a dead motorcycle. He tinkered with it and finally after hours got some truck to take him somewhere to charge the battery. He returned after dark and tinkered by the light of his flashlight for more hours. I awoke later to hear him in agony saying desperately, "Son of a bitch, son of a bitch." Apparently after all that, the damn thing still wouldn't even sputter, and there it sat out in the middle of the damn desert. I could hear his unfathomable depths of frustration and bitterness: "Son of a bitch, son of a bitch." Then he started to cry. I could hear him sniffling. This morning he was finally asleep, and I left my box of wheat thins next to him as I left.

In the Donner Party the scruples of civilization did not die quickly or easily, nor did they ever die completely. But as the press of the desperate struggle for mere survival intensified, the emigrants' priorities circled closer and closer to their immediate families and even themselves. When one's own family is threatened with death from thirst, it is not hard to imagine refusing water to another family only slightly nearer death. Would one conserve food carefully only to give it away to others in closer peril of starvation?

ALONG THE HUMBOLDT

An old man near 70 traveling alone named
Hardcoop became the first victim of inhumanity and
neglect. His feet were giving out early along the Humboldt.
With oxen weakened to near immobility, wagons were
stripped to the barest household essentials to lighten the
loads. Women carried babies, and children walked beside
the wagons, but still the going was perilously slow. Old
man Hardcoop, barely able to walk, was tolerated to ride for
stretches by some and turned away by others. The wagons
were strung out along the trail for many miles with minimal
communication between them. A thousand worries weighed
heavily on every person; Hardcoop was but one concern.
And then the inconceivable happened: turned away by
some, forgotten by others, Hardcoop was left behind. By the
time it was discovered that he was missing, it was declared
too late to return for him. Every ounce of energy in the
animals and every second of time would be needed for the
stretch ahead, and still it was doubtful they would make it.
It is testimony to their frenzied panic that the once-
respectable emigrants allowed this inhumanity to occur.
One can imagine the old man baby-stepping and finally
crawling as the last wagon receded before him. In the end
was it the Indians or the wolves or the desert heat or cold
that finally got him?

*Lots of chubby gray lizards with wrinkly necks, but
they move very fast.*

*Last night found a good place to camp. I had feared
finding nothing. The opposite I-80 lane diverged about 1/2
mile. and between the lanes was irregular gouged earth. I
crossed the crusty, cindered alkali, extremely hard to pull
(cinders sharp and alkali soft under crust) and found a pit,
deep, far from either lane. A van stopped as I headed
toward it, making me uneasy. As night fell I kept peeking*

out of the pit. Somehow I felt so vulnerable down there. Then I got up and hauled all my stuff up and out and onto the flat. But that only helped somewhat. I heard a distant car door slam. The moon was too bright in my eyes. And then, in the middle of the damn 40-mile desert where oxen and horses died from thirst by the hundreds, on came the mosquitoes. Pale beige nasties. I kept getting a very distinct odor of tea. I'd drift to sleep and then be awakened as if someone were holding a tea bag in front of my nose. Then asleep again only to be awakened by a sudden stiff breeze. Oh, to be in the pit again. The wind blew alkali into my eyes and flapped the plastic hiding my pack. On went the down jacket. The wind died down, leaving me too hot, and I awoke again to the sound of cattle bawling and fussing. Cattle??!! In the 40-mile desert? They must have been on the slopes of the brown and tan mountains rimming and ringing the desert and alkali flats. "Dear God! My nerves are shot," I thought. Nothing as serious as "seeing the elephant" but I felt weary, weary, weary, tired of being on guard and fending for myself. I wondered if I were picking up the vibes of all the horrors this desert had served up to the exhausted pioneers. Would the ghost of old Hardcoop crawl by?

After the moon went down, I slept better and awoke and left. The cooler air made the terrain seem less hostile. After a few miles I saw a fringe of trees in the distance, 12 miles, that had to be the Truckee River, the closest thing to heaven to the desperate pioneers. Meanwhile, stagnant pools of alkali water gave off a strange odor.

Approaching Fernley, the faint figure of a person walking east toward me appeared. It was a man heading into the desert. He was already shiny wet with sweat and wearing hot, dark, polyester, blue pants and shirt. He reeked and look unhealthy, relaxed abdomen yet only in his

30's. I said, "Where are you going?" "I'm trying to get to Chicago." "How far have you walked?" "Since Fernley." (2 hours). He was hitchhiking, and his unsavory appearance and smell didn't make him a good candidate to be picked up. He asked, "Have you got any water?" I unhooked the last of my gallon and then impulsively said, "If you want to carry that, you can have it." "Thank you." "Good luck." We parted. As long as I could see him (hour), he never did get a ride. I was sorry I hadn't given him some food. It strongly occurred to me that he could easily die out there; in fact, it seemed inevitable if he were not picked up very soon.

Then I realized, holy smokes! I HAVE NO WATER! My cardinal rule was always to have plenty of water, especially in the desert. Immediately a tiny panic set in, and my mouth felt absolutely dry. My realistic self said, "Well, you're not going to die and Fernley is only 2 hours away." And that was that.

Some green grass appeared and the Truckee's trees were now only 6 miles away. My now familiar high crept upon me. I found myself inexplicably singing, "Stand beside her and guide her through the night with a light from above." I didn't know what song it was but continued, "From the mountains, to the prairies, to the ocean white with foam, God bless America, my home sweet home, God bless America, my home sweet home." Some shore-like birds (peep) squeaked in the alkali marsh and their tiny running legs held the promise of water, even ocean, far beyond the mountains. Then I sang on I-80 in the desert, "Oh beautiful for spacious skies for amber waves of grain. For purple mountain majesty above the fruited plain, America, America, God shed his grace on thee. And crown thy good with brotherhood from sea to shining sea." There were tears in my eyes, emotion and happiness. I said it again, this time, "God shed HER grace on thee, and crown thy good with SISTERHOOD." And "Happy trails to you

326

*until we meet again. Happy trails to you, keep smiling until
then. Happy trails to you, till we meet again." And "We're
on the trail. My mule and I, we haven't a care." Then, "Oh
beautiful for patriot's dream that sees beyond the years
thine alabaster cities gleam..."*

But the important Truckee River? I later recalled
its beauty but could not remember more and did not speak
of it in my journal. I can only conclude that this attests to
my mental exhaustion. Although nearing the end of the
journey, large chunks of narrative were totally omitted from
my journal and lost from memory, and my moods became
more erratic.

Rest areas are used primarily for dog bathrooms.
Ninety percent of the people who stop urgently spring loose
dogs to pee and drink water. One is hard pressed to find a
place to unroll a sleeping bag. The proper people guide their
dogs to the surrounding areas which pollutes for sleeping
bags, and others pee right in the middle of things.

But one particular rest area was like going into a
theater. *A woman's baby was "choking to death" (her
words) and after stopping at the rest area (why?) she
couldn't get her car started but didn't want anyone else to
take them to the hospital. (I guess the baby had stopped
choking?) In the midst of many helping hands popping
clutches and jumper cables, the frantic mother kept trying to
light a cigarette while on a dead run. Finally the milling
crowd of concerned and wonderful people (I had teary eyes)
got her car started, and off she went to the hospital, 30
miles.*

*I became aware of a young hippy couple and their
17-month old daughter. They were relaxed and clean and
nice to their little girl. Their faces were pleasant, old tie-*

327

*dyed t-shirts, jeans and braids. But why did the young man have to LOOK so counter-culture, long skinny tight braids hanging from the sides of his head and a long wispy beard? Then they came over and gave me some fruit: tomato, banana, and apples. We started talking, and the proselytizing was on. They are from the "spiritual commune," and on and on he went about the Indians and the world, etc. etc. The word "love" was flung around with the old abandon of the 60s and the term "folks" cropped up in every other sentence. "We have to love all the folks even if we can't stand to live with them, but we still love those folks." These young hippies from the commune are good, sincere, hardworking people, but Dear God, I wish they would not preach their naive simplistic palaver, even if it is true. They gave me a book from their commune, THE FARM, Summertown, Tennessee, on **Spiritual Midwifery**. I've read it today for a few hours and after one gags, swallows and tolerates the slang— "stoned psychedelic vibes, far out" etc.— it does paint a pretty picture. All this hippy talk about the beauties of natural childbirth has always been a red flag to me. I react with an emotional anger, having suffered soundly through labor and delivery of my own kids and having seen other women similarly suffer and then pronounce it a beautiful experience the next* day. (However, 13 months later, I re-read **Spiritual Midwifery** by May Gaskin and am impressed, a rare admission for me. Maybe I was wrong. Maybe it is possible to create and interpret this into something super...)

And then two retired couples brought me a sandwich and coffee and talked radiantly and glowingly of their retired lives, vagabonding in their trailers. I slept on the pavement between their rigs. I prefer sun-sterilized dirty pavement to the sun-shaded, food-sticky picnic tables. All night the truckers pulled in and out. The street lights

*spotlighted me and the traffic roared by, but I slept deeply;
vivid dreams lately.* What a rest area stop that was...

*Today walked nearer to Sparks than I intended. It
was close to 4:00 P.M. in terribly heavy traffic when nearly
in a panic and close to tears, I found a hiding place, 30 feet
from the traffic but in a ravine deep enough to be invisible.*

*Lying in this ditch, I look up at the old fashioned
telephone lines, the pole with 4 crossbars lined with 10 blue
insulators on each bar. I remember as a child lying on the
back seat of the car riding to Connecticut, being very
impressed with the much larger number of wires down there
than I'd ever seen in East Greenbush, New York. Somehow
this was evidence of traveling far away and seeing
something important. I remember telling this fascinating
discovery to my childhood best friend, Karen.*

17

RENO

October 12 – 27

"I have not told half of what I saw."
Marco Polo on his death bed

Impatience, erratic moods, memory loss, fewer journal entries… 1978 David Hiser

Tomorrow Reno. I fumbled doubtfully, hoping for a
solution from the reporter to "what will I do when I get

there?" (As if I hadn't done perfectly well on my own for nearly 2,000 miles...) She said without sympathy, "Wing it."

I often see planes flying high on this trip. I say, childlike, "Oh, you lucky thing! Where are you going? Reno? San Francisco? Las Vegas, Los Angeles?" Now I'm close to California. It is still the land of lure and promise. Its very name conjures up images of the clearest waters, the biggest, most aromatic trees, the freshest mountain air, and the coldest, swirlingest ocean waves. California!

Today looked down to oil my wheels and discovered one of my old shoes gone. It's like losing an old friend. That shoe was with me all the way from Lawrence, Kansas.

Distances here: I've stood on the edge of valleys looking across to distant mountains 6 miles, 13 miles and 20 away, and to these untrained eastern eyes, they all look the same. The eye is much more accurate when judging distances from side to side.

Over the rim of a hill I saw Reno. What a mess! It was shrouded under a blanket of the ugliest air pollution I've ever seen, thick and brown as emptying a vacuum bag of filth. The Sierras loomed in undistinguished lumps behind the dirty valley.

The traffic increased, and as I neared town, I got lost on a cloverleaf; around and around I went. I defy anyone to go west on the eastbound lane while negotiating complex cloverleafs. Not having an advanced degree in civil engineering, I gave up and switched to the regular westbound lane and simply followed signs. Trucks blew me into guard walls, and all in all I felt little and bewildered and embattled.

In the city bustle a TV news car stopped ahead and started filming my approach. The reporter whisked me to breakfast and interviewed a thoroughly dazed and disoriented me at the busy lunch counter. People stopped me and asked for autographs, and just an hour before I had been in solitary peace in my sleeping bag in a ditch beside the road.

In a real estate office called The Donner Corporation an efficient broker drove me to an employment office. I was again ahead of the Donner schedule, so I got a maid's job at the Golden Road Motel.

I searched for the free housing that came with the chambermaid's job. The house, once elegant, looked ominous when I found it. It was surrounded by tawdry trailers and noisy drunken people. I stepped inside. A dissipated long-haired man surrounded by empty beer bottles eyed me and called me "another crazy broad." He was probably in his early 30s, but his pasty wrinkled complexion and watery eyes under tangled hair made him look desperately old. I'd been told to take a room upstairs. I tugged my golf cart up the narrow, dark stairs and took an empty closet sized room, no lock, under the eaves. I slept that night clutching my flashlight. Drunk Mexicans rattled my door, leftovers from when "the hooker lived here last week." My fear left as I learned to know and like these people who confided their stories…

Wanda, married to Tom, both 15. Wanda, pretty and dissipated at 15, sallow skin, brittle, stoned on pot, drunk, friendly, fired, lost, raging blindly. I like her. How did she sink so low so young? So soon?

Beth, 30, fat, tangled blond hair, a leader, had baby at age 15, birthed 6 children, only one still alive, age 9, running from police for $40,000 in bad checks, proud to consider herself "top maid," exploited by employer, brother *in prison 25 to 50 years for rape of daughter. I like her and respect her endurance and leadership. She had planned to marry Tony but quit the maid's job the last day I was there to marry a Filipino she'd met the day before. Why? A citizenship scam for him to get his green card.*

Ingrid, sharp-nosed, attractive, German, orphaned, stepfather brutal to submissive stepmother, married to religious fanatic, cruel, child at 15 given for adoption, 2 more children, left husband to run off with emotionally disabled woman-beater, spent entire inheritance of $15,000 buying cars for him, left after too many beatings, still "loves" him, wants to go back, suicidal, seeks tranquilizers, can't sleep, I like her but feel great pessimism around her. On my last day the "loves him" Mike arrived, clearly unstable and unemployed.

Hazel, running from husband, 40s, tough gutteral staccato statements, "My name's Hazel. Pleased ta meet ya. We help each other here. It's the only way we can survive. Here's some food and towels I stole. Ya heard me. Good luck, kid."

Outside my door at 4:00 A.M. I heard the same rapid fire flat guttural monotone. "I'm sick of Mexicans. Ya heard me. See this knife? Take one step toward me and I'll cut your guts out. Comprende? Get the hell out of here. Ya heard me." Hazel was protecting me.

Hazel said goodbye suddenly, planned to go to Washington. Next day she was still around, depressed, no money. Beth feared she'd taken an overdose next morning but said not to wake her up so early. My head reeled with the illogic of that statement.

Pat, very pretty, in late 40s but looking like an aging ridiculous Betty Grable under her long bleached-blond curls. Left home and married at age 15 after stepfather kept sexually abusing her. Married 5 times, 5 kids. Last husband "took my money, my kids, my pride."

Also running from police, bad checks. Mental breakdown and severely ill in hospital for 2 years. Now taking first shaky recovered steps. Son in prison.

Kim, 16, Pat's daughter, planned to marry on Sunday, changed to Monday when couldn't get day off, sweet 16, still a flicker of a young spirit, mostly bewildered into playing the servant to new unemployed husband. I feel hopeless pessimism. Where were you, woman's lib, to warn this young child? Sweetness taking a plunge, trapped.

Pat and Kim worked together as a pair. Pat did the cleaning and refused to dilute the cleaning solution. "I can clean faster this way." Her hands had deep cracks from the solution. How deep? At least a frightening half inch...

Lupe the Mexican woman left suddenly with a heavy white man said to be a wetback smuggler.

Mary, 57, aristocratic, well-dressed in elegant black pantsuits, 5 grown children, kicking up her heels to see the world, almost married a 70-year old multi-millionaire last year but backed out at the absolutely last minute because he was so cheap, unscrewed light bulbs, bullied clerks about a twenty-cent tax, etc. She's soon leaving. In the middle of a slave day she said to me incredulously and in amazement (me on my knees scrubbing a toilet), "Why are we doing this anyway? It's absolutely unnecessary." She drives me crazy, talks at length in a soft voice totally inaudible in the midst of a blaring TV, and on and on she mumbles. Her stories are astounding. Married 30 years to a psychopath who tried to murder her dozens of times, stealthily, smothering her in her sleep, poisoning, etc. This monster was later murdered by a 14-year old stepson. Her priest had laughed at and joked about her bruises after her beatings.

Beth told of her acquaintance with a 9 year old girl pregnant from her own father's rape, having the baby to be kept in the family and given to her when she marries some day.

Feliciano the wetback, 25, ugly beyond belief, crooked teeth, hawk nose, misshapen stomach, sings all day in heavenly melodic tones and listens to opera-like Mexican music, scrupulously clean and neat. I like him. He was a bandillero bullfighter in Mexico. I loved him when he admitted after much thought that he did feel sorry for the bulls that are killed. Knife fight with brother, Alfredo.

All the women wounded, struggling day by day, terrible health, verging between exhausting work and sickness, which becomes the only allowable relief from work. Poor diets, living on coffee and coke to pep up and pot and liquor and tranquilizers to come down. Suicide a lurking topic.

I was invited to the home of a TV man and reporter where I tried to convey the lives of my co-workers back at the Golden Road Motel. The reporter immediately stiffened and said, "Those people just don't know any better than to live like that. They could climb upward if they worked two jobs."

He then began talking on his CB, reminding me of a little kid trying to be important. I choked down embarrassed laughter at him. From then on in his lovely Sunset Magazine home, all mention of my maid friends was considered vaguely obscene.

Every day in the motel we cleaned up after privileged people who had enjoyed the splashy excitement of the big casinos. We washed their shower stalls, made their beds, emptied their trash. None of us motel help had ever been to a big casino show, so I vowed to take us all to the biggest, gaudiest, and most spectacular before I left Reno. I blew a week's very hard-earned pay on the adventure, not from altruism but from miscalculation. The free tickets I had naively counted on never materialized.

When the big night arrived some of my motel friends were too frightened or too proud or too ashamed to go, but five joined me for the big fest. I had loudly announced that considering the outrageous price of the tickets, I felt no compunction to spend even more money on fancy clothes so I would wear my trail clothes. I urged them to follow my lead. The maids were shocked. Beth had blown her paycheck on clothes for the occasion (something that saddened me). The consensus of opinion was that my trail and work clothes would never do. Somehow they dug into their wardrobes and contributed odds and ends of their own clothes to outfit me "properly." In the end the strange assortment and varied sizes felt even more peculiar than my trail clothes would have, but I tried to wear them as if Christian Dior had dressed me.

We crept into the ostentatious casino like the babes in the woods that we were. I found the decor obscenely opulent. Beth gazed in starry-eyed wonder, and the Mexican wetback, Feliciano, fighting something that offended his pride, ostentatiously threw his cigarette onto the rich red carpet and ceremoniously ground it out with his heel. We wandered among the gamblers who would lose more on one hand of blackjack than we would earn in a month at the motel.

And then our ragged little band was escorted to front row seats for the big show. Right away it became obvious to me that the front row was undesirable unless one was in a haze of alcohol. Every ripped stocking of the dancing women, every scabby elbow, and every layer of grotesque makeup quivered before my startled eyes. But Beth sat entranced as wave after wave of ostentatious display engulfed us. A dance number featuring lavender feathers was followed by a dance number featuring pink feathers. The pink feathers preceded a number with no feathers as 250 dancers shuffled about topless except for one set of drooping diamond chains. The evening became an endless blur of feathers and noise and lavish special effects, waterfalls and earthquakes and smoking cauldrons. It was the most spectacular display of bad taste I could envision. The Mexicans sat stunned. Beth sat enraptured. And the rest of us just sat through it. It was American materialism gone wild.

We went home and tried to get a few hours sleep before the grueling maid work began all over again.

Motel maid work, the lowest of low, no tips. We are instructed on how to do a room. The first room took me one hour, wiping air conditioner slots, polishing bathroom plumbing etc. and we sometimes must each do 25 rooms a day. Rooms are inspected to eliminate skimping... Impossible stress to do more than is possible. At day's end I am exhausted to the point of fever, exhausted beyond thinking, beyond reading, beyond eating, with the next day just a night's sleep away. It's enough to make a person drink just to get in a few moments of release before morning. All this for $15 to $20 per day or less. Through this I began to seethe and boil in a quiet rage at the smug bastards who wail about welfare and people who won't work. I have worked this hard at my school or real estate occasionally. Ranchers and farmers occasionally work this hard, but in every such case it is not a dead end like chambermaid's work. I feel a white fury toward anyone who would condemn a welfare recipient or anyone to this life of exhaustion, poverty, ruined health, deadened spirit, and dead-end future.

I like the maids and the wetbacks here too. I do not spend much time with them in friendship because at this point my own mental resources are exhausted. But why do I identify with them and sympathize with them so strongly? Why are my scorn and self-righteous fury toward the middle class here so raging? I have a list of names of people in Reno that I could be staying with in moderate opulence, yet I, with some kind of perverse self-righteousness of my own, refuse.

Today I ate dinner with a mid-30s smug couple from the Nevada National Guard. I pleaded the case for the people I am working with as eloquently as I could. The man said, "Your maid friends just don't have enough sense to sit down and plan their lives ahead like we do." This paunchy, bland man in his military jacket suddenly was so repulsive to me, that I could scarcely eat. In my book HE is the fat lazy slob on government welfare, sitting all day in his plush office and living smugly off taxpayers' money. Self-satisfied, useless butterball...

I was given a rare tour (the reporter told me this tour was a rare and great honor for me, ho hum...) and we watched some military planes take off. I couldn't have been less impressed or more bored, though I tried to act impressed. Marilyn the reporter, playing the role of the spunky little spitfire, kept saying how she wanted a ride in one of the planes. (I'm sure none of them can conceive of how I can't remember the name of it, F something or Ghost or Phantom or something equally juvenile). A pilot stood with us (this alone was supposed to impress me) and he was handsome in a gray-haired catalogue model sort of way, but the pilot and everyone but me had the most incredible demeanors, proud, excited, triumphant, almost sexual admiration as these noisy, stupid planes would take off. So this is the fierce pride of the Air Force, the esprit de corps, the hallowed worship. The pilots would give some jerky hand signals which seemed to impress everyone all the more. To me they looked like fools.

    A TV newsman said that it was good I wasn't a hippy spouting flower child garbage, etc. If I had done that, it would supposedly negate my whole 2,000 miles of walking.

    For the past few weeks I'm aware off and on of a yearning to find a friend who would try to understand me. I was reading **The Woman's Room** *by Marilyn French, and suddenly there it was perfectly expressed for me:*

> Loneliness is not a longing for company, it is a longing for kind. And kind means people who can see who you are, and that means they have enough intelligence and sensitivity and patience to do that. It also means they can accept you, because we don't see what we can't accept, we blot it out, we jam it hastily in one stereotype box or another.

    People ask me about the trip and then don't listen for one second when I try to express my puzzlement and disappointment at how I can't comprehend it, etc. I'm not boasting or bragging or glorifying. I'm trying to share, and I badly need someone who'll sit and listen. Why do they all clamor about how I should write a book when they won't listen now? I see no end or solution to this strange part of me that's lonely because after all, I did this alone. No one else has done it, and that sets me apart.

    The admiration I bask in is fine as long as I smile and say the expected things. When I say what is really me, I get closed off.

———

Regardless of how many times I read about the journey of the Donner Party, I find myself straining and hoping they could move just a little bit faster to make it before the snows trap them. I know better, of course, but the race with time never fails to stir me to fairly shout across the pages and years. And just as I plead with them to hurry, I react with flaring indignation whenever I hear criticism of their efforts. They came within two miles of the pass, a scant one day too late in a year, 1846, when the snows came earlier and more severely than any winter of that century.

On the south shore of Donner Lake is a monument dedicated to the first wagon train to cross the pass, the Murphy Party in 1844. They *began* their assault of the pass on November 25. November 25! One month *later* in the season than the Donner's fall arrival. The Murphy Party feat is regarded as a remarkable accomplishment, yet the difference separating their success from the Donner's failure was simply a fluke in the weather.

Way back in Nebraska, I had first run into David Hiser and Melinda Berge, National Geographic photographers assigned to an upcoming book, *Trails West.* We crossed paths intermittently throughout the west. Theirs were the only familiar faces I'd see for hundreds of miles. They gave me continuity and moments of peace.

Arranged by them (and Bob Laxalt, the Senator's brother), I had the privilege of riding for a day on an old-fashioned wagon train across part of the 40-mile desert. It gave me a vivid feeling for the struggle involved (physical for the animals and mental for the pioneers) in hauling wagons over hills and uneven roads. Even a minor incline like a child's first sledding hill was a major crisis, men wielding whips with tense shouts, women taut with held breaths, and animals churning forward only to stop in mid-hill, then everyone clambering out of the wagons to lighten the load, a brief recuperative rest for the animals, and a renewed heave at the traces. Similarly a side slant of the road was cause for yet one more tense crisis as passengers lean sideways to counter-balance the frightening tilt of the wagon bed, and on it would go for 2,000 miles. By the end of the exhausting day, tempers were short as men screamed at the animals and goaded them in frustration with prods and whips.

I rode behind the oxen in the covered wagon and could imagine the stress and futility the Donners must have felt behind the slow-laboring animals. The wagon master told me that when the oxen become overheated or overtired they simply walk slower and slower until they come to a stop, at which point it would take dynamite to move them. By the end of that day with them, a sharp stick poked into the animal's hide with the zeal of frustration came back from the oxen hide dripping with blood, yet the animal had not moved one bit faster. It was common in the 1800s for oxen to literally die on the trail from being worn out.

Is it no wonder that the Donners were nearly driven frantic with the stress of rushing the animals fast enough to beat the snows but not so fast as to kill them? The rest days snatched here and there were probably not for the whims of lazy, shortsighted people so much as an attempt to merely keep the pitiful animals alive. In the meadow around Reno they rested for a few days. With oxen that by that time resembled wobbling bones and with the rigors of the Sierras directly ahead, is it unreasonable that an attempt was made to rest the animals? No one ever claimed that oxen were faster than walking people, and in the case of pioneers, the animals probably held them back. But in the wagons patiently pulled behind them, the oxen transported a civilization.

18

CALIFORNIA

October 28 - November 7
(150 miles)

"All men dream: but not equally. Those who dream by night in the dusty recesses of their minds wake in the day to find it was but vanity: but the dreamers of the day...may act their dream with open eyes, to make it possible. This I did."   Lawrence of Arabia

Trees, forests, California...   1978 MB

After walking for weeks and months across treeless plains and deserts, I left Reno behind and approached the California border. A lovely woman, Kathy Wolcott, offered to be my guide. My calendar was in sync with the Donner Party's of 1846. At last, this was it.

October 28, First Summit, Sierra Mountains, California:
Seeing my first tree in the Sierras came as a shock. It was a long needled evergreen and there it stood shimmering in the light, a miracle of beauty, a worthy object of worship, a new but familiar old friend.

Passing the second summit I was stopped by a man who was familiar with much of the Donner Route. "You didn't cross the Great Salt Desert in Utah in the exact original route, did you!"

"No," I answered, "I could have, but I stayed closer to Interstate 80 for safety."

"Well, of course you didn't," he said, "you couldn't possibly have made it!"

And then for the first time I found myself indignant at this weak assessment of me and my abilities. "Gee whiz, don't challenge me," I heard myself saying, "Of course I could do it." And I really meant it. And it's true, I could do it for sure. I basked briefly in the feeling of my hard-won confidence.

Happiness...   1978 MB

The false promise of the Hastings cut-off had lured the ill-fated Donner Party into a trail of doom. But still somehow they had beaten the Wahsatch, survived the hellish horrors of the Great Salt Desert and, by some thread of dogged human endurance, flowed around the stubborn wall of the Ruby Mountains. They had sped across the Nevada desert at the truly remarkable rate of 20 miles per day. Considering their starving, weakened condition, the accomplishment is almost incredible. They pressed across the dreaded 40-Mile Desert and fought their way up the eighty miles of the canyon of the Truckee River, submitting to 50 crossings along its tortured course. Frightened, demoralized and ragged with internal dissention, although refusing to die, the broken and separated remnants of the Donner Party climbed deep into the Sierras. And then with exquisite cruelty, it began to snow. But still, for a few days the little people flung themselves repeatedly against the hopeless white barrier at the pass.

Five miles behind the vanguard, the Donner brothers and their families bogged down in six inches of falling snow at Alder Creek near what's now Truckee, California. George Donner, the kindly captain of the train now bringing up the rear, cut his hand trying to repair a broken axle in the midst of the snow emergency. How typical of the Donner bad luck to have an axle break at a time like that... But the crisis was upon them as they hastily threw up temporary brush huts for the night. Reports say that by morning the brush tepees sagged under 22 inches of snow, and it continued snowing without stopping for eight days. George was to die slowly there five months later of his wound and of heartbreak as the horrors mounted in those snow-buried brush tepees. Death and cannibalism would yet pass before his tortured eyes before his rest would come. Tamsen Donner, his devoted wife, would choose to remain behind at his side to the end. She was never seen alive again, her body never found.

October 29th at Alder Creek, California, with Melinda of *National Geographic*, Micky of *People Magazine* and Kathy, my guide.

We walked on to the Donner Camp. I turned into the parking lot and chuckled to Melinda, "Melinda, don't ever tell anyone that I went to the outhouse before I looked at the campsites."

I went to the restroom feeling nothing in particular. After many miles of looking for a bathroom, it did seem strange that I wasn't able to go. I walked back to the parking lot and over to the sign by the Donner Camp with no awareness of emotion...And then suddenly and stunningly there it was. In a low, broad, partially treed meadow utterly ordinary yet terribly personal, suddenly, after following the Donner Party for six months, 2,000 miles and only occasionally glimpsing them, rarely feeling them, suddenly I'd caught up with them. There they were, stopped forever in this ordinary yet throbbing place. I approached the sign, pulling my golf cart (which had become my security blanket and my friend), and I read "At this site now so peaceful and easily accessible, one of the cruelest stories in Sierra history was written, the story of the George and Jacob Donner families."

My anguished tears.   1978 MB

CALIFORNIA

At the word "cruelest" I was overwhelmed with uncontainable sorrow and grief, just as the term "suffering humanity" had moved me in South Pass, and I stood helpless as waves of tears gushed from my blinking eyes. Melinda and Micky were snapping pictures behind me, not aware of my tears. I felt caught. Finally, alone, unable to read the plaque further, I turned and sought a large boulder nearby to which I fled. I turned to Melinda and said, choked, "I can't read it. I can't get through it." Her face was puzzled and non-comprehending. I glimpsed the kind and sympathetic face of Kathy, and then I sat on the rock curled into a ball, my head buried in my arms on my knees. I did this to try to regain control, but instead deep sobs racked my body. I could feel my back and rib cage convulsing uncontrollably. I returned to my cart for tissues and tried again to read the plaque only to return to hide on the boulder again.

The Donner Party. To have come so far, so far, so far, as I had just done, and to be stopped forever in this ordinary little meadow...Surely they deserved better than this. Then it all came together, the realization and memory of those spring days along the Little Blue River in Kansas, along the Platte, across the Great Plains, through South Pass, and the terrible struggle through the Wahsatch. We had both known fear in the Great Salt Lake Desert and plodded grimly across the Nevada deserts, burning sun and biting cold, a lifetime, two lifetimes of experiences, many already forgotten. Dear God, to be stopped here in this meadow so close, so close to the goal, stopped dead. They didn't deserve this. A tragedy that knows no adequate words finalized in this ordinary little meadow, right here....

But for them, in 1846, the unimaginable worst was still to come, their ordeal by hunger.

347

Finally, the part of us that separates us from feelings began to numb me, and I began the long process of walling off the feelings that were publicly awkward; yet, tragically, I also closed off the brief and priceless oneness I had had momentarily with the Donners. Micky looked confused. I scarcely looked at him. Melinda was armored against softness, a permanent state for her. Kathy was soft and sympathetic but too inhibited to move to me. So I read the plaque with unseeing eyes two times and had no idea what I read. We took the circular path and saw the tepee sites, I in a mushy, unstable state of stiffening up and breaking down. Slowly and lonely I walked alone ahead of everyone, head down and back to the parking lot as David **(National Geographic)** *pulled up. He looked at me, and even from a fair distance I sensed that he sensed that I was crying, and his face changed from its usual secret melancholia to the deepest compassion and kindness I've ever seen or ever shall, and he simply walked up and stood beside me and put his arm around me and stroked my arm. I said "Why am I crying? I've got to stop crying."*

And he said gently. "That's what you came here for."

Such kindness and sensitivity and understanding were more than I could handle, so I stiffened and walked to the bathroom to get into my long underwear. "Maybe that will help," I had murmured.

On emerging I spotted a man whom I assumed was Steve Moore, the park ranger I'd never met but who had encouraged me by letters from the very beginning. I approached him and, fighting for control, said "Steve, I'm sorry I'm crying,"

And he with a mask of embarrassment said, "Why?"

After that I pulled myself together and conversed with animated brightness brittlely through my tear-swollen face.

One regret is that I choked off my hard-won communion with the Donners at Donner Camp. I'm a very well-trained woman in that sense anyway. When I am making others uncomfortable (crying), I automatically use all my will to remedy that, in this case at my own expense. Surely after 2,000 miles I had earned the right to cry and to feel and to commune, yet I failed to assert that earned right. So I stiffened and took charge and walked the path with Steve, asking him about his job and Proposition 13 and how it affected the parks, and he rambled on about those irrelevancies, and I smiled mightily and brightly through my tear-bloated eyes, and the world was back to normal, familiar fronts. The coming night would be the only night of the trek I spent in a tent. It felt appropriate.

Everyone left except Kathy and me. That night in her tent the wind howled in the pines. It would have been an unfamiliar and doubly ominous sound to the plains-accustomed Donners. Occasionally I could hear a feeble whack, whack, or clink, click, which sounded for all the world like a weakened person trying to chop down a tree for firewood. Otherwise all human noises were swallowed in the vast silence or occasional crescendo of howling, moaning wind. Kathy fell asleep, and I lay rigidly still on my back. I cried for all of those who died and endured here. The tears spilled at last over the side corners of my eyes, tracing rivulets over my temples, dripping steadily and wetting the hood of my jacket. Occasionally one would follow a path into my ear, feeling suddenly cold. Kathy stirred an hour later and I said tonelessly, "This is the spookiest place I ever camped." Spooky was a word choice to make light of what was sheer horror. Whack, whack, whack would go that pitiful ax sound as the cold winds increased their mournful threats.

And then snow was in the air.   1978   MP

The following morning was bitter cold, and then, appropriately and incredibly, tiny, white, hard chips of snow were in the air. The chips became flakes and it snowed with varying intensity for two days. Kathy and I left Donner Camp, and a mile beyond, I became aware of a great flooding sense of lightness as if a great weight I had unknowingly carried had been lifted. I was able to walk Kathy's slow pace without that sense of strain to go faster. Everything looked lovely, even the housing development on the logged mountain.

Steve Moore, the Ranger, met us a few miles from Donner Memorial State Park. Our approach to Donner Lake wound through a section of deeply forested emigrant trail. The white snow swirled against the dark evergreens and settled gently over us like confetti at a joyful wedding procession. My arrival at Donner Lake, unlike yesterday's soul-wrenching experience, was light and radiant and underlain with deep satisfaction and happiness.

With Steve at the Monument.   1978 MP

I found a delightful and growing rapport with Steve. We stood before the Donner Monument at Donner State Park and read its inscription: **VIRILE TO RISK AND FIND; KINDLY WITHAL AND A READY HELP. FACING THE BRUNT OF FATE; INDOMITABLE,— UNAFRAID.** *I turned to Steve questioningly and said, "I don't get it."*

After a pause, Steve said, "Neither do I." And the woods rang with our deep laughter.

351

The Pioneer Monument showing snow depth   1978 MP

Then we solemnly read the plaque on the back:
NEAR THIS SPOT STOOD THE BREEN CABIN OF
THE PARTY OF EMIGRANTS WHO STARTED FOR
CALIFORNIA FROM SPRINGFIELD, ILLINOIS, IN
APRIL, 1846, UNDER THE LEADERSHIP OF CAPTAIN
GEORGE DONNER. DELAYS OCCURRED AND
WHEN THE PARTY REACHED THIS LOCALITY, ON
OCTOBER 29, THE TRUCKEE PASS EMIGRANT
ROAD WAS CONCEALED BY SNOW. THE HEIGHT
OF THE SHAFT OF THE MONUMENT INDICATES
THE DEPTH OF THE SNOW, WHICH WAS TWENTY-
TWO FEET. AFTER FUTILE EFFORTS TO CROSS
THE SUMMIT THE PARTY WAS COMPELLED TO
ENCAMP FOR THE WINTER. THE GRAVES CABIN

CALIFORNIA

WAS SITUATED ABOUT THREE-QUARTERS OF A MILE TO THE EASTWARD, THE MURPHY CABIN ABOUT TWO HUNDRED YARDS SOUTHWEST OF THE MONUMENT, AND THE DONNER TENTS WERE AT THE HEAD OF ALDER CREEK. NINETY PEOPLE WERE IN THE PARTY AND FORTY-TWO PERISHED, MOST OF THEM FROM STARVATION AND EXPOSURE. IN COMMEMMORATION OF THE PIONEERS WHO CROSSED THE PLAINS TO SETTLE IN CALIFORNIA. MONUMENT ERECTED UNDER THE AUSPICES OF THE NATIVE SONS AND THE NATIVE DAUGHTERS OF THE GOLDEN WEST. MONUMENT DEDICATED JUNE 6, 1918.

In the Donner Museum I stood reverently before a 15-foot high tree stump taken from the Donner Camp and purporting to show the depth of snow when chopped for firewood by a Donner member. My eyes rested on the chopped end. There was a long silence. Steve was standing next to me. "Steve," I said, "that doesn't look like it was chopped with an ax to me." Had I been too disrespectful?

Then Steve answered with a loud laugh of relief. "You're astute, Barbara. That was obviously cut with a saw. But it still MIGHT have been done by the Donners, who might have had saws."

October 30 Donner Memorial State Park:

I ate dinner with Steve and Anna Moore, wonderful food where, as usual, I stopped eating at the conclusion of the meal, not when full. That night Steve and I walked to the edge of Donner Lake and gazed toward Donner Pass at the opposite end. In 1978 the edge of the lake is rimmed with twinkling lights of people's homes. A super-highway passes through the once-virgin woods. Steve said, "It's hard for me to imagine what it was like here in 1846."

But, God, I knew. The mountain silhouette back then loomed as black and impenetrable as it now appeared. I blocked out the faint roar of traffic and felt the bottomless silence that must have smothered the trapped pioneers who stood here terrified exactly 132 years ago. The wet, cold air bit as insistently now as then. The dip in the mountain silhouette, the pass, lured and beckoned now as then, but back then it might as well have been the other side of the moon for many who never lived to approach any closer than this. Steve and I paid them our quiet reverence and then turned and walked back to the car.

The next day I left Donner Lake as quietly as I came. It seemed strange to have no fanfare after reaching such a hard-won goal. So I left unannounced, content, satisfied, deeply happy, past the tightly home-packed shores of Donner Lake toward the notch known as Donner Pass.

Before my struggle up the last big mountain I stood uncomprehending and squinting with disbelief before the approaching dizzy spectacle of Donner Pass, a tousled jumble of house-sized boulders mounting a vaguely tilting sheet cliff. Way back in Ash Hollow, a man who had visited the pass had fairly shouted at me, "How did they do it?" with insistent marvel and disbelief. (The Donner Party never did but not for lack of trying.)

Bob Laxalt the day before had pronounced with scorn and near fear, "They must have been out of their minds to try to scale that sheer cliff with wagons!" They weren't out of their minds, of course, they merely saw no other choice. I had my own toiling to do to surmount the pass, so up I went on the old highway, eyes darting unceasingly, searching in vain for any even remotely possible looking wagon route. Visible high to the north was I-80. I walked on old Highway 40. Two ancient road beds were in sight below me to the south, and high, high, dizzily, barely clinging to the vertical granite walls, ran the railroad, built and paid for in Chinese blood nearly 100 years ago. Over the pass I labored, passing 2,000-year old cypress trees looking virtually identical to me as to frantic pioneer eyes.

19

BEYOND THE PASS

"A stranger is a friend you haven't met." (best lesson from the trail)

I wanted the trip to never end, so, I tacked on the last stretch of about 100 miles to Sacramento. Westward I walked for days beyond the pass. The air was fresh, cold, and luscious. I followed a lovely river in a kind of Sierra paradise but realized the arduous long descent from the pass was no picnic. The Donner Party would have been a long way from "home free" even if the pass had been scaled. After a series of ups and downs, there began the most astonishing land form of the trip: 50 miles of down-hill steep enough to give blisters and sore ankles, steep enough and long enough for me to gasp repeatedly in amazement. I descended through several ecological zones: high granite and fir to chaparral and into the darkest and wettest conifer forest imaginable. It was many, many miles before I found an accessible campsite in the steep banks and heavy undergrowth.

Then, some of the most enchanting hours of the trip. Suddenly the air was warm and benevolent, the close rounding hills as intimate as New England's. The soft beige grasses were dotted with spaced park-like scrub oak and occasional broad-leaf trees. Gradually the rolling and twisting road wound through small, established farms festooned with ancient vines over arbors. The fragrance of ripe and rotting fruit perfumed the balmy air. Small duck ponds backed up lazily behind tiny streams. Even in November, neat vegetable gardens sprouted a fresh crop of beets and lettuce. Chickens and ducks and geese scurried, unfenced, while milk cows and horses and lots of goats grazed in languor on the hills. Small orchards nestled in the hollows while tall, piny pine stands marched on the hilltops. Clearly this was the paradise image (and reality) that so many pioneers had struggled so long to reach.

Paradise beyond the pass.   1979 ES

I gradually became aware of an uncanny, eerie feeling. I felt a strong, special, and urgent responsibility to take in this "Eden Valley" completely and totally. It was as if someone else in addition to me was seeing it through my eyes and my senses. Carefully and reverently my eyes caressed every tiny farmhouse, every sparkling duck pond, every nanny goat and grapevine and old barn and wagon lane. I reveled in the paradise, murmuring in wonder and understanding, "So this is what they struggled for," and I felt it a valid struggle. I felt it and breathed it and saw it for those who came so close but died behind the Sierra wall. I walked through it, experiencing it for Tamsen Donner and Eleanor Eddy and old Mrs. Murphy and all those who were

357

left behind. It was a profoundly moving and joyful experience.

The last day of my trip was the 20-mile walk to Sutter's Fort (in Sacramento), the goal of the pioneers. For days I had felt schizophrenic, profoundly sad because my trip, almost my life, was nearing an end—and deeply happy, triumphant, even jubilant at my accomplishment. So the last day this paradox felt all the more keen. I was alternately elated and mournful, lost and found, ignored and congratulated. A man with his grade-school-age daughter stopped. The father had seen my picture in the paper. He announced with an air of historic solemnity to his daughter, "Peggy, I want you to remember this. This woman has walked across the country on the Donner Trail. You can tell your class at school that you met her." Occasionally someone would shout generously, "Congratulations!" or stop to hand me flowers to carry.

Three TV stations did their things off and on during the day. A telling incident occurred during one. While the camera and mike were being moved, a car pulled next to me in heavy traffic. A man in his 50s dressed in a garage mechanic's uniform thrust his business card and a $10 dollar bill into my hand saying, "I don't want to take your time but take this and go have dinner and champagne tonight to celebrate. I think it's magnificent what you've done." Miraculously much of this was filmed by the TV camera. A scant minute before this incident the interviewer had asked, "What have you learned on this trip?" I replied that "I used to see strangers as ominous or threatening or at least indifferent, but now to me strangers are simply nice people I don't know yet."

BEYOND THE PASS

The big bash arrival at Sutter's Fort was completely upstaged by a national story that broke in Sacramento one hour and two miles before my arrival. (Computer-operated diamond robbery, top story on national news.) A special gate was opened for me at Sutter's Fort, and a cannon was set off to welcome me—as it would have been staged for the Donner Party, had they arrived in 1846. A Mexican woman had brought her family to see me. "Everyone calls us the weaker sex," she said with feeling, "but just look what you've showed the world." It was a wonderfully confused time with lots of peculiar people jockeying for position to get into the pictures that were flashing. Comic mass confusion reigned for a while, and then it suddenly evaporated, and it was over, the end. I was happy and hyper and dazed.

November 7, Sacramento:

Alone at night I saw me on TV, and I guess that was the culmination of my personal growth during the trip, the old me and the new me viewing it together. The old me realized I wouldn't have liked the floppy pants, the rolling gait, the too high forehead, etc., etc., but the new and now real, true me was stunned with the personal perfection I had created. I loved my gestures, uninhibited, my deep firm voice in response to the interviewer's questions, my earnest and transparent straining to answer truthfully, my expressive face and hands communicating and oblivious to old society notions of pretty femininity. It was a brief and shining moment, so rare. I loved the me that I was, unique and perfect.

I slept that night tight along the edge of the fancy king sized bed, taking no more room than my sleeping bag would have. In the morning I awoke and realized the walking was over, the tension was over, the journey was over. It was time to get ready for the reporter who would

359

drive me to San Francisco. My golf cart sat faithfully in the corner of the room, the wheels tilting and worn, the rubber tread peeling off. My yellow pack was appropriately dirty with the many stains that had accumulated for two thousand miles. The blotch on the top was from the cheese that melted in Nebraska, the streak on the side from the spilled can of Three-in-One oil in Nevada. I unstrapped my water jug and then violently backed away. I couldn't bring myself to take my pack off the cart. I paced the room alternately sobbing. "Oh my God," and then laughing, "this is ridiculous." Silly or not, dismantling my pack and cart marked a poignant ending I wasn't ready to handle just yet. I thought back to that morning so very long ago (was it just six months?) when frightened and unsure I had been afraid of that same (then clean) yellow pack. Tears of thankfulness and pride blurred my vision. Crying; something I had done daily at first and then hadn't done for months until reaching Donner Camp. Hearing the crunch of a car on the stones outside, I took a deep breath, tenderly removed my pack, and went to answer the knock. I was a woman alone on the trail no more. It was finished.

Those days now only a memory....   1978   David Hiser

May the road rise to meet you.
May the wind always be at your back.
May the sun shine warm upon your face
And the rains fall soft upon your fields...
Until we meet again...   From an Irish blessing

"Don't take no cutoffs and hurry along as fast as you can."

Virginia Reed surviving member of Donner Party after her rescue.

20

HOMECOMING

"He who tells the truth will be chased out of nine villages."
                                        Turkish proverb

I took a long, unwinding Greyhound bus ride home from San Francisco to Boston, riding over much of the route that I had walked. On the bus I hummed comfortingly to myself all day and deep into the night the melodic wistful lullaby:

Home is the hunter
Home from the hills
Home is the dreamer
Safe in the arms of her love
Never more to roam
She's home.

Somewhere nearing my village of East Bridgewater, I sat staring out the window of the humming bus and spotted a beauty I had already forgotten… Brown leaves were floating edge to edge on the black surface of a still pond. It reminded me of old New England lace. I was home.

As soon as I walked into my old house, I saw with delight and relief the emerging calm maturity of my children, Paula and Cliff. But then my journey unhappily took the status of a faded dream. It was as if it had occurred 50 years before, a distant memory. Yet some part of me refused to let it be over. For a full two weeks, I almost unconsciously kept changing into my trail clothes. Despite complete cessation of exercise, my appetite continued to soar unchecked as I consumed enough food for six people. And my body rebelled and protested the trip's ending by developing dozens of psychosomatic complaints from headaches to rashes. I became accident prone, poking myself in the eye and walking into things.

The New England landscape that had carried me through deserts as a vision of heaven now looked cluttered and dirty and closed in. The people with whom I had wanted to share my deepest experiences asked politely, "Did you have a nice trip?" and clearly had time and energy only for a polite superficial answer. Naively I pressed with urgency my revolutionary message: "Hey! We don't have to be so afraid; there's a benevolent world out there, and we all can feel free to pursue any of our wildest dreams." An unbridgeable gulf, a separation would open between me and others so that the response was either a tolerant blank stare or a faint but firm hostility: "Well, it's nice for you that you can believe in such things," putting me and my trip into the perspective realm of the tooth fairy. "I think you were very, very lucky." (Stern finger wagging.) "The truth is that you can't even walk across a parking lot these days safely." Not knowing when to retire my mouth, I respond, "But surely six months walking alone on the highways can be regarded as more than a fluke and maybe even an indication of the way it really is out there."

Most of my relatives assumed the attitude that they would overlook my six-month indiscretion and do me a favor by just not mentioning it. When I spoke before groups, however, the rapport became as intensely dynamic as it was dead on a one-to-one meeting. I would look at my audience and find tears in their eyes as I related stories of exceptional kindness from strangers.

One night I had a vivid dream. Melinda and David (the two *National Geographic* photographers who became my friends) and I were standing on a huge pier in balmy brilliant sunlight. We were euphoric, basking and gazing out on an exciting creation, the world. Regretfully but with firm decision I said goodbye and walked off the pier and along the shore upstream, where I entered the water out of sight. I was sucked into the current and swept past Melinda and David. I was swept out to sea and pulled down deep into the gray depths. The people back east at home were working down on the murky gray bottom. I joined them and began telling them about sunshine and light and heaven way, way up above the surface of the water. "But there really is sunshine and breezes up there," pointing, "I've been there." But they wouldn't listen or even lift their heads to look up. The cloudy water pulled heavily at my arms and legs, and I sensed that we were more dead than alive. I strained and strained to deliver my story to the people, but they were dead to my futile entreaties. And then I realized that perhaps I was trapped down there with them forever unless we all would go up together. I woke up and wrote down the dream.

As the weeks and months slipped by I grew to doubt even my own memories and perceptions of my Donner journey. While speaking before a group one evening, I impulsively decided to drive the route, and within a week, I was gone, leaving behind a family more resigned than surprised at my erratic behavior. I was frightened. It would be a test of my fragile and precious memories and convictions. Were people really as nice as I remembered? Had I somehow idealized the whole journey? Would I be received as warmly the second time through, this time arriving unannounced in a truck and traveling with a friend instead of limping in, pulling a cart, alone?

Reverend Ashmore in Gardner, Kansas, answered my first brave but frightened knock. It was a crucial moment for me. Maybe he wouldn't even remember me.

"Barbara!!!" he shouted through a grin as wide as the west, and my joy was too big to be contained. And that was the way it was throughout the second journey. Not only were my memories of America reaffirmed—they were strengthened. The country IS as vast and magnificent; the people ARE as warm and supportive; and indeed, our pioneer heritage is alive and well.

During the interim between my two trips, three of my favorite old people had died, and three new babies were born. I returned home the second time confident and sure and above all, free: free of doubts, free of popular convention, free of fear and caution and suspicion, Free.

THE END

EPILOGUE: A STRANGE PHENOMENON

I am including this odd occurrence which happened at the conclusion of my trip while recuperating briefly with my friend. Was it caused by a nutritional deficiency in my brain, or a stroke, or a psychic visitation? I have no idea.

After reaching Sacramento, I visited Sue Williams, an old college friend, near San Francisco. A transplanted easterner, she had dabbled in the dizzying variety of mind explorations that sprout endlessly in California. She's an old hand at telepathy and converses easily about reincarnation as if it were all no more mysterious than my cat's water dish.

My trip had ended, and I was in that rare state of satisfied completion but bursting aimlessly now with the momentum of recent physical conditioning and purpose. In the aftermath of my trip relaxed and in a happy daze, I simply sat on the couch in the afternoon and passively floated with her relaxed conversation.

Suddenly I became aware that Sue's face had changed. It wasn't Sue anymore. It was the face of a plump English-looking, old-fashioned young girl. I blinked, startled, and there it was, the same old Sue talking on without a pause. Within five minutes Sue had changed again, this time to a teen-aged boy with red hair and freckles. A quick shake of my head brought Sue back again. There was no mistaking the dissimilarity between Sue's face and the others. There were the obvious physical differences, hair color, skin complexion, age, sex, but the difference that I found most arresting was the facial expression. Sue wears a perpetual guarded tense expression. The faces that had flashed so fleetingly were radiant with humor, beaming with a sense of well-being.

I waited till the next day to tell Sue about the faces. They had amused me, but inexplicably I thought little about them as the conversation had flowed to other topics. Sue questioned me closely about the faces I had seen. She had a desire that they resemble her mother who had died years before. There had been no resemblance, and the incident was forgotten with typical California acceptance without forced analysis.

In the evening after dinner we relaxed again, Sue sitting across the room and lounging happily. Her face changed, but this time I was alert and interested, not wanting to blink or shake my head to make it disappear. Scarcely moving I said, "Sue, it's there."

"What does it look like?"

"Young girl, late teens maybe, very thin, radiant but beaming through sickness."

"Still there?"

But I shook my head and the vision disappeared. I wasn't frightened, but after all, I am an easterner thoroughly immersed in a culture that scoffs at silly stories of faces or apparitions or whatever. What was I doing sitting there reporting seriously to my friend about how I saw her face change into other people? By the end of the evening, I had seen two more faces, one a woman in her 30's, another a woman in her 50's. Both were the same person as the young girl but older. As I became more confident and less embarrassed, the faces stayed longer, and I gave long descriptions to an amazed Sue. Finally, not knowing what else to do, I got up and the faces left. I will never forget them, the radiant, beaming, almost humorous and amused expressions. I had then and have now no explanation for what I saw. I do not believe in Ouija boards or anyone else's psychic stories; I believe only in what I see for myself.

I visited Sue a year later and saw nothing special or unusual. Many months later I mentioned the phenomenon to an acquaintance who, said, "I have no explanation for what you saw except that it seems obvious that something was trying to get through to you an attitude of approval or congratulations to you for the trip." Whether that something was part of myself or a combination, I have no idea, but her explanation is as satisfactory as any.

APPENDIX: ITINERARY DAY BY DAY

Daily Schedule and Mileage Log of the Journey 1978

These notes are from my original journal including all its gaps, inaccuracies, confusions, and question marks.

April 20 ? Leave home to Bridgeport, CT
April 21 Yonkers, NY, Our Lady of Mt. St. Carmal
April 25 Gerald, MO
April ? left Thurs. ? bus to Kansas City, MO
April 28 ? Independence Square, MO
April 30 with Belle
day 1   13 miles
day 2   13 miles
day 3   9 miles
May 1   day 4   9 miles
May 2   day 5   13 and a half miles
May 3   day 6   13 and a half, Lawrence, KS
May 4   day 7   0 miles, Holiday Inn
May 5   day 8   16 miles, Big Springs, KS
May 6   day 9   11 miles, Topeka, KS
May 7   day 10   5 miles
May 8   day 11, Tuesday, 17+ miles
May 9 ?   5 miles ?
May 10 ? 17 miles ?
May 11? 19 miles to Westmoreland, KS
May 12 0 miles
                plan 8 miles to Blaine, plan 40 miles to Marysville 4 days
May 13 0 miles
May 14 Sunday, Mother's Day 2 and a half miles ?
May 15 12 and a half miles
May 16 Blaine, KS
May 17 Smith's
May 18 13 miles from Marysville to Heisterman's
May 19 14 miles Rippe's
May 20 12 and a half miles to Endicott, NB
May 21 6 and a half miles to Fairbury, NB
Sunday   15 miles to Alexandria State Park, NB
Monday   13 miles to Marsh's
Tuesday 14 miles
Wednesday 12 miles a bit beyond Oak, NB Curray's

Thursday   to the Paul's
Friday   to Deweese, NB
Saturday rest in Deweese, Memorial Day Weekend
May 28   16 and one half miles
May 29   11 miles Hastings, NB
Tuesday   17 miles to Kenesaw, NB
Wednesday rest at Miller's
Thursday 23 miles to Fort Kearney, NB
Friday   0 miles, Fort Kearney, NB
Sunday   17 miles
Monday   16 miles
Tuesday   14 miles, Lexington, NB
Wednesday 16 and one half miles, Cozad, NB
Thursday 11 miles, Gothenburg, NB
June 9   14 miles, Brady, NB
Saturday 12 and one half miles, North Platte, NB
Sunday   12 miles
Monday   21 miles, Paxton area, Ella Miller
June ?   to Ash Hollow
June 17   Saturday 15 miles to Oshkosh, NB (590 miles total)
June 19   15 miles Broadwater, NB
June 20   15 miles, Bridgeport, NB
June 21   21 miles to Hickey's
June 22   rest 0 miles
June 23   17 miles, Scotts Bluff, NB
June 24   22 miles, Morill
June 26   15 miles Torrington, WY
June 27   24 miles Ft. Laramie, WY
June 28   20? Miles Guernsey, WY
June 29   18 miles, Willar
June 30   about 20? Miles to Cundall's
July 1   32!!! Miles to Douglas, WY
July 2   rest
July 3   2 miles?
July ?   23 miles Glenrock, WY
July 6   20 miles, Casper, WY
July 8   12 and a half miles, Poison Spider School
July 9   27 miles camp on Oregon Trail Rd. WY
July 10   to Independence Rock, WY
July 11   18 miles Sun Ranch
July 12   19 miles Split Rock, WY
July 13   16 miles, Jeffrey City, WY
July 15   21 miles

July 16   rest, Woolery Ranch
July 17   8 miles
July 18   21 miles, through South Pass
July 20   13 miles, Farson, WY
July 21   Cliff sick
July 22   14 miles
July 23   18 miles, Lombard Rd.
July 24   11 miles through Granger, WY
July 25   KOA
July 26   22 and a half miles, Lyman, WY
July 27   through Fort Bridger toward Evanston, WY
July 28   20 miles, Evanston, WY
July 29   20 miles Echo Canyon start
July 30   20 miles, Weber River Junction, UT
July 31   East Canyon Campground, UT
August 1 to the divide
August 2 side trip to SLC with Paula
August 3 Wahsatch divide to Salt Lake City, UT
August 4 at the "Y"
August 4 through 15, factory work Salt Lake City, UT
August 16 Wednesday, 20 miles to Great Salt Lake, UT
August 17 18 miles ? to Grantsville, UT
Total confusion of dates crossing Great Salt Lake Desert, UT and into
Nevada
September 3 resting 2 12 miles to Brown's in Clover Valley, NV
September ? 13 miles
September ? 10 miles In Ruby Valley, NV
September ? 10 miles
September ?   12 miles
September 14   ? Jiggs, NV
September ?   Spring Creek, NV
September 19   ? Elko, NV
September 20   near Carlin Tunnel, NV
September ?   camp
September ?   Friday. Dunphy
September ?   Saturday 25 miles Battle Mountain, NV
September ?   Sunday rest Battle Mountain, NV
September 26   15 miles Valmy, NV
September 27   rest
September 29   22 miles to Winnemucca, NV
September 30   rest
October 3 Tuesday   20 miles to rest area
October 4 Wednesday to Humboldt

October 5 Thursday   to outside Oreana
October ?   12 miles to Lovelock, NV

October 8 Sunday 23 miles to junction route 95
dates missing in journal
October ?   5 miles Sparks, NV
No dates for motel maid's work in Reno, NV
October 28   18 miles to First Summit
October 29   ? 18? miles to George Donner Site CA
October 30   11 miles to Donner Lake State Park, CA
No more dates in journal for last 100 miles to Sutters Fort, CA

ABOUT THE AUTHOR

2009   PM

Barbara currently lives in her happy clutter in tiny, sunny Crestone, Colorado. The landscape reminds her of the stunning Ruby Valley, Nevada, from her Donner Walk. She and Howard have burros, cats, and dogs with an abundance of wildlife surrounding them where the beauty and cruelty of mother nature can be seen daily. She has developed a passion for the urgent, screaming need for animal rights awareness.

She is an enthusiastic agnostic/atheist believing that there is a lot more "out there" than we now realize including the possibility of continuing forms of existence. "Our human intelligence and imagination within science disciplines will some day unlock these mysteries," she confides. "The rational study of evolution, archaeology, brain science, and the cosmos is most exciting to me. Education is the key to our shining future."

Profits from this book will go to animal right issues.

CPSIA information can be obtained at www.ICGtesting.com
Printed in the USA
LVOW121500060212

267318LV00018B/118/P